The Music Documentary

The Music Documentary offers a wide range of approaches, across key moments in the history of popular music, in order to define this prominent genre of filmmaking. The writers in this volume argue persuasively that the music documentary must be considered as an essential cultural artifact in documenting stars and icons, and musicians and their times—particularly for those figures whose fame was achieved posthumously. In this collection of fifteen essays, the reader will find comprehensive discussions of the history of music documentaries, insights into their production and promotion, close studies of documentaries relating to favorite bands or performers, and approaches to questions of music documentary and form, from the celluloid to the digital age.

Robert Edgar is Head of the MA programs in Film and Documentary at York St John University.

Kirsty Fairclough-Isaacs is Lecturer in Media and Performance in the School of Media, Music and Performance at the University of Salford.

Benjamin Halligan is the Director of Postgraduate Research Studies for the College of Arts and Social Sciences, University of Salford. Publications include *Michael Reeves* (2003) and *Reverberations: The Philosophy, Aesthetics and Politics of Noise* (2012).

Routledge Music and Screen Media Series

Series Editor: Neil Lerner

The **Routledge Music and Screen Media Series** offers edited collections of original essays on music in particular genres of cinema, television, video games, and new media. These edited essay collections are written for an interdisciplinary audience of students and scholars of music and film and media studies.

The Music Documentary: Acid Rock to Electropop
Edited by Robert Edgar, Kirsty Fairclough-Isaacs, and Benjamin Halligan

Music in Science Fiction Television: Tuned to the Future
Edited by K.J. Donnelly and Philip Hayward

Music, Sound and Filmmakers: Sonic Style in Cinema
Edited by James Wierzbicki

Music in the Western: Notes from the Frontier
Edited by Kathryn Kalinak

Music in Television: Channels of Listening
Edited by James Deaville

Music in the Horror Film: Listening to Fear
Edited by Neil Lerner

The Music Documentary

Acid Rock to Electropop

Edited by

Robert Edgar
York St. John University

Kirsty Fairclough-Isaacs
University of Salford

Benjamin Halligan
University of Salford

Routledge
Taylor & Francis Group

NEW YORK AND LONDON

First published 2013
by Routledge
711 Third Avenue, New York, NY 10017

Simultaneously published in the UK
by Routledge
2 Park Square, Milton Park, Abingdon, Oxon OX14 4RN

Routledge is an imprint of the Taylor & Francis Group, an informa business

Library of Congress Cataloging in Publication Data
The music documentary: Acid Rock to Electropop/
    edited by Robert Edgar, Kirsty Fairclough-Isaacs, and
    Benjamin Halligan.
      pages cm.—(Routledge music and screen media series)
      1. Documentary films—History and criticism. 2. Documentary
    television programs—History and criticism. 3. Musicians in motion
    pictures. 4. Concert films—History and criticism. 5. Rock films—
    History and criticism. I. Edgar-Hunt, Robert, editor. II. Fairclough-
    Isaacs, Kirsty, editor. III. Halligan, Benjamin, editor. IV. Series:
    Routledge music and screen media series.
    PN1995.9.D6M875 2013
    780.26'7—dc23   2012031128

ISBN: 978-0-415-52801-6 (hbk)
ISBN: 978-0-415-52802-3 (pbk)
ISBN: 978-0-203-11868-9 (ebk)

Typeset in Goudy and Gill Sans
by Florence Production Ltd, Stoodleigh, Devon

Senior Editor: Constance Ditzel
Editorial Assistant: Elysse Preposi
Production Manager: Alf Symons
Marketing Manager: Jessica Plummer
Copy Editor: Anna Carroll
Proofreader: Jane Canvin

In fond memory of David Sanjek, 1952–2011

Contents

Series Foreword

While the scholarly conversations about music in film and visual media have been expanding prodigiously since the last quarter of the twentieth century, a need remains for focused, specialized studies of particular films as they relate more broadly to genres. This series includes scholars from across the disciplines of music and film and media studies, of specialists in both the audible as well as the visual, who share the goal of broadening and deepening these scholarly dialogues about music in particular genres of cinema, television, videogames, and new media. Claiming a chronological arc from the birth of cinema in the 1890s to the most recent releases, the *Routledge Music and Screen Media Series* offers collections of original essays written for an interdisciplinary audience of students and scholars of music, film, and media studies in general, and interdisciplinary humanists who give strong attention to music. Driving the study of music here are the underlying assumptions that music together with screen media (understood broadly to accommodate rapidly developing new technologies) participate in important ways in the creation of meaning and that including music in an analysis opens up the possibility for interpretations that remain invisible when only using the eye.

The series was designed with the goal of providing a thematically unified group of supplemental essays in a single volume that can be assigned in a variety of undergraduate and graduate courses (including courses in film studies, in film music, and other interdisciplinary topics). We look forward to adding future volumes addressing emerging technologies and reflecting the growth of the academic study of screen media. Rather than attempting an exhaustive history or unified theory, these studies—persuasive explications supported by textual and contextual evidence—will pose questions of musical style, strategies of rhetoric, and critical cultural analysis as they help us to see, to hear, and ultimately to understand these texts in new ways.

Neil Lerner
Series Editor

Preface

The music documentary has risen in prominence—from a mere adjunct to music "proper" to a component fundamental to contemporary popular music, and a film genre in its own right—without ever being subject to substantial critical and academic perspectives. And yet, even at the point of embarking on such an examination, we find that the genre itself is in crisis. It was the detection of the institutionalization of the music documentary and the ways in which, of almost all categories of documentary, this genre has become so fully given over to commercial concerns, that prompted the need to identify and explore the ideological, social, performative, historical, and aesthetic underpinnings of the form. To put this in more straightforward terms: almost any commercial music store will now contain a "music documentaries" section. The genre is clearly well established. And yet to sample even a small selection of these documentaries prompts an unavoidable question: how can it be that documentary, operating in the field of popular music, has strayed so far from ideas of objectivity and reportage—ideas that represent the fundamentals of the documentary form—and has become pure promotion?

To begin this study of music documentaries, an engagement with the form of the musical documentary was understood to be necessary and, beyond that, a reacquaintance with key periods of music and the relationship between the methodologies of their documentaries and the conceptions of popular music at that time. At the same time, our intention was also to look to the alternatives to the loose canon of acclaimed ("classic") music documentaries, and to look to newer films that suggest the future of the music documentary. These were the intentions that have determined the selection of chapters in *The Music Documentary: Acid Rock to Electropop*, as outlined below.

Structure of the Book

The first section of this volume, "Evolutions of the Music Documentary," addresses the ways in which the music documentary has positioned itself as a recognised genre in its own right. Here a series of questions are raised concerning the establishment and subsequent evolutions of the music documentary, in its form and content, for television, film and radio.

In Chapter 1, Long and Wall regard Tony Palmer's documentary series *All You Need is Love* (1977) as a seminal moment in the establishment of music documentary and as the first televisual presentation of pop history at a time when little else was emerging in this field. Long and Wall posit Palmer as pop television's first documentary-maker and through an analysis of narrative and narration articulate wider questions concerning how popular music histories are turned into stories, and critically received. Palmer's *All You Need is Love* established an approach to presenting pop music history that many subsequent documentaries have emulated and so can be identified as a significant moment in the establishment of the music documentary. Palmer is presented as deviating from a straightforwardly chronological examination of pop history and instead reveals a far more complex, and ultimately problematic, exploration of the past of pop.

Likewise Saffle, in a chapter that redefines the music documentary via an examination of Hollywood's musical compilation programs, questions the very nature of what a music documentary is, or can be. Saffle's intervention speaks to well defined disagreements in academic and industrial circles concerning what can be considered a documentary, in terms of questions of formal features, of audience expectations and of the construction and conflation of history and knowledge. After a series of arresting case studies, Saffle presents the view that there needs to be critical redefinition of the types of footage, and types of construction, that can be considered as music documentaries.

Music documentary in this section is considered not only visually but also within a purely aural medium. Carter and Coley in Chapter 3 consider the music documentary on radio, an area that has received remarkably slight critical attention. They consider both the production of radio documentaries and development of participatory fan cultures in the context of the ways in which David Bowie fans responded to the broadcast of *Bowie's Waiata* documentary (a program produced by Coley). This examination raises a number of questions about the continuation of the documentary and use of the documentary by fans in the context of Henry Jenkins' work on new participatory cultures. It questions how the boundaries between producer, listener, and fan have, and continue to become, increasingly blurred.

The chapters in "Scenes from the Sixties," Part II, find a central concern in questions of communality and festival audiences, as inside the festival area and outside, "on the streets." Wright identifies two distinct readings in operation and, via a deft deconstruction, illustrates how the modish notions of good karma and bad vibes determine the films that have come to document the two most notable festival events of the era. Woodstock, from this vantage point, is presented as positively utopian since, as Wright argues, the audiences are included as equal creators in the event or happening. The Altamont concert, on the other hand, confines the audience to the role of passive consumers, to be policed and contained, and in so doing is seen to have engendered alienation, bad trips, and worse. And these readings and film documentations, in turn, go some way to shape the notion of the counterculture in the popular imagination.

Wennekes' concern in Chapter 5 is with those turbulent events "on the streets" and how they are understood to feed back into the music and performance of, and find a touchstone in, Jimi Hendrix. But this contextualization, which is found in innumerable texts that deal with the counterculture, is identified as questionable. Wennekes, and Sanjek in Chapter 6, destabilizes assumptions that are typically, and lazily, used to explain hippie cultures of this moment.

For Sanjek, Woodstock is thrown into relief by the attempt to mount a second such event, complete with festival film. In one of the final pieces of his writing to be published, characteristically incisive and resolutely determined to recover texts outside the canon, Sanjek sees, in this coda to the countercultural era, the unguarded emergence of the financial restructuring of popular culture at the turn of the 1970s. The common ground between the counter- and the dominant culture comes in the instruction to enjoy, and the assumptions that culture operates merely to provide enjoyment. Halligan, in his Afterword, finds in this train of thought a key to unlocking the ways in which the relationship between live music and event, in the context of the music documentary or the concert film, would come to be radically realigned in subsequent decades.

Part III, "Punk Cultures," moves the focus to the next period of case studies, with an emphasis on retrospective readings of films arising from punk music and cultures. For many the moment itself was so short-lived that its explosive interventions could only be considered as legacy; for others, the period only becomes palatable at some years' distance. All authors note how this legacy remains a matter of contention and subject to what Raymond Williams identified as the "selective tradition."[1] Such revisionism typically occurs in high-profile music documentaries, consciously or otherwise.

In Chapter 7, Goddard outlines and explores the mostly unmapped subgenre of No Wave films and filmmaking, closely connected to the New York punk scene, and considers the reasons for the invisibility of this distinctive collection of films. The films resonate with both the ethos and philosophies of punk, and in this respect remain as "documents" which have proven to be difficult to square with the ways in which punk has found its place in the collective imagination.

Hertz, in Chapter 8, focuses in on the ways in which the music documentary often presents the city as the essential element in the visualisation of punk music. "Dissonant" music is understood to flow from, and reflect, the experience of the musician in respect to the dangers and stresses, poverty and alienation, of city life. The punk groups typically designate or identify such a locale as their own, presented as a mark of the authenticity of their music as a *cri du coeur* born not so much of outsider-ism and marginality, but of the unenviable position of being too far "inside": conditions of alienation as endemic to, or at the very heart of, modern urban life. Once the punk group has made its exit via commercial success what then becomes of the city narrative? Hertz, in this respect, touches on tensions which find their fullest expression, and engender a variety of responses, in the music documentary.

In Chapter 9, Grant Ferguson looks to the documentaries that have emerged from the British punk scene and finds in them the beginnings of a postmodern aesthetic. The certainties of documentary form are eroded, and questions of truthfulness and untruthfulness come to the fore. Even in more contemporary documentaries looking back to this period the problem of "knowing" what "really" happened remains. But this is not a matter of unhappy confusion; these tendencies suggest a liberation from the confines of typical documentary-making, towards what could be termed a problematization of the form of the documentary (which necessarily suggests that "the truth is out there," and so can be captured and reproduced). For Grant Ferguson, this is more than just differing sides to a story: it becomes a way of questioning the elements that, collectively, could be said to make up a wider history. And the potential of punk culture is the potential of rewriting history: of refusing to accept the official version of events.

Documentaries have long produced their humorous "mock" counterparts, or abandoned documentary tropes of objectivity in order to convey a fully immersive experience of the subject at hand. The music documentary is no different, and this is the focus of Part IV, "'Mockumentaries' and 'Rockumentaries'". In recent years, much critical attention has been paid to films that lampoon the style and aesthetic tendencies of the documentary. However, there has been little consideration of the music mockumentary. This section aims to redress this balance and presents chapters that explore the need to poke fun at a genre of music that has long been associated with defiance.

Roessner, in Chapter 10, considers why rock music documentaries attract parody via an examination of *The Rutles: All You Need is Cash* (Idle and Weis, 1978), a film that revels in mocking one of the most mythologized rock bands of all, The Beatles. Using Bakhtin's notion of the carnivalesque, Roessner examines why sixties rock and roll has been read in terms of carnival and how mockumentaries that lampoon this era represent a further expression of the carnivalesque in terms of their ability to undercut rock music pretensions.

In Chapter 11, Donnelly addresses the "rockumentary" film, in particular the progressive rock live concert film in Britain during the 1970s, as a distinct subgenre of the music documentary. He considers the often unfair treatment of these films, as the target of mockery by film theorists and historians, and reconsiders their form and function. Donnelly concludes by suggesting that the unique quality of the rockumentary lies in its subordinance to the album soundtrack, and posits that fruitful analysis of such films lies in approaching them from a position of music history rather than film.

The final part, "New Directions in the Music Documentary," addresses some of the contemporary issues associated with the documentary form as and when it interfaces with music, and seeks to embrace the diversity of emergent music documentary forms.

In Chapter 12, Burke addresses the technology involved in the production of music and focuses his attentions on a "Moogie Wonderland". In looking at this development Burke notes that the documentary touches on the socioeconomic position of America in the 1960s and 1970s, which is understood as being a period of musical modernity. Burke's analysis notes the importance of the integration between different subsets of American society through the use of the Moog and thus the documentary becomes an analysis of America through an analysis of popular music.

Music and documentary education is a topic highly pertinent to the development of future documentary forms. In Chapter 13, Ballengee addresses the practicalities of music and video pedagogy through detailed consideration of his own practice. This chapter addresses the matter of music students and their understanding of the practicalities of the documentary form and opens up issues associated with the music practitioner as commodity, and as a subject of, and for, documentary-makers. Ballengee also addresses the integration of music and image for music ethnographers, an approach that differs from what might be termed "conventional" documentary production where the music or musician, or aspect of music technology, is a subject like any other which can be approached in any way.

Rather than considering *The Agony and the Ecstasy* as a documentary primarily about music, Duffett and Hackett in Chapter 14 address the cult of personality, and the specifics of Phil Spector's public downfall. In their forensic analysis of the documentary which follows, a critique of the supposed objectivity of the documentary-makers is mounted: the manipulations of documentary form at work in this film are seen to be anything but objective. Similarly, Kylie Minogue can be considered to be more of an icon than "just" a singer. In Chapter 15, Manghani and McDonald analyse the emergence of Kylie in and through the privileged access illustrated in *White Diamond*, which they then view as part of performer-centric documentary canon. However, there is something different in operation with Kylie as icon/performer which the documentary itself uncovers: the new direction is in part the music documentary as confessional. This echoes the emergence of a puritanical strain to the contemporary music documentary, as also identified in Duffett and Hackett's analysis. Such a strain would seem to represent both the dubious legacy of reality television across the first decade of the twentieth century and the ideological project of moving against 1968 and its unresolved legacies which, as Badiou has argued in a European context, found its champion in Nicolas Sarkozy.[2] Through an approach that combines the methodologies of structuralism and semiotic analysis, Manghani and McDonald come to argue that even in the case of music documentaries engaging with familiar pop stars, the music documentary cannot help but take the form in a new direction at the present juncture.

As a contribution to the *Music and Screen Media Series*, this edited collection intended to examine the clearest, indeed the most fundamental, correlation between these two elements, as found in the visual documentation of music—the "music documentary." The assumption in operation was that this subject would allow our authors to identify and expand on a number of ideas concerning what it means to film musicians and music, with that essential documentary "liveness" derived from conducting interviews and capturing concerts. In the event, we have found that the notion of a "straight" correlation between music-making and documentary-making has proved to be insufficient from the critical standpoints that our authors have taken. Music and screen media have not operated in a neat parallel, but engaged in a process of symbiosis. As each connects, each has changed the other: music has been radically altered by its incorporation of screen media over the last half century, and screen media has been deprived of its old assumptions about documentary form and techniques of documentary-making through its encounters with music. This volume sets out to track how and why this has happened, and where this leaves both popular music and documentary.

Notes

1   Raymond Williams, "Base and Superstructure in Marxist Cultural Theory," *New Left Review* 1, No. 82 (November–December 1973); republished in Raymond Williams, *Culture and Materialism: Selected Essays* (Verso: London and New York, 2010).
2   See Alain Badiou, *The Meaning of Sarkozy* (London and New York: Verso, 2009).

Acknowledgments

The editors would like to acknowledge and offer their thanks to: the Communication, Cultural and Media Studies Research Centre, and the Popular Music Research Centre, in the School of Media, Music and Performance at the University of Salford, Professors George McKay and Ben Light, Dr. Deborah Woodman; the Faculty of Arts at York St. John University, Peter Cook, Wendy Burke, Robin Small and Fiona Thompson (for their knowledge of documentary); Dr. Neil Lerner, Constance Ditzel, Elysse Preposi, and the team at Routledge; to Rick and Roger Sanjek; to Tom Attah (for the expertise); to Dr. Johannes Sjöberg and Matt Grimes; to Roger Sargent, Jeff Feurzeig, and Tony Palmer. All photographs by Benjamin Halligan unless otherwise stated.

From Rob: special thanks to Meredith (for pressing the buttons on the computer). From Kirsty: special thanks to Gordon (for his continual patience), and to Evan (for everything). From Ben: special thanks to John Hefin (who knew just when to say "don't look back!").

Robert Edgar, Kirsty Fairclough-Isaacs, Benjamin Halligan
Salford, Manchester, York: August 2012

Music Seen

The Formats and Functions of the Music Documentary

Robert Edgar, Kirsty Fairclough-Isaacs, and Benjamin Halligan

"Video Killed the Radio Star"

So sang The Buggles, in the last few months of the 1970s, on their wildly popular debut single, and their fear was precisely located: the damage that would be done by the transmigration enforced by the burgeoning mass media on the fragile and often ephemeral texts of popular mass culture. The album that followed, in the first few months of the new decade, boldly announced the termination of the Age of Aquarius. The *Age of Plastic* mined the etymology and pejorative implications of the term "plastic": the man-made synthetic, inorganic and characterlessly consistent in texture and colouration, as denoting the poor replacement to the rich and utopian hippy and New Age cultures of the Aquarian period. From this vantage point "plastic" was both an insult (as with those conformists Frank Zappa termed the "Plastic People") and intimation of things to come (Norman Mailer described futureshock Los Angeles as "the constellation of plastic").[1] The *Age of Plastic* album opened with the second single from The Buggles. "Living in the Plastic Age," in this context, suggests itself as a rejoinder to "Aquarius" from the musical *Hair*, now with plastic surgeons and "shiny serving clones" replacing cosmic alignments and "mystic crystals revelation/and the mind's true liberation."[2] In the accompanying promo video, which is framed as a vision of the dystopian future beheld by the druids of Stonehenge, cardiac arrests and Space Invaders assail a group of yuppies.[3]

Pop music mass culture, as was, for a group of the New Wave pedigree of The Buggles, would have been read as the site of victory. At its best, pop music evidenced the absorption of the countercultures of the Summer of Love, of punk and post-punk, and of the early years of rap and hip-hop, into a discourse that was diffident, critical, reflexive, and anti-establishment, and yet joyful, communal, multicultural, protean, and omnipresent. In order to conceptualize the full impact of what stood to be lost, The Buggles did not issue a straight warning ("video's killing the radio star") or a prophecy ("video will kill . . .") but, projecting themselves into the near future so as to look back, a lament. And what would be lost was lost at the behest of "video":

Figure 0.1 Both diagnosis and disease in The Buggles's promo video "Video Killed the Radio Star."

Figure 0.2 Stonehenge druids confront the city of the future in "Living in the Plastic Age."

a cheap, reproducible, televisual (rather than cinematic) technology—the paradox of a visual promotion of a sonic form, and one that would invariably reorientate popular music to look over sound.

In terms of the mainstream of popular music cultures that grew from the anti-establishment cultures of the West in the 1960s and 1970s (and that were understood as acceptable to white audiences), The Buggles were not wrong: video would come to dominate, and with this a new set of concerns, often apolitical and escapist, would come to the fore. However, the tradition that would be replaced had changed substantially since 1968. Tensions in popular music across the 1970s in relation to authenticity and musicality—as with the receptions of glam and prog rock[4] and punk, and particularly in respect to the anti-disco backlash[5]—reflected the unwillingness of the old guard to think beyond "rockist" concerns, let alone pass on the baton. And authenticity and musicality were understood to be mortally endangered by a music–video hybrid.

This is not to say that music had been a merely aural affair before: looking back to the start of the 1970s, with the full media capitalization on the popular music scene, most famously for *Woodstock* (Michael Wadleigh, 1970), as well as a number of other films discussed in this collection, the idea of music as speakers without a screen belonged to an earlier period. But in general terms the approaches to the visualization of music in the 1970s, and live music in particular, were quite different. Woodstock and its immediate predecessors and imitators were essentially musical events: the cameras engaged in reportage, the musicians primarily engaged in the live delivery of their music. Such an approach presupposes the music event as an active and nuanced dialogue between performances and audiences, and as a "one-off" and particular to a time and place, and a social and historical context. As Sheila Whiteley argues in relation to outdoor music events of the 1960s, "[m]usic brought people together, engendering participation rather than passivity . . . rather than being seen as entertainment, music was considered to say things of cultural and political importance."[6] Even when these "things" remain opaque or obscure, as with *Tonite Let's All Make Love in London* (Peter Whitehead, 1967), the idea of a coming together and a general and engulfing connection, rhizomatic if need be (to use a term of Deleuze and Guattari's),[7] a connection that sweeps the audience up and creates the event in the symbiosis of audience and performer, persisted.

For the video age, and as further enabled (and this was more often than not the "problem" with disco) by machine- or computer-generated music, image comes first, and so comes to be created first. MTV began broadcasting in August 1981. The transistor radio, in this paradigm shift, would be unable to deliver the full payload, commercial or cultural, of music, and so this radio culture would wither away. And, it was commonly feared, musicianship, musicality, and even live performance would be rendered redundant. The shaman of yesteryear would be replaced by a succession of asexual, robotic models.

Figure 0.3 Event and reportage: singer, fan, cameraman in *Tonite Let's All Make Love in London* (Peter Whitehead, 1967).

Figure 0.4 The affirmation of the masses: crowd shot from *Tonite Let's All Make Love in London*.

However, in terms of popular music as it would actually evolve in the 1980s and beyond, at the point after the post-punk coda to the previous decade, The Buggles could not have been more wrong. To retain the communal and the joyous while developing further technologies for the delivery and replay of music, to junk the diffident and anti-establishment sentiments, and to recalibrate the critical, would result—for better or for worse—in a reinvention of the old guard. The Woodstock farm land would be replaced by the global and stadia events of Live Aid in 1985, as the next era-defining big gig. And the nature of the music–video hybrid on the other side of the transmigration is arresting: the introspection and immobility of the counterculture's preferred groups, as well as their multimedia ventures, had been replaced by, in all senses, performance. To privilege performance over playing, and deliver high-energy pop hits over the murkiness and meandering of psychedelia and prog, seemed to be the undoing of Led Zeppelin at Live Aid, while Freddie Mercury's mastery of performance fully established Queen as *the* "stadium group".[8] The performance of "Do They Know It's Christmas?" which closed the London half of the event, delivered by a chorus of the new rock and pop aristocracy, established popular music as a proactive force of good: proceeds of the record, and this event, were not swelling the bank accounts of hedonistic rock stars, their dealers, managers, and groupies, but represented, selflessly, financial aid to those most in need. In all these respects, video was the savior of the radio star.

Figure 0.5 Freddie Mercury's world-wide audience: Queen perform at Live Aid.

Figure 0.6 Video redeems then saves the radio star: Live Aid, 1985.

"I Want My MTV"

Such tensions, which came to the fore in the years 1979 to 1985, characterize the concerns of this edited collection more generally. While there is no question that visually documenting or just visualizing popular music pushes various genres of film and television-making into new territories, and even creates genres of its own—as with the music documentary—a secondary problem becomes acutely apparent in the process. In visually documenting or just visualizing music, it would seem to be the idea of popular music that is assailed or problematized or propelled to enact sudden and radical change in finding itself exposed to cameras. It is as if the fear of video producers was that the visual potentially had as little to do with the experience of popular music, in terms of reproducing it, embodying it, or just capturing it, as the written: the difference between an orchestra in full flight and a few hundred pages of a bound musical score. The visual would ultimately therefore demand the reinvention of the aural and what seemed to be a crude usurping of the priorities of form, in the domination of the visual over the aural, could be read as a survival mechanism or life-support system: only by completely transplanting popular music to the domains of the visual, no matter what damage would entail, would popular music continue to exist as an essential component of popular culture. And even, by extension, and as Austerlitz argues in respect of Tupac Shakur, to ensure that (artistic) life continues after death.[9] Before briefly reviewing the contours of the problematization at hand, and in respect of this context of survival, it should be noted that the unease surrounding music film and, more especially, music television, can be understood as informed by purist, canonical, and elitist impulses: a cultural snobbishness in respect to the fragile and often ephemeral texts of popular mass culture, resulting in "that ignored artefact of contemporary culture— the music video,"[10] only to be further aggravated as MTV became "the sun around which popular culture rotated."[11]

The fear of a mass culture as determined by the masses is expressed in one of the biggest hits in the early years of MTV: the 1985 Dire Straits single "Money for Nothing." The accompanying music video, directed by Steve Barron, presents the dramatis personae that are also apparent in the different registers of the song itself. The band are viewed by two blue-collar workers, one of whom is unshaven, racist, and homophobic and, in between listing the removal jobs to be done, riddled with envy for the stars of MTV and their millionaire life-styles. The irony is, seemingly not lost on this removal man, that in order for the band to attain this level of luxury they need to appear on the heavy television sets that the two lug into other people's homes. And the worry is exacting, as embodied in this animated protagonist: questions

Figure 0.7 MTV auto-critique #1: mass culture for the unwashed masses, in Dire Straits' "Money for Nothing."

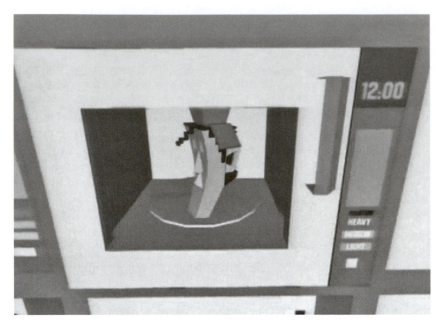

Figure 0.8 Pop music as neurological irradiation: "Money for Nothing."

Figure 0.9 Auto-critique #2: Generation X as the second generation of MTV fans, with Beavis and Butt-head.

of musicality and critique, and of the persistence of poetry and philosophy in mass culture,[12] are either ignored in favour of the baser instincts of sexual and material jealousy or, for the other removal man (who appears brain dead; at one point his head is removed and microwaved), simply do not register. Any artistic achievement is wasted, and these two represent the audience, infantile, and ignorant, to which MTV will soon pander: the song begins with an ethereal, child- or siren-like voice singing of wanting MTV (rather than, as could be expected "I want my mommy," although the words are lifted from early MTV advertising), which sucks the latter removal man into the television set itself. (And this dynamic and dramatic set-up would re-emerge in 1993 on MTV, for *Beavis and Butt-head*).

"The Great Gig in the Sky"

MTV could be said to have offered an effective but only finite solution to the question of the visualization of music. As with MTV's *ur*-text, *A Hard Day's Night* (Richard Lester, 1964), ontological questions of the performance of music took second place to conceptions of the performer.

Figure 0.10 The nonchalance of the streets, the nonchalance of the singer: The Pet Shop Boys' "West End Girls."

Figure 0.11 Morrissey cleans rain from his glasses, outside the Salford Lads Club: The Smiths' "Stop Me If You Think You've Heard This One Before."

Figure 0.12 Exotic aspirations: George Michael sings the praises of going on holiday: Wham!'s "Club Tropicana."

Figure 0.13 Taking it back to the streets: Flava Flav and Chuck D in Public Enemy's "Fight the Power."

Figure 0.14 Tourists as sirens: Aaliyah's "Rock the Boat."

And so just as Lester relocated his stars, placed them in a narrative and restaged their music, a generation later The Pet Shop Boys are found purposefully walking down London streets for "West End Girls" (1984) and Morrissey cycling the streets of Salford for The Smiths' "Stop Me If You Think You've Heard This One Before" (1987), Wham! on holiday in the tropics for "Club Tropicana" (1983) and Public Enemy staging an open-air political rally for "Fight the Power" (1990), Aaliyah and her troupe dancing on a yacht for "Rock the Boat" (2001) and Britney Spears just pole dancing for "Gimme More" (2007). The *mise-en-scène* is rarely surprising. Re-imagining

Figure 0.15 The ghost of Christmas future? Britney sees a vision of herself as a dark-haired pole dancer: Britney Spears' "Gimme More."

the song in this way, and fitting the image to the group or artist, was invariably eye-catching, refreshed the music, entered into dialogue with other aspects of popular culture (most particularly fashion) and so channelled both the singer and the song into the area of commodity fetishism (particularly when the music was rendered as aspirational). With the paradigm shift in the music business in the wake of models of digital distribution, however, such hard-hitting promotion, which had been predicated on a limited number of outlets, became redundant, coinciding with the obsolescence of music charts. MTV began to manage its decline by a partial disengagement with music while, at the same time, the commercial importance of live music or, rather, the "live music event" was revived.[13]

Within half a dozen years of the new millennium, the gig had returned with a vengeance, prompting long-since-defunct groups to reform, reissue out-of-print recordings and tour, and artists to dump managers in favour of concert promoters. The live event now occurs in the glare of a protean media apparatus: digital in form, global in reach, and instantaneous in broadcast and yet, in the live relay of images and recordings to the social media sphere, highly individualized. What live event is now not visually documented, in one form or another? On the one hand a tradition of concert films has been revived, where the concert DVD or download has become as obligatory for popular groups in the 2010s as the music video was in the 1980s. On the other hand the notion of the all-important "being there," and so only fully consuming by attending, has been bolstered by the social imperatives of social media: to report and provide evidence of oneself at the event—conceptualizing oneself therefore as part of the event. It is telling that Martin Scorsese makes

Figure 0.16 The director as worker: Martin Scorsese in *Shine a Light* (Martin Scorsese, 2008).

much of his lowly position—effectively his worker status—in respect of showing his preparation to film The Rolling Stones in concert, for *Shine a Light* (2008). The film opens with documentary footage of the flustered director, unable to secure basic information as to the event, and setting up cameras and lights as best he can for all eventualities, which is contrasted with the relaxed and louche members of the group, enjoying hotel suites rather than cramped control rooms, and socializing with the Clintons, among others, rather than (as with Scorsese), technicians. This can be read both as a gesture towards the demystification of the music documentary form but also as an acknowledgement of and reverence to, to use Auslander's term, the liveness of the event filmed.[14]

At this point the contours of the above-mentioned problematization—the way in which it would seem to be the idea of popular music that is assailed and propelled to enact sudden and radical change when exposed to cameras—have shifted again and would seem to invite a revisiting of ideas associated with the concert film before MTV, not least with a view to understanding the post-MTV music documentary. The ways in which the music documentary then remains a current concern informed the conference from which this collection arises, which was convened by David Sanjek and Benjamin Halligan at the University of Salford in Summer 2010: "Sights and Sounds: Interrogating the Music Documentary."

For this first consideration of the music documentary, it was inevitable that a limitation would occur in the predominant Anglo-American focus of the project: documentaries examined invariably looked to Western (in the sense of First World) popular music that became an essential cultural component in the lives of the baby-boomer generation, their children, and their children's

Figure 0.17 Tony Palmer with David Sanjek.

children. Non-Western traditions of music documentary remain to be explored, particularly when the tendency to marginalize or exclude the crowd remains as a central problem in Western traditions of music documentary—to the extent of the persistence of blind spots in relation to music events arising from DJ and rave cultures, and a failure to fully explore where the music "event" itself actually occurs.[15] What seems to take the place of these considerations comes with an overlap between the music documentary and acceleration of celebrity culture.

Figure 0.18 Found footage: the Northern Soul dancehall in *Fiorucci Made Me Hardcore* (Mark Leckey, 1999).

Figure 0.19 Found footage: the Acid House warehouse in *Fiorucci Made Me Hardcore*.

Celebrity Culture and the Music Documentary

Some of the most influential initial work on celebrity culture emerged from the established critical study of stardom, as conceptualized initially by Dyer.[16] Dyer posed key questions concerning the representation and ideological connotations of the star image and offered significant methodological tools for its textual analysis. Dyer's theorizing provided a basis from which much of the subsequent work concerning the star/celebrity as a cultural text has emerged. However, this approach has been steadily fragmenting alongside the growth of a celebrity culture where ideas of stardom, fame, and talent do not necessarily function together. Now that the parameters of Hollywood stardom have seeped into a more diffuse and complex celebrity culture, the new modes of analysis needed have had to expand their scope and extend their range and, it should be added, enhance their methodologies. The impact of developments such as gossip blogging, the emergence of reality television, and the increased power, influence, and reach of the paparazzi have all come to function as central concerns. Actors, sports stars, reality TV contestants, pop stars, disgraced politicians, and musicians are all subject to the same level of scrutiny.

Celebrity culture, now no longer confined to the realms of down-market gossip magazines, is to be found as fully embedded within all spheres of popular media. It is no surprise therefore that the ways in which celebrity is constructed and disseminated have altered dramatically in recent years. Alongside this shifting landscape, the work of the paparazzi, with their propensity to meet the desire for candid images, has come to destabilize the image of the star or celebrity as known. A whole new culture has been created where almost no knowledge about a celebrity's private life is off limits and where scandal appears a normalized and even expected aspect of celebrity narratives. Consequently the scale on which images of scandal are circulated and consumed has intensified. Indeed, a single shot of a celebrity can alter the celebrity persona in a myriad ways, as with impact of the iconic image of pop star Britney Spears, having shaved the hair off her head in 2007, at the height of her mental breakdown. For some this represents a democratization of celebrity, in tandem with an X-Factor-like philosophy of "anyone can be a star." Anthony Burgess noted the emergence of the non-celebrity celebrity as well established even by 1980, in his Introduction to a portfolio of paparazzi shots.[17] For others, this is understood as at best a distraction from the appreciation of genuine talent and at worse a kind of prurient pornography, full of moral comeuppance and public humiliation. For Burgess, the latter remains as transient as some of the names destined to be forgotten after their, as Warhol had it, fifteen minutes of fame. Burgess notes that the "lesson of vanity of a particular kind of fame" remains: "Callas dies but Verdi lives, and there will always be other singers to sing him ... Art lives for ever, but executants are relatively expendable."[18]

The 1991 release of *Madonna: Truth or Dare* (Alek Keshishian) very visibly shifted the landscape of the music documentary, and pre-empted these tendencies: here the suggestion is made that the key tenets of the music documentary could be both scandalous, wildly entertaining, and overwhelmingly trashy. The film was a candid look behind the scenes of Madonna's 1990 Blonde Ambition tour, cementing the image of a notoriously outrageous persona that was further exacerbated by the singer's monstrous behavior towards her crew and fellow celebrities.

Figure 0.20 "Why would you say something if it's off-camera?" Warren Beatty in *Madonna: Truth or Dare* (Alek Keshishian).

Figure 0.21 Star, entourage, paparazzi: *Madonna: Truth or Dare.*

The echoes of this documentary can be seen throughout contemporary celebrity culture, particularly in reality TV. The documentary answered, or reflected or engendered, an intense public fascination with all facets of celebrity life and, according to Madonna (seen in the documentary, interviewed on *Good Morning America*), aimed "to explode the myth that we raise up on a pedestal people we turn into icons. We make them inhuman and we don't give them human attributes so they're not allowed to fail, they're not allowed to make mistakes." But this "human" side was something that, as Warren Beatty astutely points out to her in the documentary, is rendered almost immaterial to a star that fully exists in public: "There's nothing to say off-camera, why would you say something if it's off-camera? What point is there existing?" The rise of social media in the last decade, and the ways in which self-documentation have come to the fore, in part answers Beatty's question. But these developments in themselves look back to earlier harbingers of the media matrix of stardom and celebrity, the candid and the scandalous, and the intrusive and the intimate: Fellini's paparazzi of modern Roman existence, of *La Dolce Vita* (1960), Warhol's star factory, the "indecently" private photography of David Bailey, Francesca Woodman, and Nan Goldin, and the turbulence and denunciations surrounding the British tabloid media from the point of the death of Princess Diana to the present.

This notion of reclaiming the public image from the public has since become a key trope within the music documentary. Indeed the music documentary as a vehicle for the mainstream pop star has increased exponentially alongside the global digital convergence of media, and has created a multiplicity of outlets for the distribution of the celebrity/star image. It would appear that

Figure 0.22 "I jumped at the chance to make the documentary . . . the, if you will, 'rockumentary,' that you're about to see": Rob Reiner in *This is Spinal Tap* (Reiner, 1983).

the music documentary is no longer reserved for "serious" musicians, as evidenced by the popularity of pop documentaries, often afforded a full theatrical release.[19] In the context of celebrity culture, the music documentary can be seen to operate not only in the provision of an extra layer of financially lucrative content by the pop star for the fan, but also in adding to the celebrity/ star brand via the presentation of a version of manufactured authenticity. This questionable *mise-en-scène* aims to present the "correct" version of the star/celebrity persona, away from the mutating versions seen in the blogosphere, accessed via the paparazzi, or even replacing the "banned" version: the ill-considered celebrity outburst in public or on the internet, leaked sex tapes and, in the case of The Rolling Stones, the judicial censoring of Robert Frank's 1972 documentary *Cocksucker Blues*. These developments are even visible in the more respectable quarters of the music documentary: the jaded VIP point of view that has determined Martin Scorsese's documentaries on icons of mainstream rock, where subjects narrate their own stories, often blaming society at large for misunderstanding them (as typically illustrated by the undifferentiated mass of fans) and/or getting too carried away with them, and never calling into question their own complicity in the creation and selling of their own star image, illustrates just such a tendency.[20] This is a regal rather than a people's history.

Such a biographical focus offers an individualized mode of expression that supposedly allows the real celebrity an authentically mediated, self-articulated voice that rests precariously on the commercial and promotional activity of their brand. This trend has emerged in the firmament of an intensified celebrity culture in which, for better or for worse, the music documentary has taken its place.

In these respects and many others covered in this volume, in seems clear that the music documentary remains, in its functions and formats, in a state of flux. And yet the music documentary persists as both an index of, and an access to, the certainties and the vagaries of popular culture.

Notes

1 See "Plastic People" on the 1967 Mothers of Invention album *Absolutely Free*; Norman Mailer, *Miami and the Siege of Chicago: An Informal History of the American Political Conventions of 1968* (Middlesex: Penguin Books, 1969), 83.
2 *Hair: The American Tribal Love-Rock Musical* began as a 1967 off-Broadway musical and was filmed as *Hair* by Miloš Forman in 1979.
3 The video was directed by Russell Mulcahy and was the first video to be shown on the MTV channel.
4 Hegarty and Halliwell review the suggestion that 1976 can be fingered as the year of transition, from performance (of, in this case, prog rock) to "showbiz"; see Paul Hegarty and Martin Halliwell, *Beyond and Before: Progressive Rock since the 1960s* (London and New York: Continuum, 2011), 131. In keeping with this timeline, Austerlitz argues that the promotion video for Queen's single "Bohemian Rhapsody," shot in late 1975, could be said to inaugurate the music video as it

would come to be known; see Saul Austerlitz, *Money for Nothing: A History of the Music Video from the Beatles to the White Stripes* (London and New York: Continuum, 2007), 25–26.

5 Shapiro charts this process, from the "death" of disco to the anti-disco backlash, and dates the culmination as 1979; see Peter Shapiro, *Turn the Beat Around: The Secret History of Disco* (London: Faber and Faber, 2005), 194, 226.

6 Sheila Whiteley, *Women and Popular Music: Sexuality, Identity and Subjectivity* (London: Routledge, 2000), 27.

7 See Gilles Deleuze and Félix Guattari, *A Thousand Plateaus* (London and New York: Continuum, [1980] 2004).

8 The enormity of the performance, and its persistence in popular memory, was such that Kurt Cobain, in his 1994 suicide note, complained that his dissatisfaction with his rock star status should be understood as his failure to follow the lead of "Freddie Mercury who seemed to love, relish [sic] in the love and adoration from the crowd which is something I totally admire and envy," while Lady Gaga, a stadium performer who established herself in 2010, sports a name that directly references the 1984 Queen single "Radio Ga Ga." Full text: http:// kurtcobainssuicidenote.com/kurt_cobains_suicide_note.html (accessed March 2012).

9 So that "Shakur, dead, became a bigger video celebrity than he had been alive . . . ," Austerlitz, *Money for Nothing*, 103. Plenty of recording artists have since fallen into this category or, even, have enjoyed a commercial career that only began once they had passed away.

10 Austerlitz also notes the "inherent rebuke to the obstinacy of rock snobs who insist on the primacy of the music itself . . ." in the formation of this attitude; see Austerlitz, *Money for Nothing*, 1 and 6 respectively.

11 See Craig Marks and Rob Tannenbaum, *I Want My MTV: The Uncensored Story of the Music Video Revolution* (New York: Dutton, 2011), 16.

12 The group could be said to have been unapologetic in these respects in their own output and the centerpiece of the album from which "Money for Nothing" was taken, 1985's *Brothers in Arms*, looked to the moment of crisis, tragedy, and triumph for questions of the worth of art, utilitarian, metaphysical, and (as the foundation of Western modernism) progressive and contemporary: the coming to terms with the slaughter of the First World War, and an empathy with those whose lives were lost. As if emphasizing the difference between these two singles, the accompanying music video employed a style suggesting animated pencil drawings, in black and white, rather than the garish dayglo and blocky computer animated graphics of "Money for Nothing."

13 Marks and Tannenbaum (2011) frame their oral history of MTV in respect of the idea that the channel's influence was effectively over after the end of the 1980s, as situated between the ascent of Duran Duran (whose videos for "Girls on Film" and "Rio," of 1981 and 1982, set the tone for much of what was to come) and the advent of Nirvana (where "Smells Like Teen Spirit," of 1991, is understood as the return of the repressed; outsiders over the beautiful, and dirgy "indie" music over high-energy corporate pop). However, Marks and Tannenbaum maintain, the persistent longevity of some bands can be related directly to those who were fortunate enough to become popular at the time of (and in part as a result of) the "Golden Age of music videos"; Marks and Tannenbaum, *I Want My MTV*, 17.

14 Phillip Auslander, *Liveness: Performance in a Mediatized Culture* (London and New York: Routledge, 1999). Auslander applied this idea directly to popular music, tracking the ways in which musicality versus image can be seen to play out in the immediate wake of the counterculture and then in the infiltration of radical

sexuality identities into 1970s popular music; see Philip Auslander, *Performing Glam Rock: Gender and Theatricality in Popular Music* (Ann Arbor: University of Michigan Press, 2006).

15 So that to consider Clover's study of the popular music of 1989 (roughly between the poles of grunge and rave) is to realize that much of the latter remains undocumented and so generates a critical approach to its history that can incorporate the British motorway system, entrepreneurialism, and parliamentary legislation; Joshua Clover, *1989: Bob Dylan Didn't Have This to Sing About* (Berkeley, Los Angeles, London: University of California Press, 2009). Mark Leckey's installation film *Fiorucci Made Me Hardcore* (1999) is particularly clear-sighted in respect of the absence of the audience: abstract renderings of the sounds, or the sounds of the sounds, of various musical genres, playing over a selection of found footage of dance events from the 1970s, 1980s, and 1990s. In that rave features prominently in *Fiorucci Made Me Hardcore*, not least in the marked physiological difference of the dancers, the condition of receiving rather than witnessing music becomes uppermost in unifying this patchwork of scenes evidencing the ways in which the experience of popular music had been identity- and subjectivity-forming. For Leckey, DJ culture would seem to be the route away from the consumer-consumption determinations of popular music, returning music to its underground, phenomenological origins, and its religious and ritualistic roots.

16 See Richard Dyer, *Stars* (London: British Film Institute, 1979).

17 See Anthony Burgess, Daniel Angeli, and Jean-Paul Dousset, *Private Pictures* (London: Jonathan Cape, 1980).

18 "Introduction," in ibid., unnumbered.

19 For example: Justin Bieber's *Never Say Never* (John M. Chu, 2009), Michael Jackson's *This Is It* (Keny Ortega, 2009), *Demi Lovato: Stay Strong* (Davi Russo, 2012), and *Katy Perry: Part of Me* (Dan Cutforth and Jane Lipstiz, 2012).

20 In addition to the above mentioned *Shine a Light*, *No Direction Home* (2005) and *George Harrison: Living in the Material World* (2011).

Part 1

Evolutions of the Music Documentary

Chapter 1

Tony Palmer's *All You Need Is Love*

Television's First Pop History

Paul Long and Tim Wall

Introduction

The 2009 re-release of Tony Palmer's *All You Need is Love: The Story of Popular Music*, first broadcast in 1977, allows television scholars the opportunity to reassess the status of this long-neglected documentarist, and for those interested in popular music to consider Palmer's role both in its historiography and representation. Promoted on the DVD as "Tony Palmer's Classic Series," its seventeen parts reproduced the long-form documentary approach of Kenneth Clarke's *Civilisation* (1969) or Alistair Cooke's *America* (1972–1973). Originally broadcast as prime-time commercial television in the UK, and sold to twenty-five countries, it was produced on a "Hollywood-scale" budget, in over forty countries, and the series featured over 300 musicians often in specially filmed performances.

Some reviewers saw the re-released series as a significant televisual and cultural moment, celebrating an "intelligent, adult treatment" of its subject

Figure 1.1 Television's first pop history.

and doubting that such a program would be commissioned today.[1] Others saw the series as "laughably off the mark" in seeing various international rock artists as being the future of popular music, dismissing disco, and missing out on the then emergence of punk.[2] Such evaluations are set in the context of a contemporary glut of programming on popular music and with the benefit of hindsight. Most importantly, none evaluate this ambitious and informed sweep of pop's past at a time when print histories of pop were only just emerging and television producers were first grappling with how to make long-form cultural histories.

In what follows, then, we first investigate Palmer's approach through the prism of the concluding scenes of the final episode of the series. We position him as pop television's first *auteur*, and examine the distinctive techniques of narrative and narration within this documentary series. Finally, we try to discern Palmer's core thesis on the organization of music culture in relation to art, to popularity, and to black culture.

Predicting the Future

All You Need is Love was first broadcast from February to June 1977, exactly mirroring the celebrations for the Queen's Silver Jubilee and the zenith of an attendant moral panic about punk focused around The Sex Pistols' release of "God Save the Queen." This conjunction reminds us that the most striking absence of *All You Need is Love* is the developed notion, common in Palmer's earlier work, that "pop" holds a revolutionary potential to critique the status quo. The importance of the emergence of punk as music and cultural revolution within post-1977 popular music histories, established in academic work by Dick Hebdige and Dave Laing,[3] is the basis of the common critique of the series; that it is flawed for missing this major event. This is acutely evident in the final episode. Engaging with Palmer's treatise with something approaching the "condescension of posterity,"[4] Bob Stanley, for instance, asserts:

> Disco is dismissed in less than a sentence. Kraftwerk are ignored in favor of Tangerine Dream. As for the rest (Black Oak Arkansas, Stomu Yamash'ta, Baker Gurvitz Army), it only seems proper to point out that hindsight is a fine thing. The series ends with a century of music flashing before our eyes to the soundtrack of Mike Oldfield's Ommadawn. When it was first broadcast, the Sex Pistols were simultaneously trashing their record label's offices, and pop was reborn.[5]

This notion that Palmer was in error to think that Oldfield epitomized the culmination of pop's history while it was being reborn elsewhere needs some interrogation itself. This is particularly important given that subsequent histories see the artists Palmer championed as the very ones that punk displaced. However, we want to argue that such critiques both misunderstand pop history, its televisation and how Palmer's series actually works as a meaningful text.

It is possible to construct a convincing argument that it is Palmer who understood the fundamentals of pop's development far better than his recent critics. If one looks beyond the now long-forgotten artists with whom Palmer was enamored, we are presented with a set of themes that convincingly anticipate the characteristics of twenty-first-century pop. These include the sorts of postconsumerist, collective, sustainable lifestyle music that is celebrated each year at the UK's Glastonbury festival,[6] set side-by-side with pop as a producer's medium, slickly devised with scientific accuracy in studio technologies. Palmer establishes these themes and then juxtaposes them as an assertion of pop's paradoxical and manufactured character. Highly abstract, often "symphonic," popular music is contrasted with highly personal styles, and stadium success is set against intimate retreat that, in turn, is placed aside the scale and majesty of nature. The last episode in particular highlights threads of music making which were to dominate popular music in a way punk never did. The numerous references to fusions of rock, folk, and "world music" now seem prescient, and while Palmer presents synthesizer-based, programmatic music as the product of the Muzak corporation and the Jingle Factory, as we now know, this method of music making became the basis of most post-1977 popular music genres from disco, electropop, rave, through to drum and bass, gabber and chill-out.

In this final episode these themes are personified in Mike Oldfield as a musician/composer/studio-manipulator producing a folk/world/rock hybrid using multitracked, postsong, programmatic structures. In the closing sequence

Figure 1.2 Excerpts from the final sequence of *All You Need is Love.*

Figure 1.3 Excerpts from the final sequence of *All You Need is Love*.

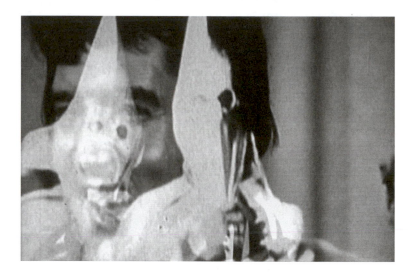

Figure 1.4 Excerpts from the final sequence of *All You Need is Love*.

of the series highlighted by Stanley, the full gallery of personalities from pop's past rush towards this present with increasing velocity, their images edited to the climax of Oldfield's "Ommadawn." The moment is then frozen as Oldfield looks out into the wild openness of the future of music like the wanderer of Friedrich Caspar David's Romantic painting[7] and we return to his studio as he contemplates the very smallest of additions to his multitracked masterpiece.

Figure 1.5 Excerpts from the final sequence of *All You Need is Love.*

Figure 1.6 Excerpts from the final sequence of *All You Need is Love.*

We do not present this argument to prove Palmer could predict the future, but to point out that the importance of *All You Need is Love* lies less in *who* he chose to represent, or in *how* successful he was in identifying pivotal moments in popular music history, but *how* he represents and engages us in the work of musicians as music makers and cultural agents. Palmer does not present a simple socially contextualized narrative of pop's breakthrough moments, and he certainly did not rely on consensus histories of pop, mainly because so few were available. Instead, he drew on approaches to documenting culture that he had established in his earlier work with more elite forms of art culture. As we discuss in more detail below, he also produced programs, which explore the potential of television as an agent of document, of investigation, and of intellectual engagement. At the same time, though, for all his interests in the genealogies of pop, we will argue that his central theses relied on received notions of cultural hierarchy which he applied to popular music, rather than comprehending pop on its own terms.

Treating Popular Music Seriously

The recent appearance of two studies of Palmer paradoxically serves to draw attention to the fact that this director's work has gone relatively unregarded in popular music historiography. In John C. Tibbetts' exhaustive appreciation, *All You Need is Love* is identified as one of Palmer's crowning achievements,[8] while Alison Huber has suggestively interpreted the series as an essay on memory.[9] Nonetheless, the long ignorance of Palmer is curious given that he produced some of the landmark moments in popular music programming over the course of a decade. These include: *All My Loving* (1968); *Cream "Farewell Concert"* (1968); *Rope Ladder to the Moon—Jack Bruce* (1969); *Fairport Convention & Colosseum* (1970); *200 Motels—Frank Zappa* (1971); *Ginger Baker in Africa* (1971); *Bird on a Wire—with Leonard Cohen* (1972); *Rory Gallagher—Irish Tour* (1974); *Tangerine Dream—Live in Coventry Cathedral* (1975); *All You Need is Love* (1976); *The Wigan Casino* (1977).

Palmer's first documentaries, mentored by Huw Wheldon for the BBC's *Monitor* (1958–1965) arts strand, were concerned with high art subjects such as Georg Solti and Benjamin Britten. He also gained contemporary renown as popular music critic for the UK's *Observer* from 1967 to 1974. His work offers an important resource for any examination of the representation and historicization of popular music. Palmer was instrumental in developing a serious critical appraisal of pop. His 1968 *Observer* review of *The Beatles* ("The White Album") insisted that "Lennon and McCartney are the greatest songwriters since Schubert," an appreciation reproduced on the sleeve of the soundtrack album of *Yellow Submarine*. This commitment was translated into his television work with *All My Loving* (1968), a film which exhibited a range of stylistic tropes established in his treatment of high art subjects for *Monitor* and which inform *All You Need is Love*. Palmer's position on popular music in 1968 was singular enough to warrant this contemporary evaluation from Tim Souster who suggested that the filmmaker-journalist was one:

> who on the strength of a moderately successful film (success of course was inherent in its subject-matter) and of some pretentious writing in the *Observer*, has been endowed with a certain "authority." For him, Pink Floyd outdo Cardew and Stockhausen in "modernity," and even The

Who's "Magic Bus" (an inferior reworking of their brilliant "Talking About My Generation") puts Stravinsky's *Symphony in Three Movements* in the shade.[10]

To label *All My Loving* 'moderately successful' is to underestimate its impact and originality. Far removed from the simple magazine format or record of performance of pop on television then dominant, Palmer took an exploratory approach to its subject. The approach was deemed to be controversial enough that broadcast was delayed several times before going out *after* the late-night "Epilogue" which signaled the end of the evening's transmission on BBC television in those days.[11] In the film, extended performances from Jimi Hendrix and Eric Burdon were intercut with interviews with musicians and industry insiders. Patrick Allen's narration posed abstract questions, not all related to the music on display, and "pop" was interleaved with footage of the Nazi death camps and contemporary atrocities. In this way, Palmer played with form and meaning in order to underline the serious way in which he treated his subject matter.

This allusive, provocative, and exploratory approach informed the style of *All You Need is Love* when filming began eight years later. Palmer once more asserted that his motivation was to take pop music seriously, arguing that "what it really means is a kind of unconscious outpouring of what it means to be alive at a particular time. When people want to know what it meant to be alive in 1965, they'll listen to The Beatles."[12]

Figure 1.7 Original footage of Paul McCartney represents the link back from 1977 to the classic Beatles era in 1965.

While the textual form is far from conventional or didactic, this series was a significant event for the UK commercial television network that commissioned it and the major record corporations, Polygram and EMI, that underwrote its production. The series was previewed extensively and hyperbolically in the ITV listings magazine *TV Times* where Cordell Marks suggested that it was "the greatest musical show ever staged on TV. It has a starring cast of hundreds and is littered with famous faces."[13] Such claims were supported by details about the £2m budget.[14] Viewed from today this looks like the indulgence and ambition of a long-lost era of broadcasting in which Palmer was authorized to follow bands on tour across the United States, making a diversion to the Sahara in order to check a theory about banjos or to Northern Ireland to film an "IRA folk singer." This investment was underwritten by the kudos of Palmer's own status as a champion of popular music and the value of his connections in the industry, citing John Lennon as a prompt for the endeavor.[15] Ultimately promoted as a documentary series that could seriously compare to the great televisual moments of British public service television, its Saturday night scheduling was another vote of faith in the series. At the time much was made of the originality and seriousness of Palmer's approach. The director was quoted extensively, outlining the breadth of his ambition to cover "jazz, swing, rock 'n' roll, folk, pop, music-hall. All of it."[16]

This was television, then, that was conceived firmly within a public service remit as a historical project that would document contemporary events and locate and rescue neglected archival material. At least 300 minutes of new musical performances were specially shot and at least a quarter of the series material came from archives, much of it not previously seen on television and some of it completely unknown. Footage of Charlie Parker was found beneath a bed, while film of Woody Guthrie came to light despite family fears that he had never been recorded in this medium. The archival values of the production shoot, as well as material unearthed, preserved and disseminated by its researchers, was a vital historical endeavor as some of the key figures featured in the series died during the time of its making, while some of the significant locations visited and recorded—Beale St, Memphis, for instance—were changed beyond recognition during the production period.

Thesis and Form

We suggest that *All You Need Is Love* can be thought of as a modernist totalizing project to understand its object "in the round" and aimed at placing contemporary music in a sociohistorical continuum, and to insist on its order and significance. Although Palmer has stated that he wanted to avoid a simple chronology,[17] his account is still organized as a temporal examination of the essence of pop as culture. Episodes thus pore over ragtime, jazz, blues, music hall, pop, musicals, swing, R&B, country, and folk revivals. Of equal note, though, is the way that Palmer deviates from the approach apparent in the first written analyses of popular music which were circulating at the time, which tended to locate rock and roll as the pivot on which pop history turned.[18] Even though he had previously championed late sixties and early seventies rock, only four of the seventeen episodes look at these forms, although The Beatles do get an episode to themselves after the birth of rock and roll is investigated, and before more commercial forms are analyzed.

In fact The Beatles are a pervasive reference point: as well as their own episode, one of their songs gives the series its title; the melody of that song is the theme tune; the logo iconically links us to the moustachioed version of the band circa Sergeant Pepper; Paul McCartney is the first person we see in the first episode and when they appear in the roll call they are presented as if they need no introduction. Of course the USA is also an omnipresent idea: its flag is the other half of the logo, all but the final episodes are primarily based on American artists and, while the theme tune melody of "All You Need is Love" signals that this investigation is rooted in a canon of then contemporary rock, it is played by a trad jazz band as an index of popular music's origins and a symbol of its American-ness. Palmer begins the book that accompanied the series with the proposal that "popular music is a paradigm of American culture."[19] He opens the series with a list of American artists and names of American cities, and presents the programs as a guided tour of popular music, both in its temporal and geographic specificities.

Figure 1.8 The *All You Need is Love* logo.

Even though Palmer was a newspaper popular music critic, it is interesting that he does not foreground himself as an expert in the way that Kenneth Clark did in *Civilisation*; he is certainly not "present" as a figure in the diegesis itself. As he explains in the accompanying book, he commissioned a series of essays on which to base the programs using a series of themes he judged to be important.[20] The existence of these diverse essays is often used to suggest that the programs themselves, and the series as a whole, "[lack] a clear narrative, and often [end] up a muddle of music, message, and meaning."[21] However, these were not used as scripts for the episodes, and though Palmer sometimes used the authors as interviewees and even, in the case of Rudi Blesh, he is one of the narrating voices, the essays, in Palmer's own words "gave me opinions with which to disagree."[22] His chosen authors were a mixture of academics, serious journalists, and participants in the events being documented. They often represented some of the key writers on popular music at the time, but not necessarily on the subjects one would expect. Blesh wrote the ragtime episode when he was best known at that time for his study of jazz (a subject allocated to George Melly and Leonard Feather) while strangely, Humphrey Lyttleton was commissioned to write about swing. More conventionally, music hall was covered by David Cheshire, Tin Pan Alley by Ian Whitcomb, and musicals by Stephen Sondheim. Essays on more recent musical styles and moments were covered by Jack Good, Nik Cohn, and Charlie Gillett.

In spite of those complaints that the series lacks coherence there is in fact a remarkable consistency of thesis and a commitment to an innovative form of narration that is notably absent in recent attempts to tell pop's story.[23] While some of the tropes used by Palmer to organize the massive assembly of visual and auditory material were mainstays of western Romantic art discourse,

Figure 1.9 Rudi Blesh narrates the ragtime episode of *All You Need Is Love*.

and are still commonly used to present pop music to this day,[24] others were striking at their time, and while they are often to be found in more recent pop documentary, they appear fresh and insightful in *All You Need Is Love*.

Strongest, perhaps, is the idea that artistry and commerciality are in some form of opposition. Of course such an approach remains common in pop documentaries, with one relatively recent examination of *Pop Britannia* building a whole narrative on the idea that "British pop has been locked in a constant struggle between the forces of art and commerce . . . [that] fuelled and crippled our pop artists."[25] For Palmer these discursive poles form pop's fundamental paradox: "the more it is musical the less it is popular; the more it is popular, the less it is musical."[26] On screen, popular music is revealed to be at its best when it is involved in a direct address to its audience and when it catches its own historical "moment" and its own sense of place.

More novel was Palmer's take on the relationship between black music and a wider definition of popular music. Again, while his earlier investigations of contemporary pop had been focused entirely on white rock artists, the first four episodes of *All You Need Is Love* establish the origins of popular music in African-American forms of gospel, ragtime, jazz, and blues, and black artists are given significant positions in the episodes on swing, R&B, and rock and roll. Here the series thesis is that as black music "crosses over" from black to white culture it often loses its ability to address us directly and falls into the trap of seeking commercial over artistic objectives. However, Palmer's strident take on jazz and blues in this way was particularly problematic for some commentators. In a damning review of his book of the same name, one reviewer described it as "a tasteless mess of misinformation, crass judgments, clichés, and ill-digested facts, not to mention plagiarism."[27] Here, Palmer was perhaps more driven by his thesis than detailed attention to history. It is further notable that this reverence for historic black musical forms is not repeated in the music closer to the 1970s. Significant artists like LaBelle, Bob Marley and the Wailers, and Fela Kuti are presented amidst a study of a hypercommercial pop music, grouped with artists like Gary Glitter and The Osmonds. This approach can be understood in the context of Palmer's sense of cultural modernity and an overarching progressive vision of improvement and achievement. While black music may have ultimately failed to avoid the pitfalls of commercial debasement, the narrative of the program tells us, it is artists like The Beatles who have reached the apogee of artistic achievement and can be compared with giants of the classical tradition.

This emphasis on the romantic narrative of artistic perfection also explains the relatively superficial manner in which the commerciality of popular music is treated, limiting Palmer's concept of what such forms might mean outside of his template of critical assessment. It is ironic that in the *All You Need Is Love* book Palmer's thesis on the incompatibility of art and commerce is preceded by thanks to EMI and Polygram for a "unique and I hope fruitful partnership."[28] Although the final episode reveals some interesting things

Figure 1.10 LaBelle, categorized as glitter rock.

about the production and design of music in the Muzak Corporation and Jingle Factory, they function to connect the commercialization of popular music to the industrial system, and are contrasted directly with the reflective and natural artistry of Mike Oldfield, even though the latter uses much the same equipment and techniques to construct his music. As in the discourse of many critics and consumers, the industrialized and capitalistic basis of popular music production can be held at bay in order to selectively determine modes of artistic authenticity and integrity.

Most striking for modern viewers perhaps is Palmer's approach to narrative and narration. As we note in the introduction, the critical engagement with the DVD release and rebroadcast often struggled with the language and rhetoric that the text deploys in pursuit of the intention to take popular music seriously. While journalist Zeth Lundy asserts in his review that "the series' potential as a watchable mess slowly devolves into a plain ol' mess with diminishing returns,"[29] similar complaints were apparent in reviews of the series' original broadcast. *Times* reviewer Stanley Reynolds noted that the seventh program, "Diamonds as Big as the Ritz," offered "a reference to the Scott Fitzgerald short story which did not appear to have much bearing here" and that "the roots of the modern musical were traced in a sloppy fashion."[30] Likewise a *New York Times* reviewer felt that "major figures are never identified clearly" and that the program's approach was thought to be potentially off-putting to viewers unfamiliar with the subject.[31]

To others, Palmer's exploratory approach was an apposite one for a subject whose complexity was often under-appreciated, if not wholly denied as the domain of ephemeral, superficiality, undeserving of serious consideration. In accord with those artists who suggested that they articulated themselves best in their playing, when discussing *All My Loving*, Horace Hudson cites Palmer as suggesting that the form of his work should be understood in total, and that "if he could describe it in words he would not have bothered to make a film."[32] In fact, Palmer's visual style in dealing with his subjects from pop, seen in performance or framed in repose or in interview, was a consistent feature of his oeuvre and which drew more or less comment depending upon how deserving of such challenging treatment the subject was. His explorations of various high cultural figures and modernist innovators such as Le Corbusier and Benjamin Britten had made an international impact, and it is productive to contextualize his pop documentaries from *All My Loving* on amidst this work. Typically his aestheticization avoids a didactic "zero-degree" style and effaces a habitual and conventional narrative realism or omniscience.

In one riposte to criticisms of his earliest aesthetic experimentation, dismissed as gimmickry by one correspondent to the *Radio Times*, Palmer suggested that:

> Pop music on television is disastrous if treated like a third-rate wallpaper sound or as some vulgar commercial, sing-along noise. The best of pop has rather more to offer in musical achievement, youthful energy, and visual excitement. The TV director tries to interpret this excitement. We make mistakes but also have our triumphs, and surely you would not have us give up trying.[33]

It is worth picking up two examples as a way of summarizing the distinctive form that *All You Need Is Love* takes. Firstly, episodes are characterized by an openness of narrative and narration. In particular there is a tendency to allow subjects to speak for themselves. We do not mean to suggest that Palmer makes no arguments of his own, but rather, episodes offer elaborated spaces in which milieu and performance are allowed to appear for leisurely consideration and reflection. Each episode of *All You Need is Love* features sequences in which artists perform in extended sequences recorded especially for the camera.

Secondly, Palmer uses counterpoint to set up an ambivalent space for reflection rather than offering consistent conclusion or coherent thesis. Thus, while he may allow his assembly of authorities and witnesses space to explore their own historical analysis and anecdote, or to expound upon their own critical perspective, he often undermines them by counterposing sequences that challenge rather than affirm what we are hearing and seeing. This is particularly notable for instance in a number of ways in the penultimate episode which deals with glam rock. Key to the narrative here is *Creem* editor Lester Bangs who effectively pronounces on the death of popular music, elaborating on its depthlessness and lack of originality. This is reinforced through the Kubrick-esque contrapuntal use of classical music. Showing the

Figure 1.11 Images from Alice Cooper's live act, screened to the audio of Berlioz's Symphony Fantastique.

mock execution of Alice Cooper in his live act, the sound of the performance is replaced with Berlioz's Symphony Fantastique, as if to affirm a comment from Bangs on the contemporary and superficial "Sturm und Drang" of musical performance. Bang's further comments about exposing the sham of rock as rebellion seem to be illustrated by an extended sequence of the egregious Gary Glitter and his band miming (the only such sequence in the series) to his hit "Rock and Roll (Part 1)." However, Palmer then shows rather convincing performances by LaBelle and Bob Marley, which we are invited to see as repetitions of the absurdity of Glitter's glam rock. Notwithstanding personal taste and the perspective of thirty years' distance, it is not clear if this is an affirmation or undermining of Bang's thesis.

Conclusions

This chapter continues our ongoing project to consider the ways in which the histories of popular music are narrativized, how the medium treats the discourses of popular music, and deals with this domain as history. In this context we recognize Palmer as a filmmaker whose work and contribution to arts television are long overdue for serious evaluation. Perhaps because *All You Need is Love* predates the print-based totalizing histories that followed, this series generally avoids an over-reliance on narratives of disruption. As interesting is the equal avoidance of an over-emphasis on the idea of musical roots which had dominated the earlier generation of popular music analysis. However, he does consistently deploy contrasts of margins and mainstream

Figure 1.12 The closing credits signal Tony Palmer as pop television's first auteur over an image of Mike Oldfield.

that are common in most pop histories, and which are particularly important for his romantic sense of pop as popular voice and individual genius.[34]

A major reservation overall is that, while the series deployed a new and relatively experimental televisual language to investigate and promote thought about popular music, the documentary text Palmer produced does not actually seem fully to understand the popular cultural practices in which it grew, and instead wants to evaluate and so judge popular music on the terms of high art. Nevertheless, both *All You Need is Love* and Palmer's larger body of popular music documentary need more critical attention. This chapter has only tentatively raised his innovation as a filmmaker, the substantial archive of carefully mediated music performances he created, and the interest in documentary work as a form of archaeology and genealogy.

Perhaps the most important contribution of this documentary series is its insistence that we seriously consider the past of pop, and the ideas it offers up to document and discuss what that past means. Here Palmer seems interested in asking questions, while more recent television histories seem more committed to reiterating an already presented answer. If Palmer was investigating how to document pop's past, too many present-day documentary makers are convinced they have the formula for a successful history. If nothing else, attention to his work asks us to radically rethink whether we have.

Notes

1 David Stubbs, "Pick of the Day: *All You Need Is Love*," *The Guide*, *The Guardian*, (July 19, 2008), 95.

2 Zeth Lundy, "*All You Need Is Love*," *PopMatters* (July 22, 2008). Online at www.popmatters.com (accessed May 2012). Bob Stanley, "The Greatest Story Never Told," *Guardian* (May 1, 2008): 23.

3 Dick Hebdige, *Subculture: The Meaning of Style* (London: Routledge, 1979); Dave Laing, *One Chord Wonders: Power and Meaning in Punk Rock* (Milton Keynes, England: Open University Press, 1985).

4 E. P. Thompson, *The Making of the English Working Class* (London: Gollancz, 1963).

5 Stanley, "The Greatest Story Never Told," 23.

6 The Glastonbury Festival of Contemporary Performing Arts is an annual UK event rooted in the free music festival movement of the 1970s, and instructs revelers whilst at Glastonbury Festival to "forget all instructions (as long as doing so involves hurting no-one) and ENJOY!" See http://www.glastonburyfestivals.co.uk/ (accessed May 24, 2012).

7 Friedrich Caspar David's 1818 painting *Der Wanderer über dem Nebelmeer* ("Wanderer above a Sea of Mist").

8 John C. Tibbetts, *All My Loving: The Films of Tony Palmer* (Houghton-le-Spring, Tyne-and-Wear: Gonzo Distributions, 2011), 169–204.

9 Alison Huber, "Remembering Popular Music, Documentary Style: Tony Palmer's History in *All You Need Is Love*," *Television & New Media* 12, No. 6 (2011), 513–530.

10 Tim Souster, "Notes on Pop Music," *Tempo* No. 87 (Winter 1968–1969), 2–6.

11 Tibbetts, *All My Loving*, 63.

12 Blaik Kirby, "Immortality of the Pop Artist: Three Hundred Lined up to Hear John [*sic*] Palmer's Message," *The Globe and Mail* (Canada) (January 26, 1978). Online at www.theglobeandmail.com (accessed May 24, 2012).

13 Cordell Marks, "They All Played a Part . . .," *TV Times* (February 12–18, 1977), 5–7.

14 The average Hollywood film budget by 1978 was around $5m, or £2.5m. See online at http://www.filmsite.org/70sintro.html com (accessed May 24, 2012).

15 Quoted in Bernard Perusse, "Labour of Love Lives Again; Lennon Collaborated on History of Pop Music, Now on DVD," *Arts and Life, Ottawa Citizen* (21 June, 2008), F4.

16 Marks, "They All Played a Part . . .," 6.

17 Tony Palmer, *All You Need Is Love: The Story of Popular Music* (New York: Grossman Publishers, 1976).

18 Charlie Gillett, *The Sound of the City* (London: Sphere, 1971); Greil Marcus, *Mystery Train: Images of America in Rock 'n' Roll Music* (New York: E. P. Dutton, 1975).

19 Ibid., 15.

20 Ibid., 12.

21 Lundy, "*All You Need Is Love*."

22 Palmer, *All You Need Is Love*, 12.

23 For a contrast see Paul Long and Tim Wall, "Constructing the Histories of Popular Music" in Ian Inglis (ed.), *Popular Music and Television in Britain* (Farnham: Ashgate, 2010), 11–26.

24 Palmer's choice of individualist producers and artists is most recently echoed in Richard King, *How Soon Is Now?: The Madmen and Mavericks Who Made Independent Music 1975–2005* (London: Faber and Faber, 2012).

25 BBC, "*Pop Britannia*: Episode Guide." See online at http://www.bbc.co.uk/musictv/popbritannia/episodes/ com (accessed May 24, 2012).

26 Palmer, *All You Need Is Love*, 15.

27 Stanley Dance, "Journal Reviews," *Music Journal* 35, No.4 (1977), 36.
28 Palmer, *All You Need Is Love*, 13.
29 Lundy, *"All You Need Is Love,"* 2008.
30 Stanley Reynolds, "Weekend Television," *The Times* (April 4, 1977), 11.
31 John O'Connor, "TV: Historys [sic] Focus on Popular Music," *The New York Times* (July 22, 1980), 19.
32 Hudson Horace, *"All My Loving,"* *Radio Times* (October 31, 1968), 34–35.
33 Tony Palmer, "Points from the Post," *Radio Times* (October 3, 1968), 62.
34 See Tim Wall, *Studying Popular Music Culture* (London: Sage, 2012) for a discussion of these tropes.

Chapter 2

Retrospective Compilations
(Re)defining the Music Documentary

Michael Saffle

Scholars disagree about what documentaries are or should be. As Matthew Bernstein observes, any given documentary may be accepted (or rejected) "in terms of its formal features, its assumptions about the construction of knowledge, its approach to narration, its assertions of authority, the expectations it evokes in the audience—or all of the above."[1] Occasionally, music documentaries are categorized entirely on the basis of their musical genres and delivery platforms—with anything about jazz available in digital format separated, for example, from anything originally distributed via television or film.[2] The following discussion evaluates existing and hypothetical music documentaries primarily in terms of accessibility, authenticity, film history, media issues, musical styles, and political–social–cultural goals ranging from avant-garde experimentation to postmodern infotainment.

Defining Music Documentaries I: Essential Attributes and Exceptional Examples

Whatever else they may be, all film documentaries are retrospective. Television and the internet are able to broadcast live news reports and radar weather images, but full-length movies, long-term TV programming, and digital recordings have to be planned, shot, and edited before being distributed.[3] Jack Ellis includes "production method and technique" as one of five ways in which documentaries "are distinct from other film types."[4] Furthermore, almost all documentaries are compiled from various sources, with each documentary representing its compiler's "purpose/point of view/approach."[5] At first glance concert films would seem to be exceptions, in that they present performative material in something like uncut form. Ellis considers *Stop Making Sense* (Jonathan Demme, 1985) a documentary, even though it consists of nothing more than a "straightforward recording of a dazzling stage performance" by Talking Heads.[6] Nevertheless, *Stop Making Sense* is subjective as well as retrospective: it embodies its director's point of view as well as his production methods and techniques.

In spite of tremendous interest in documentaries of other kinds, music documentaries have received little attention from critics and teachers, including those interested in "Marxist critical theory, feminist theory, and literary criticism" as well as efforts "directed at defamiliarization, demystification, denaturalization—i.e. the critical project of deconstructing the cultural mechanisms of hegemony in support of a dominant ideology."[7] Certainly many contemporary documentaries "interrogate the more traditional depiction of the truth as stable, objective, and knowable, even suggesting that identity itself is shifting and fragmentary."[8] At the same time, the performers and performances they depict do not necessarily challenge the "mechanisms of hegemony."[9] Student-made documentaries, for example, often focus on performers eager to advertise themselves. Music sells, of course, and films sell music. Even classical music has been marketed through film,[10] and many pop-music documentaries are manufactured in order to market the artists they foreground.

Most music documentaries differ from their political and social counterparts in terms of contemporaneity. Some of them include interviews with living performers as well as recordings of recent performances. *Woodstock* (Michael Wadleigh, 1970) reported on what, at the time of its release, was still a newsworthy event: the "Woodstock Music and Art Fair" held in August 1969 in Bethel, New York. The event was politically (counter-) cultural as well as musical, and its legacy includes at least one lengthy oral history.[11] Furthermore, the filmmaking process featured hand-held camera shots, split-screen photography, and other techniques associated with "candid filmmaking," progressive cinema, and the avant-garde.[12]

Other music documentaries, however, are deliberately, even self-consciously retrospective. *This is Elvis* (Andrew Solt and Malcolm Leo, 1981) was released four years after Elvis Presley's death. Solt's and Leo's film, which contains clips from Presley's appearances on *The Ed Sullivan Show* (1956–1957) as well as *Blue Hawaii* (Norman Taurog, 1961), *Viva Las Vegas* (George Sidney, 1964), and *Elvis* (Steve Binder, 1968; the so-called "Singer Special"), also contains re-enactments, thereby conflating fiction with fact. *Jazz* (Ken Burns, 2000–2001), a ten-part television series, is and was unusually retrospective. More than a few critics felt it emphasized "the distant past at the almost complete exclusion of the present,"[13] because Burns devoted nine of ten episodes to pre-1960s material and just one to the following fifty years.[14] In this respect, and in Burns's use of a very few narrators to tell the story of a complex art form, *Jazz* was less concerned with recent or on-going "reality" than "device[s] or format[s] conjured up by the producers" for their own purposes.[15]

Still other music documentaries conflate recent and retrospective sources and assessments. *All You Need is Love* (Tony Palmer, 1977) traces the history of rock from its origins to the present (i.e. the mid-1970s). In Chapter 1 of the present volume, Paul Long and Tim Wall describe *All You Need is Love* as a serious contribution to the historiography of pop. The 1994 and 2009 rereleases of *Woodstock* (re)presented it to its audiences simultaneously as a nostalgic memorial as well as a masterpiece of reportage. The 1994 director's cut, subtitled "3 Days of Peace & Music," includes an additional forty minutes of performances by Jimi Hendrix, Janis Joplin, and other artists as well as a list of "Woodstock Generation" dead, including Hendrix, Joplin, John Lennon, and Martin Luther King, Jr. The remastered "40th Anniversary" edition provides an additional two hours of material, including footage of five performers and groups omitted from the original release: Paul Butterfield, Creedence Clearwater Revival, The Grateful Dead, Johnny Winter, and Mountain.

Woodstock serves as an example of a remade documentary and, in its later iterations, of a retrospective compilation. Furthermore, every version of *Woodstock* contains footage of the photographers and interviewers at work, thereby documenting its own production methods and point of view. In these respects it is simultaneously informative and entertaining, authentic and self-consciously arch. *The Last Waltz* (Martin Scorsese, 1978) is another documentary Ellis considers "worthy of mention," even though its widespread appeal distinguishes it from many of the naturalist/anthropological, newsreel-like, propagandistic, and/or avant-garde films he also cites—all of them devoted to quite different subjects.[16]

Hollywood's Retrospective Musical Compilations

Of special interest to students of art music, jazz, and pre-rock pop of other kinds, as well as to aficionados of Hollywood's "Golden Age," are movies about musical performers and performances from days gone by. In most feature films, of course, entertainment is foregrounded, although naturalist scenes, newsreel (or newsreel-like) footage, and propaganda may also appear. At the same time, Hollywood-manufactured musical material, much (but not all) of it originally released during the 1930s, 1940s, and early 1950s, provides a great deal of information about movie making as well as music itself and the culture that surrounded it. Extant filmed performances range in character from Bill "Bojangles" Robinson's staircase routine with Shirley Temple in *The Little Colonel* (David Butler, 1935), to appearances by Louis Armstrong and Billie Holiday in *New Orleans* (Arthur Lubin, 1947), to Leopold Stokowski's backlit podium presence in *Fantasia* (Walt Disney Studios, 1940).

Golden-Age Hollywood, however, produced almost no music documentaries. The closest the major studios came, at least in terms of art music, was *Carnegie Hall* (Edgar G. Ulmer, 1947), a fictionalized account of a mother who wants her son to become a great composer, complete with appearances by Jascha Heifetz, Jan Peerce, Ezio Pinza, and Stokowski.

Older documentaries were devoted to a few classical stars, including conductor Arturo Toscanini. *Hymn to the Nations*, which featured Toscanini's

Figure 2.1 Stokowski as master conductor. From *Carnegie Hall* (Edgar G. Ulmer, 1947).

1944 performance of Giuseppe Verdi's eponymous anthem, was distributed by the Office of War Information and helped wrap the conductor "in the [American] flag" insofar as his patriotic reputation was concerned.[17] Much later, footage drawn from these and other films reappeared in documentaries about individual musical stars. Louis Armstrong, for example, makes posthumous appearances in Burns's *Jazz*. Clips from *Carnegie Hall* have been used in several classroom compilations, including *The Art of Conducting*.[18] Toscanini's *Hymn* performance became part of a longer documentary narrated by James Levine.[19] More recently, other conductors have been honored with documentaries of their own. Consider Herbert von Karajan, whose career was encapsulated in a film one critic called "beautiful" and praised for spelling out "in precise detail . . . how [art] musicians came to terms with the rapidly developing mediums of film and television in the mid-twentieth century."[20]

In 1974 Metro-Goldwyn-Mayer celebrated its fiftieth anniversary with a spectacular retrospective compilation entitled *That's Entertainment!* (hereafter *Entertainment I*).[21] Compiled by Jack Haley, Jr., this full-length film consists of song and dance numbers drawn from dozens of "classic" MGM movies as well as back-lit shots and interviews with some of the stars (then middle-aged or older): Gene Kelly, Mickey Rooney, and Frank Sinatra, among others. To this day *Entertainment I* remains among the most commercially successful music documentaries. *That's Entertainment Part II* (Gene Keller, 1976) appeared just two years later and, like its predecessor, featured Kelly and Fred Astaire as co-hosts. Additional sequels of sorts have included *That's Dancing!* (Jack Haley, Jr., 1985), *That's Black Entertainment* (William Greaves and G. William Jones, 1990), and *That's Entertainment! III* (Bud Friegden and Michael J. Sheridan, 1994). *Entertainment III!* made up for its predecessors' relentless exploitation of golden-oldies moments by presenting less familiar and/or more daring film clips and interviews, including observations on racism by Lena Horne and an excerpt from *Jailhouse Rock* (Richard Thorpe, 1957).[22] In somewhat similar fashion, *Festival Express* (Bob Smeaton, 2003) conflates footage of several rock ensembles on the road in 1970s Canada with much more recent interviews.

Defining Music Documentaries II: Media, Functions, Accessibility, Intentionality, Musical Styles, and Source Materials

Entertainment I and its various sequels and spinoffs raise interesting issues about what (music) documentaries are or should be, which materials are appropriate, and what place(s) music documentaries may find for themselves among increasingly specialized and savvy audiences. One issue is medium; a second, closely related to it, is function. As Mervyn Cooke explains, 1930s and 1940s documentary films "fulfilled both didactic and entertaining functions—and, in times of war, totalitarianism or national crisis, often served as powerful propaganda aimed at a captive spectatorship."[23] Music has often been employed in film documentaries,[24] but until recently it was rarely employed in commercial productions. Instead—armed "with utopian illusions" of totally transforming American taste—radio broadcasts, classroom instruction, and volumes ranging from college textbooks to trade publications like B. H. Haggin's *Music for the Man who Enjoys Hamlet* more often provided instruction as well as diversion from the 1920s to the 1950s.[25] *Fantasia*, often cited as an exceptionally educational film, was all about entertainment. Even the "lack of musical knowledge among Disney's creative staff was touted as evidence that the 'average listener should be much less humble about his ability to understand good music.'"[26]

Then, during the 1950s, "television established itself as the ideal medium for disseminating factual and current-affairs programs."[27] *Victory at Sea* (Henry Salomon, 1952–1953) was one of the first and most important historical and instructional documentary series American families watched in their own living-rooms.[28] *Victory at Sea* wasn't a music documentary, but Richard Rodgers' and Robert Russell Bennett's score remains famous, and many people today still listen to the soundtrack rather than watch the show itself. For them, Rodgers's and Bennett's music retrospectively "documents"—or at least accompanies—images of World War II. Recently, other composers of documentary "background" music have received attention from musicologists and cultural critics.[29]

Another issue is accessibility. Beginning with *Entertainment I*, music documentaries have increasingly drawn upon pre-existing sources of many kinds. Not all pre-existing material is familiar: *Entertainment III!*, for example, featured a production number by Judy Garland cut from *Easter Parade* (Charles Walters, 1948) as well as footage from *The March of Time*, an unfinished 1930 film musical. Furthermore, music documentaries may be entertaining, but with few exceptions—*Woodstock*, for instance, and mockumentaries such as *This is Spinal Tap* (Rob Reiner, 1984) and *A Mighty Wind* (Christopher Guest, 2003)—they appeal primarily to "niche" audiences. Burns's *Jazz*, for example, was "narrowcast" (rather than broadcast) originally by PBS rather than released in theaters. Commercial television networks have never been able to show *Spinal Tap* uncut; it contains far too many "forbidden" words and references.

Still another issue is intentionality. Prior to the 1960s, the word "documentary" often suggested classroom use. It also referred to anthropological and ethnographic "essays," beginning with *Nanook of the North* (Robert J. Flaherty, 1922), one of the first films ever shot on location. Anthropological films are sometimes (mis)understood to include *Mondo Cane* (Paolo Cavara, Franco Prosperi, and Guartiero Jacopetti, 1962) and other faked studies of "primitive" practices.[30] For Walter Goldschmidt, however, the best ethnographic documentaries have endeavored "to *interpret* the behavior of people of one culture to persons of another."[31] *Titicut Follies* (1967) and *High School* (1968), both compiled by Frederick Wiseman, changed all that—at least if we accept the premise that hospital workers, high-school students, and overworked teachers, members of our own culture, represented Wiseman's cultural "others." *Woodstock* and *Gimme Shelter* (Albert and David Maysles, 1970) (re)presented popular music as real-life "folk" spectacle even as they sought political–social authenticity by means of self-conscious *reportage*.

By the early 1970s, lines had been drawn between scientific or quasi-scientific documentary essays, wild and woolly *cinéma-vérité* provocations, and less challenging infotainments. Shortly after, all three kinds of documentaries began borrowing from or confronting each other. Some of the footage in the "Singer Special," for example, seems more immediate than *Woodstock*'s full-length performances, because televised close-ups include audience members and their reactions to Elvis. By the time *Entertainment I* opened in American theaters, *Gimme Shelter* had already become a cult classic and *Woodstock* was losing some of its countercultural appeal. In other words, no one subject, style, or era entirely defined "music documentary" thirty-five years ago. That is still the case today.

The Wicker Man (Robin Hardy, 1973) is an especially complex and controversial example of documentary/folk spectacle/cult-classic/mainstream entertainment. Although altogether fictional, it hints at the anthropological authenticity of *Nanook of the North* (Robert J. Flaherty, 1922). Sgt. Howie, the film's protagonist/victim, is cast as a "fieldworker," and one scholar has found "something genuine" in the film's "ethnographic impact" and "well-researched details."[32] That Hardy's film also conflates horror with local color and musical comedy-like interludes (*Nanook* and many other "salvage documentaries" lack music of any kind) may be irrelevant to its quasi-documentary reputation and character.

To what extent, however, do the MGM *Entertainment* films and other, less controversial retrospective conflations actually *document* music rather than merely (re)package it? Should documentaries be little or nothing more than sight-plus-sound record-keeping, advertisements for ambitious performers? Should they be rough or smooth, shot on site or carefully constructed in the studio? Like the World War II footage in *Victory at Sea*, almost all of MGM's "compilation tapes" were originally filmed for other purposes. Wiseman's and the Maysles' documentaries are *vérité* pastiches, but *Woodstock* is a carefully crafted feature film, "popular" because (or in spite of) its political and social commentary. At the same time, every one of these productions includes more than music. *The Wicker Man*, for example, references accounts of pagan sacrifices written by Julius Caesar and Pliny the Elder.

Nor can individual musical styles, sources, or artists be considered definitive. Palmer, for example, has filmed Frank Zappa *and* Liberace. He has also dealt with classical musicians; his *Wagner* (1983) and *Testimony* (1987)—the latter about Dmitri Shostakovich's controversial career as a Soviet composer—"view music history through the filters of biographical studies."[33] No classical music documentary will probably ever surpass *Entertainment I* in sales, but Leonard Bernstein's televised *Omnibus* (1954–1958) appearances and *Young People's Concerts* broadcasts (1958–1971) made him a household name as late as the 1970s. At the same time, "Lenny's" lectures "were televised not as 'take-home' or 'correspondence' courses," but as upscale entertainment.[34]

Clearly, any assessment of the music documentary needs to take classical, conflated, and posthumous material into account. Nor are classical documentaries quite as scarce as some pop music fans might believe. Consider *Landowska: Uncommon Visionary* (Barbara Attie and Janet Goldwater, 1997): an exploration of the life and influence of Polish harpsichordist Wanda Landowska, who died in 1959. Here we encounter another issue: that of a classical artist who also made a cameo appearance in *Pride and Prejudice* (Robert Z. Leonard, 1940), a mainstream commercial movie. Critics have often preferred authenticity (a difficult word to define) and political/social issues over high art and popular appeal, privileging "film as record" and "the idea— or ideal—of an original unadulterated truth."[35] Acting is scarcely a "record" of everyday life.

Stokowski as Subject for a Hypothetical Retrospective Music Documentary

An intriguing example of an artist-turned-potential documentary subject is Leopold Stokowski (1882–1977). More than a few classical pianists, violinists,

Figure 2.2 Stokowski as Deanna Durbin's pal. From *100 Men and a Girl* (Henry Koster, 1937).

and singers have appeared in films, but mostly as performing musicians. Bernstein, for example, played himself on TV and became known as "a great *musician* at work in a medium that was new."[36] Among celebrated pre-1960s classical artists, only Stokowski and pianist José Iturbi appeared several times both as themselves and as quasi-fictional characters in major Hollywood movies.[37]

Those movie-goers who remember Stokowski at all probably remember him from *Fantasia*. In other films, however, he is a remarkable yet "regular" guy: a genius with a heart and a smile. In *100 Men and a Girl* (Henry Koster, 1937), for example, he not only flirts with Deanna Durbin but also agrees to lead her father's home-made orchestra in a successful concert.

In *The Big Broadcast of 1937* (Mitchell Leisen, 1936), he bends to the masses simply by appearing in a movie featuring such popular co-stars as Benny Goodman, George Burns, and Gracie Allen. Stokowski also speaks: significantly, in order to introduce a new fictional performer—and a jazz musician at that. Finally, Stokowski inspired a gleefully caricatured "classical" eminence in *Long Haired Hare* (Chuck Jones, 1948) and a number of other animated sendups.

These Hollywood images helped make a special star out of Stokowski, one whose portrait once graced the cover of *Time* magazine.[38] The images are even "true" insofar as that they touch on important aspects of his cultural legacy: the new performers he introduced to professional life, for example. Stokowski really did have long hair. He really did conduct Liszt's Second Hungarian Rhapsody in concert as well as on film. In spite of his fame, however, few of his performances were ever filmed, most of them near the end of his career. Furthermore, he was one of the strangest modern orchestral conductors. Unlike Iturbi and other classical stars, Stokowski was fond of misrepresenting his accent(!), age, background, and nationality even to his friends, and he became (in)famous in art music circles for his vigorous—some might say, violent—orchestral arrangements of well-known keyboard masterpieces.

Leopold Stokowski, the only existing documentary devoted to the conductor, avoids almost all of these issues.[39] Perhaps this is because opinions of Stokowski as man and artist differ widely. In Paul Robinson's somewhat dismissive biography, for example, the conductor is described primarily in terms of his "drive to dominate" and the "perversity of many of his [musical] interpretations."[40] "He may have thought he was advancing the cause of serious music," Robinson continues, "but probably [he] achieved just the opposite result by confirming most people's suspicion that classical musicians are insufferable snobs."[41] Adam Chasins more or less agrees, proclaiming that Stokowski participated in films because the "insatiable showman" in him "loved the public adoration he received as a movie idol," and because—as a "sun-worshipper, nudist, and fruit and vegetable enthusiast"—he was "attracted to the physical characteristics of southern California."[42]

Figure 2.3 Stokowski as interview subject. From *Leopold Stokowski* (*c.* 1961).

Preben Opperby takes a different tack. A Stokowski supporter, he acknowledges his subject's "theatricality" and refers to reviews of *The Big Broadcast of 1937* to support that assertion. For Opperby, however, Stokowski "played his role" in that film "with both dignity and human warmth"; in *100 Men and a Girl* he "contributed greatly to a happy atmosphere in the studios"—so much so that Durbin, the show's youthful star, "was finally able to record her singing parts."[43]

A third, perhaps more interesting opinion is one expressed tacitly by William Anders Smith, a staunch Stokowski supporter and psychological biographer. Although he considers his idol "the greatest recording conductor ever," Smith doesn't so much as mention *100 Men and a Girl*.[44] Nor does he have much to say about *Fantasia*, although he alone acknowledges the "playful paganism and nature worship" evident in its musical selections and animation.[45] "Stokowski's god, like Jefferson's, was 'nature's god,'" Smith writes; and the "Pagan gods, centaurs, and nymphs" depicted in the Beethoven–Disney *Pastoral* symphony sequences, "coupled with the evolutionist message of the *Rite of Spring*" sequences, "smack of Stokowski's philosophical influence on the film."[46]

In spite of their differences, Chasins, Opperby, Robinson, and Smith would seem to agree both that similarities exist between Stokowski's successes or failures as conductor and actor; and that Stokowski's personality is central to any evaluation of those successes and failures—again, as conductor and screen star. Whether "real" or "phony," Stokowski was unquestionably magnetic: almost everyone who worked with him testifies to that. And he was unquestionably an actor—not only because he appeared in films, but because he acted in everyday life as well as on stage and screen.

In short, Stokowski would make an excellent (and quite colorful) subject for an innovative yet entertaining, multi-faceted, retrospective documentary compilation—one assembled in part from reminiscences, performance footage, and (re)interpretations of his career, character, and cultural influence. As Jane Chapman reminds us, "Creative people are constantly looking for a new perspective for on-going themes."[47] An intelligent Stokowski documentary might touch on the conductor's avant-garde sense of musical experimentation. (At one point Stokowski suggested to Walt Disney that aromas as well as images be employed to make a multi-sensory impression on *Fantasia*'s audiences.[48]) It might employ "Marxist critical theory," deconstructing certain "cultural mechanisms" in terms of Stokowski's unusual relationship with the hegemonic Hollywood entertainment industry and the "mindless artistry which represents what is human as opposed to the social mechanism" of capitalism.[49] It might even touch on the "heathen" practice of sun-worship. Above all, it might remind its audience of Stokowski's pioneering work with young people—work that anticipated the development of such international and intercultural projects as the West-Eastern Divan Orchestra: itself an ensemble "of young musicians" organized in 1999, located in Sevilla, Spain, conducted by Daniel Barenboim, and foregrounding "co-existence between Arabs, Jews, and Europeans."[50] Certainly all this (and more) would provide material for a cutting-edge, conflated, yet entertaining retrospective music documentary. In short: a movie about Stokowski as man and music-maker could define the music documentary as retrospective compilation.[51]

Notes

1   Matthew Bernstein, "Documentaphobia and Mixed Modes: Michael Moore's 'Roger & Me,'" in Barry Keith Grant and Jeannette Sloniowski (eds.), Documenting the Documentary: Close Readings of Documentary Film and Video (Detroit: Wayne State University Press, 1998), 398.
2   See, for example, Scott Yanow, Jazz on Film: The Complete Story of the Musicians and Music Onscreen (San Francisco: Backbeat, 2004). Yanow locates Ken Burns's Jazz (see below) among the DVDs (pp. 67–68), although it was originally broadcast on television; he also separates "Hollywood Movies" featuring jazz performances (pp. 141–213) from "Shorts, TV Specials, and More Documentaries" (pp. 214–264).
3   For a discussion of music and film that considers both documentary and non-documentary genres, and that reviews twentieth-century film music scholarship in some detail—including studies such as Claudia Gorbman, Unheard Melodies: Narrative Film Music (Indiana University Press, 1987)—see Chapter 1 of Neil William Lerner, "The Classical Documentary Score in American Films of Persuasion: Contexts and Case Studies, 1936–1945" (dissertation: Duke University, 1997), 9–49.
4   Jack C. Ellis, The Documentary Idea: A Critical History of English-language Documentary Film and Video (Englewood Cliffs, NJ: Prentice-Hall, 1989), 1–3.
5   Ibid.
6   Ibid., 295.
7   Stan W. Denski, "Critical Pedagogy and Media Production: The Theory and Practice of the Video Documentary," Journal of Film and Video 43, No. 3 (Fall 1991), 3–4.
8   Grant and Sloniowski, Documenting the Documentary, 22.
9   Ibid.
10 See Mervyn Cooke, A History of Film Music (Cambridge: Cambridge University Press, 2008), 424–425.
11 See Joel Makower, Woodstock: The Oral History (New York: Doubleday, 1989). See, too, Andy Bennett (ed.), Remembering Woodstock (Aldershot: Ashgate, 2004).
12 Robert Drew quoted in Dave Saunders, Direct Cinema: Observational Documentary and the Politics of the Sixties (London and New York: Wallflower, 2007), 5.
13 Yanow, Jazz on Film, 68.
14 For a review of Burns's series from both positive and negative perspectives, see Steve F. Pond, "Jamming the Reception: Ken Burns, Jazz, and the Problem of 'America's Music,'" Notes 60, No. 1 (September 2003), 11–45.
15 Jane Chapman, Documentary in Practice (Cambridge: Polity, 2007), 2.
16 Ellis, The Documentary Idea, 295. See, too, 7–13.
17 Joseph Horowitz, Understanding Toscanini: How He Became an American Culture-god and Helped Create a New Audience for Old Music (New York: Alfred A. Knopf, 1987), 179–180.
18 The Art of Conducting: Great Conductors of the Past (Hamburg: Teldec, 1994). Originally The Art of Conducting was a television series, accompanied in its videotape release by Alan Sanders' essay of the same name. Stokowski footage,

in some cases including portions of his *Carnegie Hall* performance, also appears in *The New American Orchestras* (Princeton, NJ: Films for the Humanities, 1994); *Carnegie Hall at 100: A Place of Dreams* (West Branch, NJ: Kultur, 1990; rereleased in 2007); *Chicago Symphony Orchestra Historic Telecasts*, Vol. 1 (New York: Video Artists International, 1999); *Fritz Reiner, Leopold Stokowski, Paul Hindemith* (New York: Video Artist International, 2003); *Leopold Stokowski* (Pleasantville, NY: Video Artists International, 1999); *The Maestros of Philadelphia* (New York: Thirteen/WNET, 1993); and *The Music of Man*, Program 7: "The Known and the Unknown" (Boston: Home Vision, 1987). *Leopold Stokowski* was originally produced in 1961 or 1962; *The Music of Man* was produced by the Canadian Broadcasting Company and other agencies.

19 *Toscanini The Maestro, Plus Verdi: Hymn of the Nations* (New York: Video Artists International, 1985). A shorter version, entitled *Toscanini the Maestro*, omits the filmed performance of Verdi's *Hymn*.

20 Alicia M. Doyle, [review of] *Herbert von Karajan: Maestro for the Screen*, in *Notes* 67, No. 1 (September 2010), 176. The Karajan documentary was released on DVD in 2009 by the German firm Arthaus Musik.

21 Spelled both with and without an exclamation point. See, for example, the 2004 DVD rerelease, which lacks the added punctuation.

22 Commodification of all three "That's Entertainment" documentaries includes shops located in Fitchburg and Worcester, Massachusetts, as well as online at http://www.thatse.com/ (accessed September 2011). The same holds true for *Woodstock*: in additions to dozens of outlets selling books, photos, and T-shirts, the Woodstock Trading Company in Cherry Hill, New Jersey, handles "Rock & Roll Merchandise" of many kinds. See http://woodstocktradeco.com/ (accessed September 1, 2011).

23 Cooke, *A History of Film Music*, 265.

24 For a discussion of music and the "documentary aesthetic," see John Corner, "Sounds Real: Music and Documentary," *Popular Music* 21 (October 2002), 357–366.

25 Frank Biocca, "Media and Perceptual Shifts: Early Radio and the Clash of Musical Cultures," *Journal of Popular Culture* 24, no. 2 (1990), 1, quoted in Michael Saffle, "Toward a Semiotics of Music Appreciation as Ownership: Bernstein's 'Young People's Concerts' and 'Educational' Music Television," in Erkki Pekkilä, David Neumeyer, and Richard Littlefield (eds.), *Music, Meaning and Media* (Helsinki: Hakapaino, 2006), 119. Haggin's book was originally published in 1944 by Alfred A. Knopf of New York City.

26 Mark Clague, "Playing in 'Toon: Walt Disney's 'Fantasia' (1940) and the Imagineering of Classical Music," *American Music* 22 (Spring 2004), 92.

27 Cooke, *A History of Film Music*, 265.

28 In 1954 all twenty-six half-hour episodes of *Victory at Sea* were edited and rereleased as a feature-length film.

29 For example, see Alfred W. Cochran, "The Documentary Film Scores of Gail Kubik," in K. J. Donnelly (ed.), *Film Music: Critical Approaches* (New York: Continuum, 2001), 117–128.

30 See Jay Ruby, "Toward an Anthropological Cinema," *Film Comment* 7 (1971), 36.

31 Walter Goldschmidt, "Ethnographic Film: Definition and Exegesis," *Program in Ethnographic Film Newsletter* 3 (1972), 1, quoted in Sharon R. Sherman, *Documenting Ourselves: Film, Video, and Culture* (University Press of Kentucky, 1998), 32 (italics added).

32 Donald V. L. Macleod, "Anthropological Investigations: An Innocent Exploration of 'The Wicker Man' Culture," in Benjamin Franks, Stephen Harper, Jonathan

Murray, and Lesley Stevenson (eds.), *The Quest for the Wicker Man: History, Folklore, and Pagan Perspectives* (Edinburgh: Luath, 2006), 74, 81.

33 John C. Tibbetts, *All my Loving? The Films of Tony Palmer* (Tyne and Wear: Chrome Dreams/Voiceprint, 2009), 342.

34 Saffle, "Bernstein's 'Young People's Concerts," 124.

35 Stella Bruzzi, *New Documentary: A Critical Introduction* (London and New York: Routledge, 2000), 11. For many students of documentaries, edginess and even danger are especially intriguing aspects. See, for example, Daniel F. Showalter, "Remembering the Dangers of Rock and Roll: Toward a Historical Narrative of the Rock Festival," *Critical Studies in Media Communication* 17, No. 1 (2000), 86–102. For Showalter, *Woodstock* and *Gimme Shelter*, with their "excess" and "dangerous, exposed, unpleasant nakedness" (p. 93), seem more interesting than the "valuable, critical tool" (p. 100) that is *Monterey Pop* (D. A. Pennebaker, 1968).

36 Quoted in Saffle, "Bernstein's 'Young People's Concerts," 125; italics added.

37 Iturbi (1895–1980) had a more successful film career than Stokowski as well as a less successful and less prestigious musical one. In most of his movies Iturbi conducts, or plays the piano, or converses with other musicians; consider his encounter with Sinatra in *Anchors Aweigh* (George Sidney, 1945). Interestingly enough, Iturbi not only studied the harpsichord with Landowska but made several short instructional films about that instrument.

38 The date was November 18, 1940. Reproduced in Oliver Daniel, *Stokowski: A Counterpoint of Views* (New York: Dodd, Mead, 1982), 388.

39 See note 18 above. This forty-three-minute black/white film was produced almost fifty years ago by WGN TV of Chicago; it does not include clips from either *100 Men and a Girl* or *Carnegie Hall*.

40 Paul Robinson, *Stokowski* (New York: Vanguard, 1977), 4, 6.

41 Ibid., 41.

42 Abram Chasins, *Leopold Stokowski: A Profile* (New York: Hawthorn, 1979), 160–161.

43 Preben Opperby, *Leopold Stokowski* (New York: Hippocrene, 1982), 65–67.

44 See William Anders Smith, *The Mystery of Leopold Stokowski* (Cranbury, NJ and London: Associated University Press, 1990).

45 Ibid., 179.

46 Ibid., 179–180.

47 Chapman, *Documentary in Practice*, 4.

48 See Daniel, *Stokowski: A Counterpoint of Views*, 385. Disney vetoed the idea, pointing out that it would take a long time to change odors in theaters.

49 Theodor W. Adorno and Max Horkheimer, "The Culture Industry," in Meenakshi Gigi Durham and Douglas M. Kellner (eds.), *Media and Cultural Studies: KeyWorks*, rev. ed., (Malden, MA: Blackwell, 2006), 85.

50 See Rachel B. Willson, "Whose Utopia? Perspectives on the West-Eastern Divan Orchestra," *Music & Politics* 3, No. 2 (2009), 1–21.

51 The author would like to thank Virginia Polytechnic Institute and State University, especially the College of Liberal Arts and Human Sciences, for support toward both the completion of the present article and attendance at the "Sights and Sounds" music documentary conference held at the University of Salford during June 2010.

Chapter 3

Sound and Vision

Radio Documentary, Fandom, and New Participatory Cultures

Oliver Carter and Sam Coley

Introduction

David Bowie has become one of the most mediatized figures in popular music with many writers focusing on his diverse musical output and the deft manipulation of his public image. Previously published work has often blurred the line between academic and fan, such as biographer David Buckley's *Strange Fascination* in which he calls Bowie "one of the most important artists of the twentieth century."[1] The limited amount of semi-academic analysis that exists in such publications tends to drift between traditional biography and textual analysis, such as James E. Perone's *The Words and Music of David Bowie*.[2] Building on Nick Stevenson's academic study on David Bowie, this article seeks to explore new territory in the analysis of Bowie's influence.[3] It will investigate the online practices of his fans in relation to content produced for a series of radio documentaries that focused on Bowie's visit to New Zealand in 1983. David Bowie released his fifteenth studio album *Let's Dance* in April 1983. This marked the beginning of the most commercially successful period of his musical career with the eponymous title track becoming Bowie's fastest-selling single, and his first to reach number one on both the UK and US album charts.

According to Chet Flippo's book, *David Bowie's Serious Moonlight*, the world tour that accompanied the album played ninety-six shows in fifty-nine cities across fifteen countries, performing to an estimated audience of nearly three million people.[4] The tour travelled through the South Pacific, reaching New Zealand in November 1983. The audience for Bowie's concert in Auckland was estimated to be 80,000.[5] This represented the biggest single crowd gathering in New Zealand and was credited in the *Guinness Book of Records* as "the largest crowd gathering per head of population anywhere in the world."[6] Shortly after his arrival in New Zealand, Bowie was invited to visit Takapuwahia Marae in Porirua, a sacred meeting place of the native Maoris, becoming the first rock star to be officially welcomed onto a Maori Marae. Twenty-five years later, Bowie's radio documentary producer, and self-confessed David Bowie fan, Sam Coley, documented this event in two radio documentaries: *Bowie's*

Waiata and *Down Under the Moonlight*. Members of the Ngati Toa tribe and professionals involved in the tour were invited to reflect on the event that Bowie himself praised in the press of the time as uniquely hospitable. The documentary featured the previously unheard song "Waiata" that Bowie wrote especially for the occasion, as well as the reaction to it of Bowie backing singer Frank Simms who had last heard the song while singing it live, twenty-five years earlier.

This chapter discusses the production of these and other related radio documentaries and audio slideshows, which this chapter will refer to as the "Bowie project," along with the activities of the Bowie fan community prior to and following the AM broadcast and webstream of the documentary by Radio New Zealand. The fan website Bowie Down Under[7] promoted the documentary on its front page, discussion fora and Facebook page, bringing it to the attention of both the antipodean and global Bowie fan community. Following the airing, a member of the Bowie fan community uploaded a recording of the documentary to a file-sharing website. This led to a number of different fan edits of the documentary appearing on YouTube, offering their own interpretations of the broadcast documentary. Drawing on Henry Jenkins' recent work into "new participatory cultures"[8] and "convergence culture,"[9] the relationship between the fan and radio producer as well as fan practices that surrounded the documentary will be critically examined. Particular attention will be awarded to the activities of the David Bowie fan community, namely the ways in which fans promoted, captured, and finally reappropriated the documentary. This highlights how audiences were able to continue the story of the documentary through their own forms of media production.

Radio and the Music Documentary

It is worth pointing out that this is the only chapter in this publication to give attention to the radio documentary. When contrasting the amount of academic work on television or film studies compared with that on radio it is easy to see how academics have tended to favour the moving image over audio.[10] Therefore, it is necessary to clarify differences and similarities between radio and television documentaries and the role of the radio producer. While this chapter draws from a specific case study relating to radio documentary production, many comparisons can be drawn with the production of television and film documentaries. Some of these parallels are demonstrated in the book *Speech, Music, Sound*, where Theo van Leeuwen observes that sound dubbing technicians in the radio and film industries follow similar approaches to the categorization of audio production.[11] Both, for example, divide their respective soundtracks into three zones—close, middle, and far distance. Similarly, Sarah Sherman's online article *Real(ly) Good Stories* noted the comparison of the structure and concept in both radio and film documentary, which achieved "a singular texture and strength." Sherman observes how certain film documentary production techniques can also be found in radio documentary production, such as the use of stock footage (or audio), interview segments, narration, and scene recording.[12]

However, the radio producer can often enjoy far greater creative input than their television counterpart. David Hendy (2004) describes radio production as a less technically complex process than television.[13] He goes on to suggest that radio is more of a producer's medium than television since various roles such as researcher, director, editor, sound recordist, and presenter are often combined into one role—a multiskilled radio producer. Robert McLeish notes how this multiskilling has led to reduced production costs and is part of a production "convergence" enabling more radio programs to be made by fewer people.[14] This freedom has allowed the radio producer to exert a great deal of creative control as their production decisions do not require the approval and assistance from the numbers of coproducers often required for television and film productions. Of course, the obvious difference between these two forms of media is radio's absence of visual information, leading Andrew Crisell to refer to it as a "blind medium."[15] The listener is required to create their own "pictures" which, as Gulson Kurubacak and T. Volken Yuzer contend, gives them the ability to control and extract their own meanings in their minds.[16] This creative participation from the listener, coupled with the ability of music to trigger emotion, can add substantial intimacy to a production and help build a sense of trust between a documentary and its audience.

In the preface to her publication *Why Music Moves Us*, Jeanette Bicknell recounts listeners being "overwhelmed or overpowered by music, reduced to tears, and experiencing chills or shivers and other bodily sensations."[17] By exploiting the strong emotion a fan feels towards certain elements of a favorite song, such as instrumental sections, choruses and bridge sections, the radio producer generates peaks and troughs in the listener's interest which, in turn, drives the narrative forward. The producer, by demonstrating their own fandom for the subject, establishes a connection with the listener, earning or conversely losing their appreciation of a production's worth. The producer acknowledges the fans' intelligence by selecting rare tracks, obscure live recordings, twelve-inch remixes, archival recordings, and other non-mainstream content, thereby flattering their attention to detail. As we are exploring the relationship between fandom and radio documentary production, it is necessary to consider how profoundly an audience can shape the initial stages of the production process. Guy Starkey sees the radio documentary as a means of communicating a story, to which the producer expects an audience to be receptive.[18] This empathy towards the expectations of the fan as well as the general listener can be said to underpin most aspects of the production process.[19] Hendy contends that the selection of an appropriate approach which takes into consideration the context and audience of a documentary is of equal importance to the proposal stage of a project as the actual choice of subject and content.[20]

Bowie's Waiata[s1]

The origin of the Bowie project began in 2001 when a unique audio file of Bowie singing live at the Takapuwahia Marae in 1983 was located in the digital news archives of The Radio Network, Auckland, New Zealand. Any further information, regarding the source or context of the audio, was not available. This audio formed the starting point for two AM/FM radio documentaries, one online version with copyright music removed, eight YouTube clips and four on-demand web featurettes. The authors of this chapter have identified four audio slideshows created by the Bowie fan community, along with a file-shared copy of a documentary captured from the webstream and a file-shared excerpt containing Bowie's song "Waiata," also taken from the initial webstream. All of these artefacts were created to acknowledge the twenty-fifth anniversary of Bowie's Serious Moonlight tour. One of the main documentaries, Bowie's Waiata was produced for the public service broadcaster Radio New Zealand, while the second documentary Bowie Down Under was produced for The Radio Network's commercial rock station, Radio Hauraki. As both of these stations have very different identities and attract different audiences both documentaries required a separate approach to production.

The quarter-century milestone of the event was utilized as an opportunity to improve the chances of the project being commissioned. The relative freedom of radio programming allowed the documentaries to be scheduled around the twenty-fifth anniversary of the subject matter. An example of this is the programming of Bowie Down Under, which was broadcast on Radio

Figure 3.1 Sam Coley interviews members of the Ngati Toa tribe.

Hauraki on the same date and hour as the concert began, exactly twenty-five years after the Auckland show, November 22, 1983. Both documentaries utilized the same pool of contributors as well as interviews specific to the Marae visit and Auckland concert. These interviews were carried out in New York, Auckland, Wellington, and Christchurch and edited in Birmingham, UK. The content was mostly captured between August 2007 and September 2008, using a Marantz PMD660 digital recorder, a Beyer Dynamic M58 microphone and was edited using an Adobe Audition 3.0 multi-track digital editor. The soundtrack to the documentaries included tracks taken from the *Let's Dance* album along with various related Bowie hits. Live recordings from the tour were sourced from the DVD release *Serious Moonlight* (2006) directed by David Mallet. Members of the Ngati Toa tribe singing were recorded on location at the Takapuwahia Marae in January, 2008.

The *Waiata* documentary was commissioned to play on Radio New Zealand as an episode in the series *Music 101*. The documentary was twenty-six minutes in duration and was broadcast on Radio New Zealand's AM/FM transmission signals from 4:10 p.m., November 22, 2008. The *Bowie Down Under* documentary was created in six sixteen-minute sections for Radio Hauraki FM which, including commercial schedule and news considerations, ran across a two-hour duration, starting at 7:05 p.m. on November 26, 2008. Both stations were networked across the length of the New Zealand, reaching a national audience. The documentary project has received generally positive feedback via direct email, posted user comments and personal messaging. In June 2009, the documentary *Bowie's Waiata* was nominated as a finalist the New York Radio Festival 2009, in the "Culture and The Arts" and "Community Portraits" categories.

The New Participatory Culture

After the above outline of the production of the documentary, the discussion will now turn to how the documentary was consumed by David Bowie fans. In his 2006 publications *Fans, Bloggers, and Gamers* and *Convergence Culture*, Henry Jenkins considers new practices, particularly how the relationship between fandom and technology is changing in the digital age. In *Fans, Bloggers, and Gamers*, he suggests moving from the De Certeaunian approach he used in *Textual Poachers*[21] and instead draws on the ideas of French scholar Pierre Levy.[22] Now, rather than primarily seeing fandom as a form of resistance, Jenkins uses Levy's concept of "collective intelligence" to understand present-day fan activity. From this perspective, audiences work together in order to produce texts, sharing knowledge, ideas, and approaches. According to Jenkins, such collaborative activities have come to fruition because of the proliferation of home computing software and the continuing rise in internet access. Jenkins coins this new stage in fan activity the "new participatory culture" and identifies it as having three distinct trends:[23]

1. New tools and technologies enable consumers to archive, appropriate, annotate, and recirculate media content.
2. A range of subcultures promote DIY media production, a discourse that shapes how consumers have deployed those technologies.
3. Economic trends favoring the horizontally integrated media conglomerates encourage the flow of images, ideas, and narratives across multiple media channels and demand more active modes of spectatorship.

It is the first of these two trends that are of particular significance when examining the fan response to *Bowie's Waiata*. The increasing affordability of home computers and components, the open-source software movement and broadband internet access have all been enabling factors in amateur media production. In the analogue age, media audiences had the ability to engage in forms of production but the high costs of editing equipment and need for specialist training could be prohibitive to those who wished to participate. The rise in home computing, however, changed this. Many home computers come with basic editing software that allows the user to engage in media production. Other creative software can be downloaded from the internet both legally and illegally. Audiences can now have access to software and hardware that is used by media professionals to create their own productions and reappropriations.

However, not everyone has the knowledge or skill required to participate in such forms of production. Unlike professionals, they may not have gone through any formal education that has instructed them how to use such technology. This is where the second of Jenkins' trends is important, as there are numerous websites and online communities that are purely devoted to promoting and encouraging amateur production. Through a simple Google keyword search, advice can be obtained on how to use software and perform complex tasks that would usually be limited to those who have been trained to use such software. These communities adopt a discourse that promotes and encourages DIY production, producing tutorials that take you through a step-by-step process and offering troubleshooting advice. In the instance of the Bowie project, fans posted comments about where they could source the copies of the documentary which other fans had managed to capture. These fan communities operate on a global level, meaning that users from all over the world are able to collaborate. It is worth indicating that within specific fandoms there will often be a specialist subculture that is primarily devoted to DIY production. These are usually fans with a higher level of attachment than other members of the community. We might see these as the experts of community. Jenkins uses the example of Manga and Anime to demonstrate how the internet has enriched production within this specific fandom.[24] In Manga and Anime fandom, some fans outside of Japan have undertaken Japanese language courses in order to be able to both understand Anime and also to produce English subtitles for those films. This illustrates the lengths that some fans are willing to go to in order to participate in their fandom at a much greater level than casual fans.

An important issue surrounding the new participatory culture is that of intellectual copyright. Jenkins suggests that the regulation of copyright laws confuses fans on how they can interact with media. This confusion stems from the lack of understanding mass media producers have for interactive audiences. Fans might be aware of the legal ramifications of reappropriating and recirculating mass media but still actively engage in the activity. Despite this somewhat militant approach fans take, Jenkins is quick to separate fan production from alternative media production, seeing fan production as celebrating media rather than directly opposing it. Lawrence Lessig adopts a similar view but suggests that in the digital age copyright law has become outdated and now serves to limit the creative opportunities offered by new media technologies.[25] He refers to the case of an American mother who uploaded a video of her infant son dancing to a Prince song, "Let's Go Crazy," to YouTube. Universal, the rights owners for song, and infamous for their litigious nature, had the video removed from YouTube as it breached copyright and threatened the mother with legal action. Now, whilst this video does not display any real technical skills it still shows how copyright can impact upon an individual's creativity. But for every instance where a video is taken down from YouTube or an individual is threatened with legal action there are numerous other instances that go by undetected. If anything, the amateur producer has more freedom from copyright than the media professional and has the opportunity to operate free from any limits. This allows for texts to be produced in a whole variety of ways.

The blurring of the boundary between amateur and professional production is a key issue associated with convergence culture. Using the example of amateur producers of fan films entering the mainstream, Jenkins sees convergence culture as the result of media audiences and their use of digital technology.[26] He believes that we are all participants in convergence culture but not all audiences will share the same role; some may have greater levels of participation than others. Convergence culture is primarily concerned with the ways in which the use of digital technology is empowering audience members and challenging the dominant forms of mass media production. The World Wide Web, for example, has provided a distribution network for fan-produced material. Before the rise of the internet, distribution of fan-produced texts would be confined to "underground" networks such as mail order or fan conventions and fairs. Jenkins suggests that the "covert" nature of distribution in this period meant that it escaped the wrath of mass media producers. However, in the internet age, fan production is more overt; it can reach a global audience. In the words of Jenkins, the web has "allowed folk culture to flourish" and has created a "creative revolution."[27] Mark Deuze believes that convergence culture is not just about technology and the "technological process" but it also has a "cultural logic" where the boundaries between production and consumption and passive and active consumption become increasingly blurred.[28] He also notes that the relationship between producers and consumers has changed as a result of digital technology. For example, mass media producers are encouraging audiences to interact with television programming by offering them channels for communication online. This can be seen in the websites for popular television shows that encourage discussion and debate as well as encouraging fan writing. But also, as indicated earlier in this chapter, producers are increasingly aware of the fan dimension when producing media texts, encouraging response and participation.

The Fan Response

After defining the terms new participatory culture and convergence culture this section will examine the different ways in which David Bowie fans responded to the *Bowie's Waiata* documentary. Fans responded in three main ways to the documentary: promotion, capturing, and reappropriation. The remainder of this section will focus on each of these areas. It will closely interrogate how fans managed to recirculate the *Bowie's Waiata* after its initial broadcast and consider how this shows evidence of the "new participatory culture."

Promotion

Before the advent of the internet, fans would often be alerted to upcoming radio documentaries through promotional commercials and by way of announcers "trailering" an upcoming item on the station of broadcast, through publications such as the UK's *Radio Times* or the radio listings section of newspapers. The development of online chatrooms, dedicated fan-sites, Facebook, and RSS feeds has offered fans highly detailed information about upcoming programming specific to their particular fandom and provides easy access to previously broadcast radio documentaries that have been unofficially archived by fans. The online promotion of *Bowie's Waiata* began when a member of the website Bowie Down Under saw the documentary listed in the New Zealand publication *The Listener* and alerted the fan community to its upcoming broadcast. On noticing this activity, the website was contacted to promote the *Waiata* documentary and its sister project *Bowie Down Under* to a target audience of fans who had already demonstrated their interest in Bowie's Australasian activities. The site identifies itself as "the David Bowie community of Australia and New Zealand" and was a rich source of preproduction information and photographic content for inclusion in the accompanying audio slideshows. Adam Dean, the webmaster of Bowie Down Under, was clearly enthusiastic about the project, posting a number of alerts on the site. These posts detailed program content, musical track listings and new photographs taken during the production process of Bowie's associates from 1983—often holding items of memorabilia from the *Let's Dance* period.

Figure 3.2 The Bowie Down Under website promoting the documentary.

These promotional postings provided an international audience of Bowie fans with specific broadcast information, such as links to the Radio New Zealand and Radio Hauraki websites where the documentaries could be streamed live. The site also provided a simple computer program that enabled fans to convert New Zealand's standard time zone into that of their own country, in order to hear the documentary streaming at the correct time. Other Bowie fan websites picked up on the Bowie Down Under story and their chatrooms and fora featured several postings in which fans questioned certain aspects of Maori culture, such as the meaning of the word "waiata" (song). These online communities gave the producer the opportunity to interact with the fan audience and respond to questions about the production. This included the clarification of song titles and authenticating certain facts contained in the documentaries. There was also fan activity noted on the fora of the official David Bowie website,[29] although, as an unsanctioned documentary, the project was not officially referred to on this site. The majority of the discussion relating to the documentary found on the official site was focused on the inclusion of the unreleased Bowie song "Waiata." Though only short in length and of poor audio quality, it would appear that this was the "hook" to draw fans to the documentary playing on the completist nature of music fans.[30] From this evidence we can see fans as being promotional agents. By posting in these online fora, the producer was able to build a relationship with the fans and in turn rely on them to promote the documentary to a global audience rather than just its original broadcast location. But rather than simply just promoting the documentary, a select section of the online David Bowie fan community captured the audio from the broadcast and made it available online for those outside of New Zealand to experience.

Capturing

Capturing audio from radio is not a recent practice. Radio listeners have been capturing broadcasts since the audiocassette format made home recordings common in the mid-seventies. However, as many stations now stream their live content online, international audiences are able to capture audio using streaming audio capturing software such as Total Recorder, StreamRipperX, and Audio Hijack. Some of these applications allow fans to record a direct digital signal with no discernable loss of audio quality. Users can then save these recorded files into wav or mp3 formats with various codec and compression options. These files can then be uploaded to online file-sharing sites or to web content providers, as was the case in the Bowie project.

In an effort to combat copyright infringement, Radio New Zealand asks that producers provide a separate mix of their documentaries: one that contains copyrighted music and another that has all copyright music removed. Although the station has a license to play documentaries with commercial music content on their terrestrial AM/FM broadcasts, this does not cover their listen-again content which is made available on their website. By making a music-free version available online, fans still have access to the bulk of the spoken word content. This avoids potential legal issues with record companies and is hoped to pacify the fan into not illegally capturing content paid for and owned by Radio New Zealand. However, this clearly did not work in the instance of the Bowie project. Several audio files were found to have been captured by Bowie fans from the streaming of the *Waiata* documentary on Radio New Zealand's website.[31] These were then uploaded to the internet for listeners outside of New Zealand to hear the documentary in full. The documentary was made available on the direct download site *4shared*[32] and it was also hosted directly on the Bowie Down Under website. Having the documentary available on the former website was important as it gave fans the opportunity to access an audio file that they were able to reappropriate.

Reappropriation

Following the broadcast of the Bowie documentaries, several examples of fans gathering and reusing the content to create new media artifacts were identified.

Figure 3.3 Screenshot of Bodacea1's YouTube web page.

Although, as previously mentioned, some had secured the audio by capturing the Radio New Zealand webstream, other fans resorted to more creative means of obtaining content for their own productions. Once the initial documentary had been broadcast, several emails were received, offering feedback and requesting further information. An email from a listener using the name "Kristi" provided a nostalgic backstory to assist her request for a CD version of the documentary.

> I look forward to hearing the Down Under documentary. I heard your Waiata one and thought it was very well made and just fascinating to hear about, especially as I was a little 7 year old who lived up the road from the Marae he visited in Porirua. I ran down to have a look at this Bowie guy that everyone was going on about. Thanks again. Kristi

A copy was duly posted to the address given and nothing more was heard, until a series of three YouTube uploads[33] were noticed approximately one month later. These took the form of three audio slideshows using related archival photographs, apparently sourced from the internet, combined with high quality audio from the *Waiata* documentary. The producer of these unofficial features had credited the original writer and producer along with Radio New Zealand as the initial broadcaster and accompanied these credits with the date of production and the international copyright symbol. The username for these audio slideshows was credited as "Bodacea1". On contacting "Bodacea1" via YouTube messaging to compliment them on their production work, it was revealed that the producer was "Kristi," a Bowie fan who had used a certain amount of subterfuge in order to gain a CD copy of the *Waiata* documentary. This ensured the audio content of her YouTube clips were of a high standard. The YouTube user "MrDavidBowie" is credited as the producer of another audio slideshow[34] based on content sourced from the original *Waiata* documentary. However, this version used inferior audio, which can be assumed to have been captured from RNZ's online streaming of the documentary. In the examples provided by "Bodacea1" and "MrDavidBowie," both had reappropriated the original audio by selecting new edit points, dividing the audio into chapters and adding their own accompanying visual elements.

Following the presentations of this paper at three different conferences audience members have questioned the producer's response to having their work reappropriated and often uncredited. In regards to the case study provided by the Bowie project, the producer views reappropriation as an ultimately positive practice that has added new interpretations and greater depth to the initial story. It should be noted that the original Bowie documentaries themselves contained elements of reappropriated audio taken from previously produced Bowie documentaries. Fan-generated reappropriations of the story can be seen as inevitable byproducts of online media distribution and its consumption. As these fan-generated productions have not been financially motivated and have only generated a relatively small amount of online activity, no known legal action has been invoked, to date.

Conclusion—The Story Continues

This chapter has highlighted the ways in which David Bowie fans responded to the broadcast of *Bowie's Waiata* documentary. It has been identified that both prior to and following the broadcast of this documentary fans were engaged in the practices of promotion, capturing, and reappropriation. These activities can be seen as evidence of the new participatory culture where fans make use of new media technology to work collaboratively and reappropriate media content. It also suggests the boundaries between producer and fan are becoming increasingly blurred as the producer of this documentary, a self-confessed Bowie fan, drew on his own fan knowledge in order to produce the documentary. In reverse of this, some Bowie fans who consumed the documentary became producers of media by producing their own interpretations of the documentary. But perhaps it is this aspect that prompts the most interest. By having fans reappropriate the documentary and add their own interpretations the story presented in the original documentary does not end, it continues. Some of the reappropriations of *Bowie's Waiata* discussed here add images to the audio, giving further context to the audio. They also edit out pieces of the original documentary, choosing to use audio that is of particular relevance to them.

But this is not the only way the story is able to continue. Shortly after the documentary was broadcast, an Auckland-based journalist, Greg Ward, contacted Radio NZ who in turn forwarded his email to the producer. This communication revealed him to be the original sound recorder of the *Bowie's Waiata* song at Takapuwahia Marae, 1983. Ward kindly agreed to write an online article detailing the story behind his capturing of the audio. This additional text content is currently accessible alongside audio and pictorial images from the documentaries and, in a sense, can be seen to continue the story by providing added depth and clarity to the narrative. In his email to the producer, Ward commented, "listening to the *Bowie's Waiata* documentary, I was so pleased to hear Frank Simms' surprise and delight at hearing the recording after 25 years. I know how he felt! It's been a quarter century since I last heard it as well."

The initial forms of the Bowie documentaries were broadcast to a wide terrestrial audience that fell within certain AM/FM transmission signals and were consumed live in one simultaneous "listening" along with their live global streaming on the internet. Currently, in their online "on-demand" form, they exist to be heard one at a time, gradually accumulating individual listeners in the form of "hits," incrementally building a continuous audience throughout the duration of the documentary's online lifespan which engages with the documentary in a variety of interesting ways and continues to add to the story.

Notes

1 David Buckley, *Strange Fascination. Davie Bowie: The Definitive Story* (London: Virgin Books, 1999).
2 James E. Perone, *The Words and Music of David Bowie* (London: Praeger, 2007).
3 Nick Stevenson, *David Bowie: Fame, Sound and Vision* (Cambridge: Polity Press, 2006).
4 Chet Flippo, *David Bowie's Serious Moonlight, The World Tour* (New York: Dolphin, 1984).
5 Unknown, "Major Bowie Controls 80,000" in *The Herald* (November 28, 1983), 3.
6 Norris McWhirter, *Guinness Book of Records* (New York: Bantam Books, 1984).
7 www.bowiedownunder.com (accessed May 2012).
8 Henry Jenkins, *Fans, Bloggers, and Gamers: Exploring Participatory Culture* (New York: New York University Press, 2006).
9 Henry Jenkins, *Convergence Culture: Where Old and New Media Collide* (New York: New York University Press, 2006).
10 Peter Lewis, "Private Passion, Public Neglect: The Cultural Status of Radio," *International Journal of Cultural Studies* 3, No. 2 (2000), 60–167. Jo Tacchi, "The Need for Radio Theory in the Digital Age," *International Journal of Cultural Studies* 3, No. 2 (2000), 289–298.
11 Theo van Leewen, *Speech, Music, Sound* (London: Palgrave Macmillan, 1999).

12 Sarah Sherman, *Real(ly) Good Stories*. Available from: http://www.mediarights.org/news/really_good_stories (accessed March 1, 2012).
13 David Hendy, *Radio in a Global Age* (London: Wiley Blackwell, 2000).
14 Robert McLeish, *Radio Production* (Oxford: Focal Press, 1999).
15 Andrew Crisell, *Understanding Radio* (London: Routledge, 1992).
16 Gulson Kurubacak and T. Volken Yuzer, "The Building of Knowledge Networks with Interactive Radio Programs in Distance Education Systems" (paper presented at the Proceedings of World Conference on E-Learning in Corporate, Government, Healthcare, and Higher Education, Chesapeake, Virginia, 2004).
17 Jeanette Bicknell, *Why Music Moves Us* (London: Palgrave Macmillan, 2009).
18 Guy Starkey, *Radio in Context* (London: Palgrave Macmillan, 2007).
19 Ibid., 207.
20 Hendy, *Radio in a Global Age*, 206.
21 Henry Jenkins, *Textual Poachers: Television Fans and Participatory Culture* (London: Routledge, 1992).
22 Pierre Levy, *Collective Intelligence: Mankind's Emerging World in Cyberspace* (London: Basic Books, 1999).
23 Jenkins, *Fans, Bloggers, and Gamers*, 146.
24 Ibid., 141.
25 Lawrence Lessig, *Remix—Making Art and Commerce Thrive in the Hybrid Economy* (London: Bloomsbury, 2008).
26 Jenkins, *Convergence Culture*.
27 Ibid., 136.
28 Mark Deuze, *Media Work* (London: Polity, 2007), 74.
29 www.davidbowie.com (accessed March 1, 2012).
30 Roy Shuker, *Wax Trash and Vinyl Treasures—Record Collecting as a Social Practice* (Surrey: Ashgate, 2010).
31 www.radionz.co.nz (accessed March 1, 2012).
32 www.4shared.com (accessed March 1, 2012).
33 These audio slideshows can found here: http://www.youtube.com/user/Bodacea1#p/u/47/dv5sjMjT-kE (accessed May 2012).
34 This audio slideshow can be found here: http://www.youtube.com/user/mrdavidbowie#p/u/3/t66_6jBPjFE (accessed May 2012).

Part II

Scenes from the Sixties

Chapter 4

The Good, The Bad, and The Ugly '60s

The Opposing Gazes of *Woodstock* and *Gimme Shelter*

Julie Lobalzo Wright

Introduction

Two of the most significant events in American popular culture in the 1960s occurred in the later part of 1969 and were immortalized in successful music documentaries: the Woodstock Music and Arts Fair and the Altamont concert. These events, in themselves, have come to represent the highpoint of the 1960s American counterculture movement and its symbolic end, respectively. The documentaries drawn from the events—*Woodstock* (Michael Wadleigh, 1970) and *Gimme Shelter* (Albert and David Maysles, 1970)— helped shape both the "Direct Cinema" movement and the "rockumentary" genre. The Woodstock festival, which took place over the three days of August 15–18[1] was instantly deemed to be a cultural phenomenon through news reports and commentaries in the United States and worldwide,[2] including a special September issue of *Life* magazine devoted to the concert. Altamont was billed as "Woodstock West," an obvious attempt to recreate the festival concert experience four months later in San Francisco, with The Rolling Stones as the focus of the day-long event. Various planning permission issues surfaced for the hastily planned Altamont concert (originally set to take place in San Francisco and moved to the Altamont Speedway less than forty-eight hours before the concert was due to begin). In addition, the inability of the principal organizers to agree about the share of the filming rights for the to-be-released Maysles brothers documentary also caused logistical problems.[3] The planning of Woodstock was also somewhat haphazard (Woodstock was moved from the original Wallkill, New York location to Bethel, New York, over forty miles from Woodstock) and both concerts were envisaged as profit-making ventures for the organizers. Woodstock, however, quickly became eulogized, as the pinnacle of the hippie movement, while Altamont became known as the event that "put the nail in the coffin of the sixties."[4]

The concert films follow a similar narrative, presenting *Woodstock* as the zenith of the counterculture movement and *Gimme Shelter* as its violent end. Both films were released months after the events (*Woodstock*, eight months later; *Gimme Shelter*, twelve months later), allowing popular opinion about the events to dominate the cultural memory of the concerts, which the films then confirm. Although many mainstream media outlets reported traffic jams, and a lack of food, water, shelter, and proper medical attention, by the last day of Woodstock it was heralded as "both the *defining* and *last great moment* of the 1960s."[5] The word "Woodstock" has come to represent not just a festival attended by 300,000–500,000 people (various figures have been quoted), but a generation, as characterized in the spirit of the people who gathered on Max Yasgur's farm, bound by common anti-authority, pro-drug, peace and love sentiments, and the millions who then experienced the festival through a movie or television screen.[6] As festival coproducer Joel Rosenman recently noted, "Woodstock has endured for its music and its stunning demonstration of the true power of community. Those were troubled times, and Woodstock was a beacon for a generation who believed that things could change for the better."[7]

The violence that erupted at Altamont was also widely reported at the time. However, most accounts suggested that even with logistical difficulties and despite the aggressive nature of the policing of the event by the Hell's Angels,[8] the concert was generally perceived, in news reports after the event, as a moderate success.[9] Six weeks after the event *Rolling Stone* magazine devoted an entire issue to what the magazine referred to as "The Rolling Stones Disaster at Altamont."[10] The magazine began with a first-hand account of the murder of Meredith Hunter, an attendee stabbed by a Hell's Angels member mere feet from the concert stage. *Rolling Stone*'s commentary was especially apocalyptic, stating:

> It was such a bad trip that it was almost perfect. All it lacked was mass rioting and the murder of one or more *musicians*. These things *could* have happened, with just a little *more* bad luck. It was as if Altamont's organizers had worked out a blueprint for disaster.[11]

The immediate cultural success of Woodstock, conversely, highlighted the failings of Altamont through inevitable comparisons. As Paul Schrader wrote in 1971, Altamont became the event at which "the fragile Woodstock peacelove [*sic*] bubble dramatically burst."[12]

The narratives, structures, and moods of *Woodstock* and *Gimme Shelter* are clearly informed by the reception of the Woodstock and Altamont concerts. Both films are concerned with representing an experience, but while the Woodstock experience was deemed positive, the undercurrent of negativity associated with Altamont and Hunter's murder causes *Gimme Shelter* to come to function like a murder mystery—more than just a concert film. The impending film was mentioned in many reports about the concert, raising expectations that the Maysles brothers may have captured the murder on film.[13] Thus, before *Gimme Shelter* was even completed, the film was already expected to explain what happened at the one-day concert. *Woodstock*, on the other hand, was a film that sought to demonstrate what made the event so special and unique. Ticket prices were higher than normal ($5) due to the lengthy running time (over three hours) and the film was successfully marketed as something of a concert event rather than a pure documentary;[14] posters for the film even proclaimed "No One Who Was There Will Ever Be the Same. Be There."

Michael Wadleigh expressed his approach to editing *Woodstock* as such, "we never thought we were 'editing a film.' We thought we were editing an experience, that we wanted to 'take you there' . . . ."[15] The Maysles brothers perceived their film as a document of the Altamont concert, a film that "tries to say what's happened at Altamont."[16] Both films achieve their goals through differing gazes that also promote the two festivals as embodying a binary of good and bad. While the narrative of both events sets up the binary opposition, it is within the filmic texts that visual gazes emerge, causing Woodstock to be perceived as a peaceful, organic gathering at a farm in Bethel, as opposed to the dark, violent chaos at the orchestrated Altamont concert. The term "gaze" is not used here in the ideologically loaded sense as proposed by Laura Mulvey,[17] but to suggest that the audience-to-film relationship, dictated by the filmmakers' assemblage of shots, places the audience in a position to see the two films in the ways suggested above. The *Woodstock* and *Gimme Shelter* gazes add to the mythology of not just the festivals, but also the opposing myths of music either as engendering a communal experience or as divisive. Though the sonic elements of both films are vital to understanding the filmmakers' intentions (music is central to both films), the visual gaze determines the audience's perception of both events that the sound further confirms.

In this chapter, I will demonstrate how *Woodstock* employs a "communal gaze," emphasizing the natural environment and community, while *Gimme Shelter* displays a "disconnecting gaze," emphasizing the artificial, man-made environment and individualism. This will be done by comparing these two gazes in respect to three vital areas: setting, crowds, and performances (although all areas intersect with each other in both films).

The importance of sight (for the diegetic audience and filmic audience) is signaled at the very beginning of both films through, curiously, aural means. *Woodstock* begins with Sidney Westerfield, a local antique merchant speaking directly to the camera, recalling the event and suggesting that the film audience will "really see something" when the film is released. This beginning places the concert in the past, already a nostalgic event, but Westerfield's words are significant, placing emphasis on what the audience will see. *Gimme Shelter* begins with Sam Cutler (the manger of The Rolling Stones) asking the Madison Square Garden audience, "Are you ready?" before the image of Mick Jagger and Charlie Watts shooting the cover for *Get Yer Ya-Yas Out!* appears on screen. This is followed by Jagger telling the concert audience, "We're gonna have a look at ya." Sight is prioritized but, as opposed to *Woodstock*, this event (Altamont itself) is not referenced. Instead, the beginning of *Gimme Shelter* separates sight and sound, suggesting that the film may not present a cohesive experience of the event. The first reference to the Altamont concert itself is six minutes into the film, as Watts listens to a San Francisco radio station reporting on the concert. The absence of the image of the concert during this sequence confirms the concert's importance, and in a similar way to the comments made by Westerfield in *Woodstock*—the audience hears about the event before they see it, instilling the later images from Altamont with added value.

Setting

Woodstock's communal gaze begins just after Westerfield's comments with the first impressions of Bethel. The first few frames of this sequence promote human beings as in accordance with the natural environment, placing significance on the environment more than the people living there. From the first shot of a farmhouse on top of a hill (Figure 4.1), the bucolic setting is foregrounded, dwarfing the people, homes, and tractors in these images. Each shot helps to establish the environment as idyllic, peaceful, and agrarian, something the film continues to promote throughout (one of the posters for the Woodstock concert even stated the event would be "an agrarian explosion"). This opening also conveys a sense of wonderment with the setting, especially through a medium shot of a group of people on a hill, looking down on what is below (Figure 4.2). A woman in the group opens her arms wide and the camera zooms out to show their insignificance against the natural environment. The film eventually pauses on a picturesque long shot of the lake (where later we see hundreds of people swimming and bathing) before

Figure 4.1

Figure 4.2

tilting down to reveal the stage for the festival. This one shot encompasses what the entire sequence is attempting to establish—that the relationship between the environment and the festival was one of harmony. Dave Allen has even suggested, "the Woodstock festival was almost the last very public celebration of the rural within popular music."[18] The rural landscape is emphasized throughout the film, visually and even sonically—an early montage of people arriving at the concert is accompanied by Canned Heat's "Goin' up the Country," a song that celebrates leaving the city for the countryside.

In *Gimme Shelter*, the first time the film audience sees Altamont is via a helicopter shot, displaying the dry brown landscape that surrounds the raceway. This first shot of Altamont conveys a sense of speed (rather than stationary contemplation), claustrophobia, and a desolate man-made environment, as opposed to the greenery displayed in *Woodstock*. The helicopter zips along the highway that cuts through the natural landscape (Figure 4.3), as a vista of man imposing modernity on the environment, in sharp contrast to *Woodstock*, where man lived in harmony with the rural environment. The *Gimme Shelter* camera acts like a predator, stalking its prey, as it follows the highway and the lines of parked cars and the masses walking towards the concert. The film cuts to a close-up of Jagger, looking out of a window, followed by a cut to Jagger's assumed point of view, looking down at the concert space. There is a palpable claustrophobia induced by the tight framing of the racetrack to the right and the crowds assembled to the bottom left. The camera tilts to create a slanted frame, altering our perception of the image (Figure 4.4). Quite simply, there is nothing grand or beautiful about this environment.

Figure 4.3

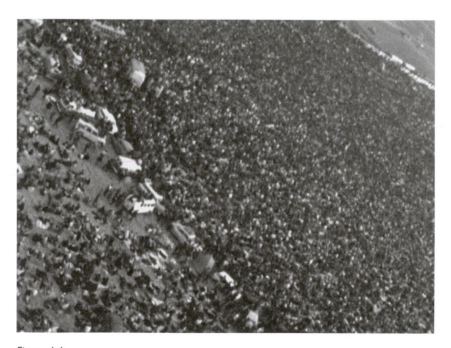

Figure 4.4

Crowds

The first shots from the helicopter in *Gimme Shelter* also illustrate the claustrophobia of the crowds gathered at Altamont. *Woodstock* features many shots of packed crowds too, but the framing of these shots differs substantially from the framing of crowd shots in *Gimme Shelter*. In *Gimme Shelter*, claustrophobia is established throughout the Altamont section through tight frames, close-ups, and zooms. While *Woodstock* featured expansive shots of lakes, woods, and farmland, *Gimme Shelter* features few shots that include anything other than crowds in tight frames: a *mise-en-scène* overloaded with people in both the foregrounds and backgrounds. These shots are generally static, with movement found in the dancing crowd members or achieved via the zooming of the static cameras. In this visual field there is nowhere for the crowd to escape, causing the masses to look like animals trapped in an enclosed area. Furthermore the camera rarely zooms out; it predominantly zooms in to focus on particular individuals in the crowd. This adds to the feeling that this crowd was trapped and its individuals were disconnected from each other. *Woodstock*, on the other hand, generally features frames with a greater depth of field, often including the horizon in the distance. The crowd shots also contain movement through zooms out from single people featured in the crowd, dissolves between one crowd member and another, the split-screen technique that connects people at different locations and times, and a fixed camera time-lapse sequence that shows the crowd movement over a long period of time.

The crowds at *Woodstock* are united through a common purpose, alluded to through the multiplicity of voices in the film (statements about "proving something to the world," interviews that suggest people are present to "find themselves"). *Woodstock*'s communal gaze also illustrates unity. *Woodstock* often uses the crowd, as Jonathan Romney has pointed out, as the components of a "lavish spectacle, the panoramic tableau of the supposed 'nation.'"[19] The film represents the crowd as not *just* an audience, there to view a concert, but *also* a community that has gathered to eat, sleep, and commune together for three days. In fact, many of the performance sequences feature wide shots, taken onstage and from behind the performer, with the vast audience becoming the true spectacle of the event (Figure 4.5). The audience often dwarfs the performers, demonstrating that the essence of the event was really the coming together of the "Woodstock generation" and not the entertainment provided by the musicians.

This is in stark contrast to the sense of disconnection achieved in the gaze of *Gimme Shelter* where individuals are singled out from the crowd, creating a perception that individuals attended this concert, and not a nation of young people en masse, united by a cause. Throughout the Altamont section, the film quickly cuts between individuals (again, in tight close-ups) that display various reactions to the music and environment. These shots, edited together, convey a sense of apathy—of individuals disunited. This could be said to be

Figure 4.5

a reason why Altamont is remembered or conceptualized as the end of the American counterculture: because *Gimme Shelter* exposed this movement's lack of unity and purpose at the close of the 1960s.

Performances

A sense of unity is displayed in *Woodstock* through the crowd, but also through the communal exchange between performer and audience. Performances in *Woodstock* create a link between the festival audience and the performers themselves through editing that suggests they are both part of the creation of music. This is especially so during the Richie Havens set. At one point Havens, in tight close-up, sings "clap your hands!" The film then cuts to a medium shot of the crowd, focusing on one man standing and clapping along to the beat. The camera then zooms out to reveal more of the audience. As the shot expands to become a wide shot more people in the crowd begin to clap and stand up. The film then cuts to a long shot of Havens on stage (who has elicited this collective response from the crowd) and then cuts to an extreme close-up of his face, as expressing his passionate performance. The performer and audience are unified through the musical spectacle that both produce. *Woodstock* editor Thelma Schoonmaker stated that Michael Wadleigh, who was often at the front of the stage filming performances from a tilted-up perspective (including Haven's performance), "had an unbelievable ability to make a camera move at exactly the right time in a song, because he knew a particular chorus was coming, or a powerful lyric was about to be sung." [20] This infers that Wadleigh was purposefully directing certain shots with dramatic intentions in mind. Most of the cameramen, however, were unable to communicate with the director or producers due to technical difficulties with headsets and walkie-talkies.[21]

The unification between the performer and audience occurs again during Santana's set. "Soul Sacrifice" begins with a medium shot of the bass player clapping that then cuts to a medium close-up of another member of the band, and then a cut to an extreme close-up of a crowd member's clapping hands. The film then cuts to a split-screen composition of the conga player and drummer building the beat. The opening of the song ends with three images on the screen: 1) of the crowd, 2) of the drummer, and 3) of the conga player, as if the crowd helped to create the beat, and so becoming significant contributors to Santana's performance (Figure 4.6).

The reading of the crowd as contributors reaches its high point more than halfway through the film with Country Joe McDonald's "I-Feel-Like-I'm-Fixin-To-Die-Rag," which includes cross-cutting between McDonald singing and members of the crowd singing along. The filmmakers here attempted to recreate this communal sing-along for the film audiences too with the use of the bouncing ball, picking out the on-screen lyrics during the second part of McDonald's song.[22] This sequence begins by cross-cutting between shots of young concertgoers and McDonald as he asks the audience to spell the word "fuck," one letter at a time. The audience members are shown walking around at the concert site, staring blankly and with one even sleeping as McDonald continues to ask the concertgoers to shout each letter. The sequence culminates with a helicopter view of the entire audience as the crowd shouts the "k," followed by a close-up of McDonald repeatedly asking, "What's that spell?" This sequence, especially as it follows John Sebastian's sweet lullaby about the generation gap ("Younger Generation"), positions McDonald's performance as the turning point in the concert: the moment that directly references a united cause for most of those attending Woodstock (opposition to the Vietnam war), but also a direct bond between the performer and audience. The climax of the song features shots of the crowd standing to sing, most of these over-the-shoulder shots from McDonald's point of view. This

Figure 4.6

sequence positions the performer and audience as part of the same community, unified through music that defined their attitude to one of great social issues of the era.[23]

Whereas *Woodstock* emphasizes collaboration between audience and performer, performances in *Gimme Shelter* feature individuals, generally in close-ups dancing to the music, but with few singing along, and no shots of the entire crowd clapping or rising to dance. The first performance featured in the film is from The Flying Burrito Brothers (the third band to play on the day after Santana and Jefferson Airplane),[24] setting up this pattern of disconnection between the audience and performers. There are sixteen shots between the establishing medium shot of the band before cutting to the audience and returning back to the band. All of the shots that follow are medium shots or close-ups, signalling individuals out from the crowd, but not as components of a united whole. Some individuals are dancing while others do not even appear to be paying attention to the music, or even seem bored. The final shot, before returning to the band, features a man crowd surfing, rolling his body over individuals sitting on the ground. This medium shot zooms out to one of the few wide shots during the Altamont section of *Gimme Shelter*, illustrating how distracting the one crowd surfer is to those around him, but also how disengaged the audience are since many people attempt to push their way through the throngs sitting on the ground, while others are standing, and even more seem to be facing away from the stage.

The disconnecting gaze comes to a climax during The Rolling Stones set, as does the violence including the murder of Hunter.[25] Obviously, violent altercations between all the attendees (band members, concertgoers, Hell's Angels members) led to the greatest sense of disconnection and detachment at Altamont, as illustrated in *Gimme Shelter*. It is notable, however, how few establishing shots are included in the Altamont section, producing a disjointed sense of time and place and adding to the viewer's confusion. This is especially true during Jefferson Airplane's performance, which includes numerous shots (all tight, medium to close shots) of various people from different locations, creating a disorienting perspective.

While the outright violence at Altamont has been well documented, it must be noted that the entire Altamont section features countless examples of aggression from concertgoers pulled off stage, numerous close-up shots of concertgoers under the influence of drugs and forcing their way through the crowd (Figure 4.7). Though *Woodstock* includes the famous announcement about "brown acid"[26] and an entire sequence showing people taking drugs, there were no obvious shots documenting a "bad trip," while *Gimme Shelter* frequently shows concertgoers aggressively "tripping out." These shots, in addition to the numerous shots of the Hell's Angels fighting with the crowd, construct an environment of aggression and individualism. The disconnect between performer and audience reaches its zenith during The Rolling Stones set, as various members in the crowd (in close-up shots) look up to Jagger

Figure 4.7

and plead with him to stop the performance, pleas which he ignores as he carries on regardless.

The violence and claustrophobia of *Gimme Shelter* is communicated to and engendered in the viewer. This is quite opposed to *Woodstock*'s communal gaze, which works to integrate the viewer with the music festival by making the event a communal experience—even for those who were not there. Tellingly, the only time *Gimme Shelter* features wider and less claustrophobic shots of the crowds at Altamont is as the crowd leaves the event, as though the people who attended now share the horrible experience of the concert. Still, even these shots emphasize how Altamont was the opposite of Woodstock—the man-made environment of the speedway and its barren surrounding areas are again emphasized. *Gimme Shelter* ends with a shot of four people walking over the horizon (Figure 4.8), as a symbol which suggests itself, in this context, the end of the counterculture. This wide shot contrasts with the last vision of *Woodstock*—the helicopter shot that circles around the united crowd.

Although *Woodstock* ends with this triumphant shot, the preceding section casts a darker light on the festival through the juxtaposition of Jimi Hendrix's music and the muddy, abandoned fields after the festival. Hendrix played to a skeleton-sized audience on the Monday morning, after many concertgoers had already departed. The last scenes featuring Hendrix anticipate Altamont

Figure 4.8

through a disconnecting gaze that emphasizes disunity and destruction. In contrast to earlier performances, Hendrix's set features no separate shots of the crowd or audience. Instead Hendrix is the main focal point, through close-ups of his face, hands, feet, and body. There were only two cameras that remained on site for Hendrix's performance, one manned by Wadleigh, hence the nature of the editing of this sequence.[27] However, this is the only sequence in the film to include moments shot *after* the concert that do not include interviews with people eulogizing the event (as the first interview with Sidney Westerfield illustrates).

During Hendrix's performance of "Purple Haze," the film cuts to a shot of the tarp that hung above the stage, tilting down to reveal the muddy and abandoned farmland in front of the stage. The aural soundtrack features Hendrix singing, "is it tomorrow or just the end of time?" as the film cuts to a shot of microphone stands, a piano on stage, and another two shots of the trashed land. This sequence acts as an epilogue for the film, especially as it follows Max Yasgur's statement from the Woodstock stage to the crowd ("you people have proven something to the world") accompanied with a wide, panning shot of the crowd and ending with a freeze frame of Yasgur with his arms aloft. The Hendrix section focuses on the performer alone, with close-ups that suggest he is lost in his own music. Without cutaway shots of the audience (and especially by including shots of the festival after Hendrix's performance), the communal spirit is missing, and has been replaced with the destruction of the ravaged rural land, with a scattered group of concertgoers searching for food (two men eat the remains of a watermelon), shoes (a man and woman try on a pair), and those attempting the arduous task of cleaning up all the waste (Figure 4.9). Still, this scene is completely undercut at the very end of the film: a cut to a helicopter shot of the crowd in all its glory (presumably at its peak number) (Figure 4.10), the footage of which is slowed down for the final focus on the crowd and stage before the last cut to the beginning of the credit sequence, featuring the film's first shot (just after Westerfield's comments) of a farmhouse in the distance.

Figure 4.9

Figure 4.10

Conclusion

As music documentaries, *Woodstock* and *Gimme Shelter* are shaped by the events they captured. Both film productions employed camera operators that often had to work with faulty equipment, difficult lighting circumstances, and the challenging expediencies of capturing a live event. Both film crews, however, took large quantities of footage, allowing the opportunity for the editors and directors to choose how to frame the events.[28] The popular imagination of the two events has been greatly informed by the two films as they counterpoint each other with a precise symmetry, just as the concerts did by representing the positive (Woodstock/*Woodstock*) and negative (Altamont/*Gimme Shelter*) aspects of the hippie period. As such, both films have become as famous or infamous as the events they capture, but it remains essential to acknowledge how the film texts are organized to fulfil very clear intentions. Fundamentally, our shared memories and impressions of the concert events derive from these two gazes, apparent here, as argued. This is not to suggest the films misrepresented either festival, but our memories of these events have been shaped by the nature of these aesthetic strategies. Even Woodstock performer Barry "The Fish" Melton of Country Joe and The Fish acknowledges the power of the films in respect to popular imagination, stating, "When [people] tell me it [Woodstock] was great, I know they saw the movie and they weren't at the gig."[29]

Notes

1   Although promoted as a three-day festival, Woodstock actually took place over four days due to the run-over of performances and a thunderstorm that took place after Joe Cocker's set on Sunday afternoon, delaying the festival for hours.
2   See Simon Warner, "Reporting Woodstock: Some Contemporary Press Reflections on the Festival," in Andy Bennett (ed.), *Remembering Woodstock* (Hampshire: Ashgate, 2004), 55–75.
3   This is the primary reason the Sears Point Raceway did not hold the concert after the raceway's owner, Filmways Inc., could not agree as to the filming rights with the management of The Rolling Stones.
4   Amy Taubin, "*Gimme Shelter*: Rock-and-Roll Zapruder." http://www.criterion.com/current/posts/103-gimme-shelter-rock-and-roll-zapruder (accessed February 2012).
5   Andy Bennett, "Introduction," in Bennett, *Remembering*, xiv. Italics in original.
6   Ang Lee's 2009 film, *Taking Woodstock*, based on the memoir of Elliot Tibert, illustrates that this image of the "Woodstock nation" still persists, focusing on the transformative nature of the event for many who lived in Bethel, New York, including Tiber. The film also ends with a knowing wink to Altamont when Woodstock and Altamont organizer Michael Lang mentions his future project, a free concert in San Francisco featuring The Rolling Stones.
7   Michael Lang and Joel Rosenman, "Foreword," in Joel Makower (ed.), *Woodstock: The Oral History* (Albany: State University of New York Press, 2009), vii.
8   The Rolling Stones had used the Hell's Angels as "security" for their Hyde Park concert in London in the summer of 1969 without any violent incidents. The Grateful Dead and other San Francisco bands had also used the Angels for years at their gigs and suggested to the organizers of Altamont that they should be hired.

See Jonathan B. Vogels, *The Direct Cinema of David and Albert Maysles* (Carbondale, IL: Southern Illinois Press, 2006), 188.

9 John McMillian suggests there was a discrepancy between how the Altamont concert was reported in underground publications such as the *Berkeley Tribe*, with its headline of "Stones Concert Ends It, America Now Up For Grabs," and the *San Francisco Examiner* that declared, "But for the stabbing, all appeared peaceful at the concert." Most mainstream publications noted the violence that occurred at the concert, but still positively assessed the event. John McMillian, *Smoking Typewriters: The Sixties Underground Press and the Rise of Alternative Media in America* (New York: Oxford University Press, 2011), 2–3.

10 "The Rolling Stones Disaster at Altamont," *Rolling Stone* (January 21, 1970).

11 Lester Bangs, Reny Brown, John Burks, Sammy Egan, Michael Goodwin, Geoffrey Link, Greil Marcus, Eugene Schoenfeld, Patrick Thomas, and Langdon Winner, *Rolling Stone* (January 21, 1970, 20); italics in original.

12 Paul Schrader, "*Gimme Shelter*" in *Cinema* 7, No. 1 (Fall 1971), 52.

13 Although the fee The Rolling Stones paid the Maysles brothers to film the concert was set after the concert was announced, indicating, as Norma Coates notes, that "the concert was not arranged in order to accommodate the movie," many people still believe the concert was planned solely for the Maysles brother's film. Norma Coates, "If Anything, Blame Woodstock. The Rolling Stones: Altamont, December 6, 1969," in Ian Inglis (ed.), *Performance and Popular Music: History, Place and Time* (Hampshire: Ashgate, 2006), 64.

14 R. Serge Denisoff and William D. Romanowski, *Risky Business: Rock in Film* (New Brunswick, NJ: Transaction Publishers, 1991), 714.

15 Michael Wadleigh, "Triumph of the Will," in Dale Bell (ed.), *Woodstock: An Inside Look at the Movie That Shook Up the World and Defined a Generation* (Studio City, CA: Michael Wiese Productions, 1999), 12.

16 "Stones: 'The Money is Superfluous to Them,'" *Rolling Stone* (September 3, 1970), 6.

17 Laura Mulvey, "Visual Pleasure and Narrative Cinema," *Screen* 15, No. 3 (1975), 6–18.

18 Dave Allen, "A Public Transition: Acoustic and Electric Performances at the Woodstock Festival" in Bennett, *Remembering*, 111.

19 Jonathan Romney, "Access All Areas: The Real Space of Rock Documentary," in Jonathan Romney and Adrian Wootton (eds.), *Celluloid Jukebox: Popular Music and the Movies since the 50s* (London: BFI Publishing, 1995), 89.

20 Thelma Schoonmaker, "Overwhelmed but Undaunted," in Bell, *Woodstock*, 152–153.

21 Ibid., 150.

22 The "bouncing ball" was added after a test screening of the film confirmed that McDonald's words were difficult for audiences to understand. Martin Scorsese, one of the film's editors, suggested audiences should "follow the bouncing ball." See Vincent LoBrutto, *Martin Scorsese: A Biography* (Westport, CT: Praeger, 2008), 109.

23 It is worth noting that Vietnam is rarely mentioned or alluded to in the film, outside of the Port-O-San sequence (a spontaneous interview with a Port-O-San cleaner) and a short scene featuring two towns people who debate whether the Woodstock festival should have taken place.

24 Both *Gimme Shelter* and *Woodstock* feature performances in different orders from the actual daily line-ups, suggesting that these performances are sequenced for dramatic effect.

25 There are a number of theories as to why The Rolling Stones began their performance so late at night: some have suggested the band continued their touring

habit of building up anticipation by making their audience wait; others believe Mick Jagger would only appear on stage after the sun went down. See Philip Norman, *The Stones* (London: Pan Books, 2002), 392. Alan Passaro, a member of the Oakland chapter of the Hell's Angels, went on trial for the murder of Meredith Hunter, but was acquitted mainly on the grounds of Hunter's possession of a loaded gun at the time of the stabbing. *Gimme Shelter* was used by the police to identify Passaro and screened for the trial jury. See ibid., 400–401.

26 From Chip Monck, a lighting technician and announcer for most of the festival: "The brown acid that is circulating around us is not specifically too good."

27 Thomas F. Cohen, *Playing to the Camera: Musicians and Musical Performances in Documentary Cinema* (New York: Columbia University Press, 2012), 43.

28 Various unconfirmed figures exist regarding the number of cameras and cameramen at Woodstock. *Woodstock: An Inside Look at the Movie That Shook Up the World and Defined a Generation* contains an anonymously authored "list of things we took" that includes nine Eclair NPR cameras, one converted Auricon 16mm camera, three Bolex cameras, and three Arri S cameras, totaling sixteen cameras; "Our Arsenal," in Bell, *Woodstock*, 72–74. In a recent interview, Albert Maysles recalled that that there were somewhere between fifteen to eighteen cameras at Altamont, including the one he operated, which was positioned to the left of the stage for most of the concert before being moved onto the stage to film The Rolling Stones. Brian Lynch, "Albert Maysles on *Gimme Shelter*." http://perspectivesfilmfestival.com/archive2010/?p=172 (accessed March 2012).

29 Thomas M. Kitts, "Documenting, Creating, and Interpreting Moments of Definition: *Monterey Pop*, *Woodstock*, and *Gimme Shelter*," *Journal of Popular Culture* 42, No. 4 (August 2009), 722.

Chapter 5

"Let your Bullets Fly, My Friend"

Jimi Hendrix at Berkeley

Emile Wennekes

Some four months before his sudden death in a London hotel room at the age of twenty-seven, Jimi Hendrix gave two Memorial Day concerts in Berkeley, California.[1] These stage performances provided the primary source material for the movie *Jimi Plays Berkeley* (Peter Pilafian, 1971).[2] For diehard watchers of rock concert footage, this very first film to feature Hendrix as its principal subject could be—at first glance at least—of little interest. In pop musicological literature the movie is usually marginalized, if not neglected. It might not be Hendrix's best recorded performance; some involved qualify it as "sloppy" and "wasted" even, because Hendrix talked a lot between songs.[3] In Shapiro and Glebbeek's *Jimi Hendrix: Electric Gypsy* the qualification is simply: "This could have been a five star film if only they had presented some of the songs in their entirety."[4] Nevertheless, this 1971 Peter Pilafian "rockumentary" is a unique artifact within the "Hendrixology" of (concert) films, rare TV show appearances, and posthumously created documentaries. The movie is generally referred to as "a more or less straightforward concert film," to cite biographer Charles Shaar Murray,[5] and although it contains perhaps "some of the best Hendrix concert footage" ever—a qualification by biographer Charles R. Cross[6]—authors marginalize the fact that the film includes images of protesters trying to get free admission to these concerts, as well as some striking footage of politically motivated rioting. These inclusions place the performance concert registration in a hybrid category of music documentaries, one in which observational documentary characteristics are featured in a "Direct Cinema" style, typical of the time. One need only cite the hand-held camera documentaries by contemporary D. A. Pennebaker, the person behind the 1967 Monterey Pop Festival documentary, *Monterey Pop* (1968), featuring Hendrix's iconographical and spectacular guitar "sacrifice" within the rendition of the song "Wild Thing," during which he set his Fender Stratocaster on fire.

Becoming Involved in a New Medium

Like the Hendrix discography, much of his audiovisual legacy is now available in different presentations, remediations, compilations, and contextualizations.

Footage is constantly issued, re-issued, and ripped off in various formats and distributed under comparable titles. Although his career was short lived and his repertoire easily surveyed, a relatively large amount of audiovisual material featuring Hendrix has survived, varying from lengthy concert presentations to shorter performances, some interviews, even some backstage footage.[7] This is due to the fact that Jimi Hendrix was on the verge of becoming involved "in the making of concert films/documentaries for distribution in cinemas and other outlets—something being done by relatively few rock acts at the time, The Beatles' *Let It Be* being a notable exception," as Ritchie Unterberger rightly points out in his small but informative Hendrix guide.[8] The film *Jimi Plays Berkeley* was the first opportunity to watch Hendrix perform at length on screen. In spite of its mere forty-nine minutes' length, the movie presents much more live footage of Hendrix than the iconographical, yet shorter appearances in the documentaries about Woodstock (Michael Wadleigh's *Woodstock*, 1970), in which Hendrix performed "Voodoo Child," "Star-Spangled Banner," and "Purple Haze" and *Monterey Pop*, in which he performed "Wild Thing."

Hendrix's manager, Michael Frank Jeffrey, played a crucial role in the decision to get involved in the relatively new medium of concert films. A controversial figure, Jeffrey made a name as business manager of The Animals and subsequently Jimi Hendrix, the artist he comanaged with former Animals bass player and producer Chas Chandler.[9] It was Jeffrey who assigned Peter Pilafian to the job of producing the Berkeley footage. Cinematographer Pilafian was at that point a busy musician himself; he had been performing the electric violin with The Mamas and The Papas (most notably on the hit album *The Mamas and The Papas*, 1966), acoustic bass with Ry Cooder and Taj Mahal and was heavily involved in the Greenwich Village folkscene of the 1960s. Pilafian's concert footage would eventually evolve into his first film. Pilafian recollects that Jeffrey "agreed to pay me to produce a film (at my insistence) which later became *Jimi Plays Berkeley*. He had never sent me a check for the shooting, but then when Jimi died, Jeffries phoned me within 24 hours and said he would pay what he owed and he wanted the footage right away."[10] This is consistent with a remark made by John McDermott, the catalog director of Hendrix's estate, who wrote: "like so many entities associated with his rich legacy, *Jimi Plays Berkeley* took form in the turbulent vacuum created by Hendrix's untimely death in September 1970. That it became a commercial property when other footage of Hendrix concerts languished elsewhere in vaults or left unclaimed was due entirely to the maneuvering of Jimi's manager Michael Jeffrey."[11]

A Multimedial Interaction between Music and Body Movement

Pilafian and his crew had full access to Hendrix, he underlined in the booklet of the 2003 DVD, but: "We were there to get concert coverage, not to make

Figure 5.1 Peter Pilafian in 1981 (photo: John Sidle).

a behind-the-scenes, personal documentary about Jimi." It is nevertheless exactly this mixture of concert footage with the behind-the-scenes, eyewitness filming that makes this movie such a compelling historical document. As a brash young filmmaker, Pilafian recognized an opportunity to do something more significant than merely process the exposed 16mm footage. Pilafian: "So my response was, 'Not so fast. How about if you pay me to make this into a complete film, since you probably have a lot on your hands with the estate etc. right now anyway.'"[12]

Jimi Plays Berkeley takes us back to the time of the initial major open-air festivals, with their spirit of free love, "Flower Power," their drug consumption and massive yet usually peaceful protests. This specific atmosphere is documented in the film, but its central focus remains a highly gifted musician and performer at the summit of his physical strength, dressed in a psychedelic outfit, designed by his spiritualist friend Emily "Rainbow" Touraine.[13] Hendrix, a left-handed player, and so consequently playing his white, regular right-hand

Fender Stratocaster upside down, embodies a striking multimedial interaction between music and body movement. He uses his body in "a genuine counterpoint with the music," Nicholas Cook noted in *Analysing Musical Multimedia*: "his stage performances were as much dance as music." His physical motions "became an independent dimension of variance."[14] It is poignant to note that the display of virility captured here occurred so shortly before Hendrix's untimely death.

Although some involved argue that the Berkeley concerts were not really part of an extended tour itinerary,[15] they belonged to a series of concerts that is usually referred to as The Cry of Love Tour. The tour commenced on April 25, 1970 at the (Great Western) Forum in Inglewood, a suburb of Los Angeles, and would last until August 1 of that year, when Hendrix gave his last official American concert in Honolulu.[16] For this tour or series of concerts, Hendrix was reunited with former Band of Gypsys bassist Billy Cox and the British drummer Mitch Mitchell, an original band member of The Jimi Hendrix Experience. The "fly-outs," as the band called the weekend concerts during this tour, "required them to fly out at the last minute,"[17] leaving weekdays for recording in Hendrix's New York Electric Lady Studios.

The Film Soundtrack versus the Audio Album

The Berkeley concert footage was shot during the two performances the trio gave on Saturday May 30 in the Community Theater. The first commenced at 7:30 p.m., the second at 10 p.m. The film is an editorial mix of both concerts and offers nine songs:

1. "Johnny B. Goode"
2. "Hear My Train A-Comin"
3. "Star-Spangled Banner"
4. "Purple Haze"
5. "I Don't Live Today"
6. "Hey Baby (New Rising Sun)"
7. "Lover Man"
8. "Machine Gun"
9. "Voodoo Chile" (or "Child").

For an unknown reason, the song that plays under the opening screen credits, "Straight Ahead" (at that time still known as "Pass It On"), is not listed anywhere, neither in the film's credits, nor the tracklist, nor the DVD booklet nor its cover. It should be noted, however, that this particular performance is the opening song of the audio album with the same title as the documentary; this specific audio album presents the entire second concert of the evening and is not identical to the film soundtrack.[18] During this second set, numbers 3 to 9 were performed, combined with "Pass It On," "Stone Free," and "Foxy

Lady," all three missing from the film. The audio of the concert was recorded by the famed American soundman Wally Heider with his mobile, eight-track remote recording truck. Abe Jacobs was the engineer. Strikingly, two of the eight audio tracks were reserved for recording the audience in stereo, in spite of the fact that the original video was mono.[19] Track 8 was for the film sound synchronization (60 Hz). The instruments of Mitchell and Cox were both recorded with (only) one channel, the vocal back-up used one, and Hendrix got two, one for his guitar and the other for his voice.[20] The audiotape was remixed at Heider's famous sound studio C in Hyde Street, San Francisco. In the actual released version of the video, Pilafian and Howard Chesley are credited for the sound, while the South-African-born Eddie Kramer signed for the remix produced in Hendrix's Electric Lady Studios at Greenwich Village. From 1970 to 1974, Kramer was director of engineering at Electric Lady Studios, where he produced Hendrix's posthumous albums.

Go With the Flow

The Berkeley event was captured by Pilafian's crew in an improvisational, even reactive way. The camera crew consisted of four cameramen: Joan Churchill, Eric Saarinen, Peter Smokler, and the uncredited Baird Bryant.[21] Peter Smokler filmed from the balcony of the theater, sometimes freakishly zooming in and out, from a total stage shot to a blurred Hendrix close-up shot. He gave "a wide cutting option at any time."[22] Eric Saarinen filmed at the front edge of the stage. He even appears briefly in the song "Machine Gun" (at the passage "Let your bullets fly, my friend") in an on-stage, over-the-shoulder shot by Baird Bryant. Joan Churchill filmed from stage left. There was no stage-based script for the concert footage, no clear plan beforehand for takes and cuts, no diagram of camera position. Typical of the day, they just assigned rough "zone coverage." Pilafian's crew had to react to everything as it happened, parallel to the two musical sidemen who had to react to what their leader was up to: Hendrix did not decide in advance on set lists, but opted "instead to operate solely by feel, reading his audience and reacting accordingly."[23] In turn, the cameramen reacted spontaneously to the events on stage and in the audience, Smokler even wildly shaking his camera during a stretched tremolo during the rendition of "Star-Spangled Banner." Since the crew was predominantly coming from "a cinéma vérité documentary film background," it was natural for them to "go with the flow" in any situation, including unpredictable real-life dialogue exchanges. Observational filming requires improvisational skills.[24] Cutting and editing were done in a comparable way, not directly "subsumed within the song hierarchy"—for that matter becoming more a parameter of the event itself rather than being "a parameter of the music"—to touch base with Nicholas Cook once more.[25] So the edited material shows no clear, cut-on-the-beat shot changes from the song's refrains, or strictly musically motivated zooming in and out; however, the film does

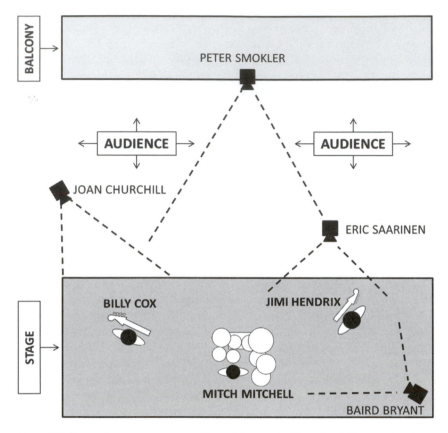

Figure 5.2 Stage diagram: camera positions (diagram by Tom Attah from a sketch by Emile Wennekes).

show rough, off-beat cuts: from total to low-angle shots to close-ups from different perspectives and cameras.

A Taxonomy of Footage

The film *Jimi Plays Berkeley* comprises seven types of footage:

a)   concert footage from the four cameras, also capturing shots of the audience;

b)   backstage footage:
   – rare, intimate shots of Hendrix in his stretched limousine, accompanied by his friends Devon Wilson and Colette Mimram;
   – the arrival of the group at the artist's entrance of the Community Theater;

– the comprehensive sound check, scrupulously done in the knowledge that everything would be recorded.

In addition to these two concerns, the film includes footage that was originally intended as periphery augmentations: glimpses of what was happening around Berkeley at the time. It is this supplementary material, documenting the place and period of the concerts, that makes the footage unexpectedly poignant. One can deduce five additional categories from it:

c) receptional Hendrix footage, for example street interviews;
d) footage of (illegal) break-in attempts before and during the concerts by people demanding free concert admission;
e) indirectly related off-stage footage;
f) footage of *Woodstock* admissions protesters;
g) Berkeley riot footage.

With these seven categories of audiovisual material *Jimi Plays Berkeley* addresses the viewer in ways situated between the "observational" and the "interactive"—in cautious reference to a typology suggested by Bill Nichols to represent reality in documentaries.[26] The observational approach can be seen in the footage of and around the performances (categories a and b), the indirectly related off-stage footage (category e) as well as in the shots of riots (category g). The more interactive angle is apparent from the receptional footage (category c) and in the break-in attempts to enter the venue (category d). The topical footage of residents protesting the showing of Wadleigh's Academy Award-winning *Woodstock* film (category f) was shot outside, in front of a nearby cinema theater. This material includes receptional remarks about Hendrix by participants (thus overlapping with category c)—like "Jimi's fame has not whirled his head." The *Woodstock* footage is the most humorous and certainly captures the sign of the times: youngsters postulating that "all music must be free," accompanied by a pet mutt bearing a proclamation that reads "The people made Woodstock, Warner Bros. makes profit." The protesters argued that three-and-a-half dollars was too high a price for a movie ticket, especially a ticket to *this* movie. This sequence becomes thrilling when someone, who is obviously not sympathetic to this point of view, starts an argument that could be paraphrased as: "hey, you simply have to work in order to go to the movies, protesting won't help you." This hyper passerby nearly generates a scuffle. All these images capture fundaments of the period's political atmosphere, but have nothing directly to do with the Hendrix concerts in town. As in *Woodstock* however, Hendrix did perform his revolutionary rendition of the "Star-Spangled Banner" during the Berkeley Community Theater concerts. This fact cannot be interpreted as a conscious narratological wink on Hendrix's part. Hendrix—the hero of many a revolutionary of the time—had not suddenly joined the capitalist camp of Warner Bros.

Protesters

The admission ticket price of the Hendrix performances—between $3.50 and $5.50—also triggered the attempts to illegally enter the concert venue by jumping over the fence and breaking in through the roof. Within this specific category of footage the perspective—unintentionally—changes from observational to interactive, not only in answering the motivation about the illegal break-in, but especially in the protesters' attempt to engage the film crew as their accomplices. The protesters suggest that they should all crash the venue together, pretending they are members of the crew. It is this particular footage that illustrates one of the most fundamental anthropological dilemmas on a documentary level: it is impossible merely to observe. To be there is to be already "part of the scene," and so subsequently to be an influence on that scene, and therefore to become a component of the film's narrative.

The Berkeley riot footage is the final category to be discussed here. This material is, in a way, even more of a strange element in the documentary concert film than the previous category. Hendrix was by no means present at the riots, and in fact he had not been in Berkeley since he was a small child. Furthermore, the material was not even filmed by Pilafian's crew, but was purchased several months after the concerts from a news cameraman, Johann Rush, who is credited separately for his material. It was not Pilafian who championed the incorporation of Rush's material, but filmmaker and writer Baird Bryant. Pilafian recruited Bryant, giving him a free hand in the editing process. Bryant had previously been one of the twenty camera operators involved with the Maysles brothers' shocking Rolling Stones documentary *Gimme Shelter* (1970). He also shot the cemetery trip scene in Dennis Hopper's *Easy Rider* (1969).

Pilafian's Berkeley footage was not intended for use as or in a finished theatrical film. Its use was to be determined later. But in the process of turning this raw material into a theatrical film, Pilafian was then confronted with a lack of concert material and, as Hendrix was already deceased, Bryant suggested the possibility of broadening the film's scope, to pad out the limited footage, with a political message: it was Bryant who spliced footage of the student demonstrations into the performance of the song "Machine Gun."

Johann Rush's footage of civil unrest shows the University of California campus, and other locations in Berkeley, in the weeks preceding the concerts—a period in which these areas were effectively a battlefield where students, armed with stones, metal rods, and a huge catapult, were engaged in fierce fighting with the National Guard, which was equipped with full battle gear: helmets, shields, and gas masks. Berkeley had grown into an icon of student protest, dating back to the Free Speech Movement of 1964. These more recent riots were triggered by then Governor Ronald Reagan and his ominous response to student protests, such as the one at Kent State University in Ohio the previous year: "if it takes a bloodbath, let's get it over with."[27] These student protests ultimately resulted in 128 injuries and one death. The Rush material offers very dynamic eyewitness footage and is present even during Hendrix's introductory dedication of the song "Machine Gun." A former paratrooper himself, Hendrix dedicates the song to "all the soldiers fighting in Berkeley . . . you know what soldiers I'm talking about . . . I dedicate it to other people that might be fighting wars too, but within themselves, not facing up to the realities." Note that there is no reference made at all here to the Vietnam War, something Hendrix did however address in his second set with the words: "and oh yeah, the soldiers fighting in Vietnam too."[28] The lyrics differ in each performance of "Machine Gun"—Hendrix clearly had some compositional building blocks for every tune and text, the components of which are slightly altered with each rendition.

Let your Bullets Fly, My Friend

In many respects the "Machine Gun" sequence is the most adventurous and most telling of the *Jimi Plays Berkeley* film, alternating diegetic and non-diegetic use of the music, changing from on- to off-stage images and back, sometimes even using different audio material from the concerts as the soundtrack to the footage of the live performance.[29] At the start of Hendrix's verbal introduction, we immediately see shots of the riots and these continue to be underscored by the guitar riff that forms the musical opening of the song. As soon as Hendrix starts singing his first stanza, however, the visual attention returns to him. This occurs with heavy zooming into often unfocused details, all covered in a blue stage lighting that lends the scenery a blurred, psychedelic effect. With the first guitar intermezzo, the riot images rapidly return and the next vocal passage ("I pick up my axe") is also accompanied by the riots. Hendrix is once again in view when he starts his guitar solo, this time rotated ninety degrees, as if the screen has been turned on its left side. For the last stanza ("Let your bullets fly"), Hendrix remains the principal visual subject. During the song's climactic closing guitar solo with its "crash-and-burn extravaganzas,"[30] feedback, and virtuoso whammy bar technique, Hendrix remains the primary subject on screen.

The Berkeley protests, although initially focused on the Vietnam War, were to expand in scope, eventually becoming a general antiwar and antigovernment movement. The fact that Hendrix—at least in the film—failed to specifically address Vietnam signifies that he was perhaps tuning in to an even higher level of abstraction. "Machine Gun" is then a song, for Unterberger, that is in "protest against all pointless death"[31]—a distressing fact in regards to Hendrix's own sudden death. Yet by cutting in concrete riots scenes, editor Baird Bryant cut away alternative "readings." At other moments, however, the documentary-like inserts not only illustrate or comment on the performances, they introduce additional components, and remain open to a variety of possible narrative interpretations. A striking example is the "Star-Spangled Banner" track, which includes indirectly related off-stage footage in which a black boy receives a saxophone lesson, somewhere in the street—an obvious hint of the civil rights movement. Although he was a hero for many left-wing intellectuals, Hendrix remained an African-American who, at that moment in time, would barely have been allowed to enter the front door of Southern State theaters.[32] The saxophone-playing kid in the street echoes enigmatically Hendrix's own words, elsewhere in the film, where he introduces himself as "yours truly on public saxophone." While the images show the boy, Hendrix lets his guitar scream across the lyrics "and the rocket's red glare, bombs bursting in air."

Neither Concert Film nor Documentary

The numerous narratives, many only tentatively suggested, make *Jimi Plays Berkeley* an intriguing film. Should the film have been constructed solely around the backstage footage and the concert footage, Charles Shaar Murray's previously quoted qualification of "a more or less straightforward concert film" would indeed make sense. But due to the incorporation of the extra five peripheral categories, as suggested, the film must be situated within a hybrid framework. The film represents a subgenre: it is neither a straight concert film nor a straight documentary. The film's title surely leaves room for multiple interpretations and classifications. Even the title was only finalized at the very last minute. Pilafian recalls: "Baird and I were walking into the lab to deliver the edited work print for negative matching, and we still did not have a title. As we approached the window, we knew we would have to come up with something in the next few minutes. In one of those unexplainable flashes of inspiration, one of us said: 'why not keep it simple?' We spontaneously agreed, and it seems to have been a good choice."[33]

Immediately afterwards, a new phase in the production history of *Jimi Plays Berkeley* commenced. In general terms, the "making of" history continued as follows: dissatisfied with the material Pilafian and Bryant offered him, the manager of the deceased Hendrix hired John Jansen, sound engineer at the Electric Lady Studios, to recut the material once more and to better synchronize the images with the sound. Jansen, however, is not credited. Michael Jeffrey—credited as executive producer—apparently finished the job and ultimately launched this movie with a running time of well under an hour, presenting it in an extended network of colleges and independent theaters where it rapidly gained cult status. The film was distributed by New Line Cinema, at that time a relatively small company that handled art films and booked people to give guest lectures at universities. Pilafian recalls, "While I was in New York, I took the film to Bob Shaye, president of New Line Cinema. He liked it and wanted to make a deal. However, since Mike Jeffries subsequently maneuvered me out of any profit participation, it was up to him to deal directly with Bob."[34] Through New Line the film became a cult hit, initially triggered by midnight screenings in California (as in Venice, Santa Barbara, in a theater on Lincoln Boulevard, and other venues). In the early seventies, the film could be seen in many theaters across the US and Europe, sometimes as part of music film double-bills (as with New York's Garrick Theater on Bleecker Street). In the Edinburgh Picture House, *Jimi Plays Berkeley* was programmed as a "support act" to a live concert by the rock group Gentle Giant.

Neither an Idol nor a Star

In 2003, a digitalized picture transfer of the original film was released on DVD, produced by John McDermott and Janie Hendrix (Jimi's half-sister) for Experience Hendrix LCC. The soundtrack was once again remixed by Eddie Kramer, this time in the Clinton Recording Studios in New York in both stereo and 5.1 audio surround sound. The mastering was done by George Marino and the video postproduction by Sony's Paul Furedi.

Jimi Plays Berkeley has retained its cult status. For almost half a century after the "shootings," the images of the Berkeley protests have become as historic as the images of Jimi Hendrix performing in the Berkeley Community Theater. In contrast to most rock- or pop-orientated films, this star-oriented movie was originally *not* intended to promote, market, or sell the musician(s) featured, but merely to document a phenomenon. Or, as Peter Pilafian phrased it: "Since we came from a *cinéma vérité* background, and worked in Hollywood, we saw this young guitar player as a fascinating subject for a film, rather than worshipping him as an idol or a star."[35]

Notes

1 The author would like to acknowledge the assistance provided by Peter Pilafian, Steven Barncard, and Cynthia Wilson in the preparation of this article, and thank them for generously sharing their experiences.
2 The footage is issued on different formats and editions:
   Jimi Plays Berkeley (VHS); USA 1971: Westron Music Video
   Jimi Plays Berkeley (VHS); UK 1971: Palace Video
   Jimi Plays Berkeley May 1970 (VHS); USA 1990: Warner Reprise Video (cat. #38223-3)
   Jimi Plays Berkeley (VHS, PAL & CD, EP); UK 1990: BMG Video, Gravity 5 (cat. #791 168)
   Jimi Plays Berkeley (DVD-V, NTSC), USA 2003: MCA/Experience Hendrix (cat.# 062498611272). For this chapter the 2003 DVD adaptation is used for analysis.
3 Email correspondence with Stephen Barncard, January 29, 2012. Back in the seventies Barncard was assistant engineer at Heider's Studios in San Francisco. For further information see www.wallyheider.com.
4 Harry Shapiro and Caesar Glebbeek, *Jimi Hendrix: Electric Gypsy* (London: Heinemann, 1991), 704.
5 Charles Shaar Murray, *Crosstown Traffic: Jimi Hendrix and Post-War Pop* (London: Faber and Faber, 2001), 70.
6 Charles R. Cross, *Room Full of Mirrors: A Biography of Jimi Hendrix* (New York: Hyperion 2005), 295.

7   For more information about Hendrix on film, see: Shapiro and Glebbeek, *Hendrix*, 704–705; Richie Unterberger, *The Rough Guide to Jimi Hendrix* (London: Rough Guides Ltd, 2009), 199–208; Andy Aledort, "Rock Me, Baby! A Complete Guide to Jimi Hendrix's Album and Video Catalog," *Guitar World* 20 (November 2000), 68–69; Robert Christgau, "Music: Jimi Plays History: Redigitalizing Hendrix for the '90s," *Village Voice* 42 (May 6, 1997), 69–71; Steve Rody, "Black Gold: The Lost Archives of Jimi Hendrix," *Goldmine* 26 (September 8, 2000), 14–18.

8   Unterberger, *Rough Guide*, 199.

9   William Saunders, *Jimi Hendrix: London* (Berkeley, California: Roaring Forties Press, 2010), 19–20.

10   Email correspondence with Peter Pilafian, January 31, 2012.

11   John McDermott, "Jimi Plays Berkeley: The Long Strange Cinematic Trip," MCA/Experience Hendrix DVD booklet, 2003.

12   Pilafian to the author, January 31, 2012.

13   The fact that the footage comes from both concerts can also be surmised by Hendrix's different outfits. For Touraine, see Wade James Hollinghaus, *Currencies of Rock Performance: Youth, Electricity, and Capital* (University of Minnesota, 2008), 115.

14   Nicholas Cook, *Analysing Musical Multimedia* (Oxford: Oxford University Press, 1998), 263.

15   DVD booklet.

16   Shapiro and Glebbeek, *Hendrix*, 421, 693–695. There were some cancellations within the tour due to Hendrix's "glandular problems" (ibid., 422, 425).

17   Cross, *Room Full of Mirrors*, 297.

18   The audio album with the second set gave the program as: "Pass it On," "Hey Baby (New Rising Sun)," "Lover Man," "Stone Free," "I Don't Live Today," "Machine Gun," "Foxy Lady," "Star-Spangled Banner," "Purple Haze," "Voodoo Child."

19   Pilafian comments: "back then it was normal to do real-time mixing onto only a few tracks, relying on the mixer's skill during a performance or even a studio session, rather than doing big multi-track mixes later on, essentially postponing many decisions about balance, etc." Pilafian to the author, February 1, 2012.

20   Barncard to the author, January 29, 2012. The bass sound might be a mix between track and direct sound.

21   Pilafian to the author, January 31, 2012.

22   Pilafian to the author, February 1, 2012.

23   DVD booklet.

24   Cf. Michael Chanan's "Putney Debater" blog:http://putneydebater.wordpress.com/2010/06/10/music-documentaries/(accessed January 29, 2012).

25   Cook, *Analysing Musical Multimedia*, 165.

26   Bill Nichols, *Representing Reality: Issues and Concepts in Documentary* (Bloomington: Indiana University Press, 1991), passim.

27   Marlee Richards, *America in the 1970s* (Minneapolis: Twenty-First Century Books, 2010), 12. General information in: Philip Caputo, *13 Seconds: A Look Back at the Kent State Shootings* (New York: Chamberlain Bros., 2005).

28   On these political dimensions, see Lauren Onkey, "Voodoo Child: Jimi Hendrix and the Politics of Race in the Sixties," in Peter Braunstein and Michael William Doyle (eds.), *Imagine Nation: The American Counter Culture of the 1960s and 70s* (New York and London: Routledge, 2002), 189–213.

29   Sound and images in the film are sometimes out of sync. At the end of the first stanza, Hendrix's voice can still be heard even though he leans back, far away from the microphone, while starting a different guitar solo than the one his fingers

actually play. This is more often the case in this film, especially when Hendrix is seen from his back; one repeatedly sees him playing different notes than the ones heard.

30 Shaar Murray, *Crosstown Traffic*, 263.
31 Unterberger, *Rough Guide*, 195.
32 Onkey, "Voodoo Child," 207.
33 Pilafian to the author, January 30, 2012.
34 Pilafian to the author, February 1, 2012.
35 Ibid.

Chapter 6

"You Can't Always Get What You Want"

Riding on The Medicine Ball Caravan

David Sanjek

It must have seemed like a good idea at the time, a veritable no-brainer.[1] You can imagine the confidence that permeated the pitch meeting at Warner Brothers in the spring of 1970. The confounding success of their recent release of Michael Wadleigh's *Woodstock* (1970), returning over $50 million on a $500,000 investment, confirmed to the media conglomerate not only the marketability of youth culture but also the seeming insatiability of that generation's appetite to see themselves depicted on screen. Some criticized this inclination as little more than narcissism on an epic scale, yet the studio felt disinclined to engage in character analysis. They simply saw their role as to provide the necessary mirror. Fred Weintraub, Vice President of Youth Markets, spearheaded this project for Warner Brothers. Tom Donahue, one of the progenitors of free-form radio, orchestrated the day-to-day activities and supervised the talent. Francois Reichenbach, an Academy Award-winning French documentarian, captured all that ensued on film. The Medicine Ball Caravan proposed to sponsor a sequence of cross-country musical performances in which the artists and those who stage manage the events would receive equal billing. The participating bands would be recruited from Warners' stable, thereby in-sourcing the talent and excising the need to reward another corporation. Tack onto that a peripatetic narrative structure that echoed literary models, like that of Kerouac's novel *On The Road* (1957), or recent cinematic achievements, most notably *Easy Rider* (Dennis Hopper, 1969), and place the participants in the geographic midst of a volatile nation whose social seams were only barely stitched in place. Film the results on the run, drawing on the tactics of *cinéma-vérité*. Hope for a frolic, but prepare for a fiasco. Either way the final product would be nothing less than far out and fill up seats at your local theater.

A year later, aspirations collided with actuality. Sometimes during this period of experimentation on virtually all fronts, the effort to graft together seemingly disparate agendas resulted in something that would test preconceived limitations. Norman Mailer, for example, successfully conflated the novel and history in his investigation of the march on the Pentagon, *The Armies of the Night* (1968). Other times, the results collapsed into something as ungainly and god-awful as the drive-in "classic" *The Thing with Two Heads* (Lee Frost, 1972). The image therein contained of Ray Milland's head surgically affixed to black athlete Rosie Greer's body literalized the collision of the races to the point of absurdity. *The Medicine Ball Caravan* may not have transgressed the limits of credulity so nakedly, but it certifiably strained both the beliefs about young audiences as well as the balance sheets of Warner Brothers. What the corporation assumed would be, in the words of the event's chronicler John Grissim, "another road-show version of Woodstock" metastasized into "a month-long party that will probably go down as the most bizarre, if not the funniest, event in the media world that year."[2] The executives did not share the joke however, as the project lost $1.5 million, required a wholesale re-edit, opened and closed in New York City after only a week, got lambasted by the critics, and was speedily withdrawn from circulation. While a soundtrack album appeared, Warner Brothers to date have failed yet to release a VHS, DVD, or Blu-Ray edition of the motion picture. Grissim concludes about the escapade that "in all likelihood the adventure will end up as a historical footnote of passing interest," a characterization that quite possibly grants *The Medicine Ball Caravan* more substance than its 90 minutes can bear.[3]

Nonetheless, the act of paying attention to this cinematic shambles amounts to something more than misplaced *Schadenfreude*. What resonates throughout the film at the present time is not simply the misjudgements and oversights of the participants so much as the coincidence of a number of factors, both intrinsic and extrinsic to the events, that contributed to its calamity. This chapter proposes to examine three of those influences. First how the institutional dynamics of the music industry in 1970, specifically the augmentation of the corporate approach to commercial culture, collided with the lingering desires on the part of some of the participants to avoid being co-opted and, in turn, conning their audiences. Secondly how the absence of a discernable narrative trajectory in Reichenbach's footage left the editors in a sorry state as this lack virtually obliterated any kind of dramatic arc, resulting in an often redundant and far from resonant body of images. Thirdly how certain traumatic fractures in the ideological ambitions of the counterculture corrupted the potentially altruistic motives of some members of the Caravan and led them to misjudge the interests of their audience. If Donahue and some others ostensibly aimed to bring alternative viewpoints to the youth of Middle America, their motives unfortunately betrayed a lamentable state of consciousness that Mailer adroitly characterizes in his analysis of the 1972 political conventions as "a complacent innocence altogether near to arrogance."[4] Grissim somewhat blithely says of the Caravan, "It was a little of everything: a capitalist venture, a noble purpose, a tripster fantasy, a plot, even an immense joke."[5] Endeavouring to be so many things to such a multiplicity of constituencies, *The Medicine Ball Caravan* ended up defusing whatever musical, cinematic, or ideological ambitions it might have achieved such that its virtual erasure from the public record may be lamentable but remains altogether understandable.

The considerable success of the film *Woodstock* and the considerable additional profits accrued from the soundtrack released by Cotillion Records reinforced the importance of the youth market to corporate balance sheets. Boardroom residents had just newly awakened to these opportunities, beginning with the Seven Arts purchase of the Warner Brothers brand in 1967 and their speedy acquisition shortly thereafter of Atlantic Records. The degree to which the fiscal stakes had risen was also confirmed by the bidding wars that ensued at the Monterey Pop Festival that same year and only increased in size subsequently at Woodstock. Signing bonuses ballooned, as when Capitol Records put forth the then unheard-of figure of $40,000 each for Quicksilver Messenger Service and The Steve Miller Band. The Kinney Corporation, led by used-car and parking-lot magnate Steve Ross, engineered a prominent place in the process when they absorbed Warner and Atlantic in 1969 only to add two other prominent independent concerns: Jac Holzman's Elektra and David Geffen's newly founded Asylum. The principal players in the industry contracted in short order, as the leading four (Columbia, Warners, Capitol, and RCA Victor) sewed up 50 percent of the marketplace. Profits rose incrementally. By 1973, the music industry reported $2 billion in yearly income. Enumerating these figures and mergers does not aim simply to echo Adorno's animosity against the culture industy in a knee-jerk manner. Rather it is to echo the account of history. To assert therefore that a system that once offered considerable opportunities for individual entrepreneurs who sometimes combined visionary and fiscal propensities had succumbed to profit-motivated objectives amounts to the same kind of commonplace as to argue that potatoes contain ample carbohydrates.

The ambition to unseat the forces that served as the foundation of this enterprise would prove to be as daunting as to convince the average adolescent of the benefits of a well-balanced diet. It collided with the corporation's seemingly transparent attempts to abscond with the rhetoric of the counter-culture and alter that discourse into a marketing tool. Most memorable of these efforts was the 1969 Columbia campaign that trumpeted the injunction "The Man Can't Bust Our Music," seemingly either unaware of or unembarrassed by the statement's oxymoronic dimensions. Just such a divisive and potentially self-destructive pursuit of seemingly antithetical ambitions lay at the core of The Medicine Ball Caravan. Some of those on the bus might have convinced themselves that they could circumvent the corporate agenda, but most did so by absenting it from their awareness. Consequently, when the outside agitator/underground journalist/White Panther spokesman Tom Forcade interjected his admittedly propagandistic critique into the mix by challenging the endeavour's intentions, he was dismissed by Tom Donahue as advocating "Maoist, moralist horseshit" driven by a constitutionally narrow definition of revolution.[6] Donahue, and others, refused to concede the artificial construction of the Caravan and its somewhat confounding ambitions. Their position bracketed off and bailed out on inquiring, as John Grissim observes, "whose reality is being filmed, or, in other words, whose movie is it?"[7]

You would think that Donahue might have proved more prescient about and provoked by these conundrums, for he had been one of the groundbreaking stage managers of the transformation of the airwaves and adoption of a more inclusive playlist through his administration of San Francisco-based KMPX. He recognized and thereafter institutionalized a dialogue with radio audiences that paralleled the collective discourse emanating from the counterculture. Consequently, "the governing principle was to play music—any cut from an album, not just the song the record company designated as a single—as you would for your friends."[8] Donahue succeeded in acquiring his requisite share of that target audience without talking down to those consumers by recognizing that they collectively inhabited an alternate frequency. Forcade's fulminations, unfortunately, came across as just so much static, notwithstanding the fact that Donahue had only recently been sensitized to competing concepts of commerce. During the summer of 1969, he clashed in San Francisco with a host of alienated constituencies who felt locked out of a proposed Wild West Festival of which Donahue was one of the producers. Those who assumed cultural labor could not be severed from an expansive definition of civic consciousness argued that this event imperilled the integrity of their community, such that to gain a stake in the profits would invariably thrust a stake into their very souls. One flier announced, "Long Hair Is Not Enough! Is Your Soul Shaggy Too?".[9] Donahue did not carry the conundrums raised by this debate along with his cross-country baggage onto the Caravan, yet that did not mean the fissures it illustrated had been left at home beside the San Francisco Bay.

If the intentions and ambitions of many of the travellers on the Caravan remain ill-defined, those that impelled the filmmakers prove to be similarly imprecise. Francois Reichenbach perceives his young subjects through a haze of romantic stereotypes as impenetrable as the pot smoke that surfeited their surroundings. The serial enumeration of one shot after another of glazed-over adventurers in his 130 hours of footage might at best incrementally illustrate their *joie de vivre*. However, it fails to ascribe any nuance or texture to their behaviour. Reichenbach observed to John Grissim, "I can't see young people being wrong. Even if they are wrong they put in life."[10] Such an approach all too easily risks infantalizing his subjects, thereby transforming their promotion of the pleasure principle into little more than a risk-free reflex. It also dissolves any distinguishing characteristics between individuals, making it hard to think of the Caravan as other than a homogeneous mass. While that approach is reinforced by the fact that the film begins and ends with a group photo of the characters, intimating their unity of purpose and point of view, one nonetheless cannot help but imagine the probable presence of contradictions obscured and collisions overlooked.

The cutting out of collisions between the characters evaporates anything that might be particularly dramatic or dynamic and thereby saps any narrative integrity from an arguably listless 90 minutes. The Caravan may move transcontinentally from place to place, but paradoxically comes across as virtually standing still. It furthermore renders the confrontation that occurs in Yellow Springs, Ohio and concludes the film even more opaque. Reichenbach's cameras fail to convey what John Grissim recognizes: "the symbolic significance of those twenty or thirty seconds stands out with crushing irony—the Caravan of Love has just pulled a knife."[11] The students from local Antioch College reject the Caravan's presence and debate the event's motivations, albeit in the form of a dialogue that rapidly descends into an empty exchange of slogans. Brought along by Tom Forcade, David Peel, the Lower East Side performer of audience-friendly agit-prop, interjects himself into a fevered debate yet only succeeds in pouring kerosene on an already raging blaze. Broadcaster and caravan crew chief Chan Laughlin loses patience with Peel and draws out his weapon. Temporary chaos ensues. By not foregrounding the event's array of motivations, The Medicine Ball Caravan transforms the complex cultural dynamics dramatized by their confrontation into caricatures. This allows Grissim, and others, to dismiss the interventions of Forcade as the blatherings of "a politically righteous Captain Bad Vibes."[12] This temporary surrender of serenity just before the final credits roll consequently leaves the audience with the impression that ideology amounts to a virtual afterthought, something you indulge in when you cannot pharmacologically alter your consciousness.

The failure to interrogate their own motives and methodology goes to the very core of the Medicine Ball Caravan's raison d'être. What were they hoping to achieve by criss-crossing the nation and what did they hope to offer to the audiences they encountered? The document that Tom Donahue presented to Warner Brothers when they shopped the project characterizes the event as follows:

> We have formed a Caravan of love, discovery and sharing that will retrace the steps of the pioneers from West to East and on to the Europe of our forefathers. We do not return to seek old philosophies or values but rather to bring a new life-style and new attitudes accompanied by the music that best of all expresses the new world in which we live—a new world in which Margaret Mead has said the older generation must think of themselves as Migrants.[13]

Effusive and engaging as this rhetoric might sound the leaders of this venture seem to have been deaf to the echoes of the less than vaunted imperatives that inspired the pioneers whom they emulated. Their distinction between advancing the ambitions of a new counterculture and ignoring any value in the pre-existent beliefs or social practices of those they encountered along the way might possibly be thought of as a kind of day-glo grafting of imperialism upon a smiling facade. For one might well ask, as did the students at Oberlin in addition to Tom Foracade, just what was the Caravan advocating and were they at all concerned whether their intended audience might spurn their gifts? Might there be an unintended totalitarian dimension to the advocacy of transcendence, and can one feel liberated as a matter not of ambition but obligation if not insistence?

The activities of the Caravan bring to mind the often-quoted admonition espoused by Ken Kesey and the Merry Pranksters as a means of promoting the virtues of the Acid Test—the pharmacologically induced alteration of conscious they championed: "You're either on the bus or off the bus." Inviting as that phrase might be, it can be thought equally to combine an element of both inclusion and exclusion. Much as it welcomes acolytes, it shuns the apostate. Tom Wolfe's 1968 classic narrative of the group's efforts at enlightenment, *The Electric Kool-Aid Acid Test*, illustrates the author's undeniable fascination with Kesey's charisma but simultaneously acknowledges his subject's affinity for manipulating others, albeit in the name of purportedly desirable ends. Kesey certainly aspired to control his environment, and those who joined him in it. Wolfe writes, "Control . . . and it was so plausible, the way it sounded in Kesey's Oregon drawl. So few humans have the hubris to exert their wills upon the flow, maybe not more than forty on the whole planet at any given time."[14] Kesey believed in the benign motives of his manipulation of circumstances, assumed that he was not unintentionally mimicking the brutal tactics of his character, Nurse Ratched, in her management of her patients' mental health.[15] Others in his circle ratify that agenda and argue that his charisma always served transactional ends and changed those who chose to enter his orbit for the better. However, if we make joy not an objective but an obligation, don't we risk diluting if not dissolving altogether the alterations in our being that it provides?

The late British film critic Raymond Durgant wrote dismissively of what he called "fun morality": "the post-puritan attitude whereby it's your duty to have fun, and if you fail you feel not only sad, but positively guilty . . . the puritan conscience devoted to post-puritan goals, and as preoccupied with one's own salvation."[16] With Durgant in mind, when is it therefore possible, as Nancy Reagan advocated in quite another context, to just say no?

"You're either on the Bus or off the Bus"

The Medicine Ball Caravan ultimately failed as both an endeavour and a motion picture for any number of reasons, but chief amongst them was the absence of any consideration of what it meant to get on board and the cost that entailed. Others have certainly paid their figurative as well as literal fare, for themselves and ultimately for all the rest of us, in order to be able to take their places. Rosa Parks certainly comes to mind, and the "new life-style and new attitudes" she helped to put in place more than made the fare she incurred worth the price. Some other occasions, and The Medicine Ball Caravan certainly seems to be one of them, lead you to think that in the end you have just been taken for a ride.

Afterword by Benjamin Halligan

A cliché among British jazz fans of the 1950s and 1960s was that the vinyl record was only able to communicate a fraction of the artistic prowess and abilities of their icons. It was the live experience that was the actual measure of, and true encounter with, the jazz musicians whose work was often understood to be predicated on authenticity. Arguably the fundamental aspect of the counterculture's moments of authenticity and freedom—of the be-ins, the love-in, the open-air festivals, the happenings—was derived from the way in which such events were understood to be essentially collective. It is the high-security zone, complete with crash barriers, electrified fences and security guards, as branded by advertising sponsors and/or charity Non-Governmental Organizations, as backed by multinational conglomerates and captains of industry, as understood as product promotion, as surveyed by CCTV and serviced by merchandisers, that typifies today's open-air music event. This is a far cry from its path-breaking predecessors. In this current set-up authenticity is an imperative mostly in respect of a contracted delivery of specified goods over a pre-agreed time period: for the musicians or performers to now appear as they do in their mediated images. This familiarity occurs both in terms of clothing and styling and the delivery of the pre-arranged set-list, and to the ends of the simultaneous relay of the performances to screens at the events themselves (whose portrayal of the gig sometimes results in an arresting disparity between the crash-edit "action" on the screen and the immobility of the band), or as simply broadcast, or as disseminated through social media. Such total commodification, in respect of reading each concert-goer as an individual with specific purchasing potential and tendencies, an economic analysis that begins long before the event occurs,[17] would seem to be a recent development, and perhaps represents the full, if belated, flowering of the Live Aid concert of 1985 where music for money became a rallying cry—Bob Geldof's cri du coeur, during a studio discussion broadcast from the event, of "Please—stay in and give us the money; there are people dying now, so give me the money!" Even in 1991, as evidenced in 1991: The Year Punk Broke (David Markey, 1992), the outdoor music festival had barely progressed beyond the chaos and exposure-to-the-elements of the famous Isle of Wight festival of 1970 (filmed by Murray Lerner as A Message to Love: The Isle of Wight Rock Festival, eventually released in 1996). There is a sense that the planning authorities will tolerate a temporary autonomous zone-style festival as long as it is safely away from urban centers and the revellers are consigned to a demarcated area. But this penning in, akin to a border camp for apprehended

Figure 6.1 Kurt Cobain in close proximity: *1991: The Year Punk Broke* (David Markey, 1992).

Figure 6.2 Crowd shot: *A Message to Love* (Murray Lerner, 1970/1996).

Figure 6.3 1960s-style crowd: *1991: The Year Punk Broke.*

immigrants, would need to move to the chicken battery model by the late 1990s: not the fenced-in masses of the festival, but individual cells of friends and families, or just individuals, so as to tap into specific, stratified, purchasing opportunities.

In this history, the conceit of the Medicine Ball Caravan initiative suggests that the project was more than just an aberrant footnote or coda to the great era of outdoor popular music events. While the initiative was clearly an exception, it would be an exception that would establish a rule: the flipping of the classic paradigm of the culture industries effectively consigned to a secondary, parasitical role of supporting the new cultural zeitgeist as it suddenly breaks surface. Failure to do so, as apparent in Clover's discussion of the British rave scene,[18] allows self-appointed middle-managers from that milieu to capitalize on the market, and dissolving this stubborn layer then becomes a matter of pre-emptive policing and retrospective legislation. The Medicine Ball Caravan was not entirely an aberration in its opportunism; as argued elsewhere in this volume, the already existing capitalization of the counterculture (particularly for Woodstock and Altamont, but it is apparent too in Hollywood's attempts, notably in respect of Michelangelo Antonioni's film *Zabriskie Point* of 1970) was problematic on a number of fronts. But an uneasy alliance between hipsters and money-men could be maintained as long as it remained mutually beneficial to both parties—those who created the sixties, and those engaged in selling the sixties. The Medicine Ball Caravan, then, can be read as a fatal melding of these roles to the end of manufactured goods: the attempt to create the sixties solely to sell these sixties. The glosses are unfortunate, to say the least, in that they speak of the notion of attaining a "natural" state that was central to the counterculture (drawing from writers such as Wilhelm Reich, D. H. Lawrence, R. D. Laing *et al.*): the folkie and bucolic, and the universal command to enjoy. And what seems to have sunk the exercise is ethnographic structuring and aesthetic: the happy masses of *Mondo Hollywood* (Robert Carl Cohen, 1967), *Tonite Let's All Make Love in London* (Peter Whitehead, 1967), *Revolution* (Jack O'Connell, 1968) or *Woodstock*, or even the unhappy masses of *Gimme Shelter* (Maysles brothers, 1970), a presence that could be traced back at least to *Rock Around the Clock* (Fred F. Sears, 1956), were missing from The Medicine Ball Caravan. Their absence altogether, as with the empty amphitheater of *Pink Floyd: Live at Pompeii* (Adrian Maben, 1972/2003), is preferable to their indifference.[19] In these respects, The Medicine Ball Caravan can be claimed as that unusual, and often obscure, cultural artefact: evidence of indifferent or miserable hippies in the eye of the countercultural storm, with the concomitant suggestion that the dream was illusory anyhow, as with *Eden miseria* (Jacques Baratier, 1967), *Vite* (Zanzibar Group/Daniel Pommereulle, 1969), *More* (Barbet Schroeder, 1969), *Say Hello to Yesterday* (Alvin Rakoff, 1971), *The Holy Mountain* (Alejandro Jodorowski, 1973) or, in its nostalgia and hindsight, *Withnail and I* (Bruce Robinson, 1987).

Figure 6.4 The empty amphitheater of *Pink Floyd: Live at Pompeii* (Adrian Maben, 1972/2003).

Figure 6.5 Summoning the dead in *Pink Floyd: Live at Pompeii.*

After the failure of The Medicine Ball Caravan, although in all likelihood not *directly* related to this failure, the relationship between live music and event, in the context of the music documentary or the concert film, would be radically realigned. Now the cameras were trained on the stage, or actually positioned on stage, with cutaway and atmosphere-shots culled from an alien vantage point: peering down into the crowd from the sky or, more recently (via techniques and technologies developed for live sports events) sweeping over the crowd, as a kind of crash zoom, on the way to the stage. This retreat to the performance and VIP areas of the event would seem to go hand-in-hand with the ascendency of a new (that is, post-Beatles) supergroup aristocracy, from the *Concert for Bangladesh* (Saul Swimmer, 1972), via *Cocksucker Blues* (Robert Frank, 1972), to *The Last Waltz* (Martin Scorsese, 1978), whereupon punk would come to represent a class-based critique of the bunker mentality of this old guard. Simultaneously, the "show" element of the live event would come to the fore (narrative and themes, dance and set design, elements of the catwalk)—a revelling in the very inauthencity that, Auslander notes, marks the point of departure from the counterculture in the beginnings of glam rock,[20] so that groups like Genesis, The Electric Light Orchestra and Queen and artists like Elton John, Marc Bolan, Gary Glitter, and David Bowie were quintessentially 1970s in their aesthetics, performances, and public personae. The rock film of this decade, as with *Pink Floyd: Live at Pompeii* (and then, in 1982, for *Pink Floyd: The Wall*, Alan Parker, from the 1979 album), Marc Bolan (*Born to Boogie*, Richard Starkey [Ringo Starr], 1972), Slade (*Flame*, also known as *Slade in Flame*, Richard Loncraine, 1974), David Essex (*Stardust*, Michael Apted, 1974), The Who (*Tommy*, Ken Russell,

1975), Led Zeppelin (*The Song Remains the Same*, Peter Clifton and Joe Massot, 1976), The Bee Gees and Peter Frampton (*Sgt. Pepper's Lonely Hearts Club Band*, Michael Schultz, 1978), and Frank Zappa (*Baby Snakes*, Zappa, 1979), only further illustrates the abandonment of the audience as the concept aspect of the "concept album" began to require theater and celluloid in addition to vinyl and gatefold art.[21] The return of the communal and collective music-orientated event in the 1970s, in the early years of disco and then rap and hip-hop—the music of the inner cities during the acceleration of deindustrial-isation and onset of asset-stripping, of the squatted building or underground gay nightclubs—remains, tellingly, with little visual documentation.

Notes

1 This is the text of a paper delivered by Professor David Sanjek for his co-convened international conference "Sights and Sounds: Interrogating the Music Documentary," which ran at the University of Salford, Greater Manchester, June 3–4, 2010.

2 John Grissim, Jr., *We Have Come for Your Daughters: What Went Down on The Medicine Ball Caravan* (New York: William Morrow, 1972), ix.

3 Ibid., 250.

4 Norman Mailer, *St. George and the Godfather* (New York: Arbor House, 1972), 33.

5 Ibid., 33.

6 Grissim, *We Have Come*, 118.

7 Ibid., 147.

8 Marc Fisher, *Something in The Air: Radio, Rock, and the Revolution that Shaped a Generation* (New York: Random House, 2007), 164.

9 Quoted in Michael J. Kramer, "The Lost Labor History of Hippies: The KMPX and Wild West Festival Strikes," unpublished article.

10 Grissim, *We Have Come*, 35.

11 Ibid., 156.

12 Ibid., 148.

13 Ibid., 14.

14 Tom Wolfe, *The Electric Kool-Aid Acid Test* (New York: Quality Paperback Books, 1990), 207.

15 Editor's note: Nurse Ratched was a fictional character in Kesey's 1962 novel *One Flew over the Cuckoo's Nest*, filmed by Miloš Forman in 1975.

16 Raymond Durgant, *The Crazy Mirror: Hollywood Comedy and the American Image* (New York: Delta Books, 1969), 214.

17 So that not having, say, the "right" credit card or mobile phone contract ultimately results in the penalization of poorer seats. Those with their payment papers in order are often granted the favour of the chance of an earlier purchase of tickets.

18 See Joshua Clover, *1989: Bob Dylan Didn't Have This to Sing About* (Berkeley, Los Angeles, London: University of California Press, 2009).

19 Hegarty and Halliwell note that the concert film was conceived in this fashion; Paul Hegarty and Martin Halliwell, *Beyond and Before: Progressive Rock Since the 1960s* (New York and London: Continuum, 2012), 125. This absence was understood to make way for the ghostly presences for or to whom Pink Floyd performed (and, more interestingly, to expand the band's sound); for a full discussion of the film, which exists in more than one version, see ibid., 125–127.

20 See Philip Auslander, *Performing Glam Rock: Gender and Theatricality in Popular Music* (Ann Arbor: University of Michigan Press, 2006).
21 On "performance and visuality" during this period, in relation to the rock film, see Chapter 7 of Hegarty and Halliwell, *Beyond and Before*.

Part III

Punk Cultures

No Wave Film and the Music Documentary

From No Wave Cinema "Documents" to Retrospective Documentaries

Michael Goddard

Introduction

The phenomenon of New York "No Wave" music, along with related tendencies in film and art, and its setting of New York City (or, more precisely, the downtown area of the Lower East Side that is known today as the now gentrified East Village), has recently received considerable critical attention, giving rise to numerous documentary and publication projects.[1] These have included books ranging from the quasi-academic, like Marc Masters' *No Wave* or Marvin J. Taylor's collection *The Downtown Book*, to "coffee table" publications dominated by photographic documentation, as with Byron Coley and Thurston Moore's *No Wave: Post-Punk Underground, New York 1976–1980* or *New York Noise*. The latter accompanied the release of a series of music compilations of No Wave and post-No Wave bands. Such attention is in addition to lower-profile and more archival publications that intersect with No Wave, such as *Captured*, that presents a "film/video history of the lower east side."[2] This retrospective interest has not been restricted to books, however, as is borne out by the fact that one of the above texts is in fact an exhibition catalog, while another accompanied a similarly archival series of music releases. Several cinematic releases also engage with the same phenomena. The documentary and fictional treatments of the life of the late artist Basquiat could be included in such a filmography,[3] together with more specifically No Wave-influenced documentaries including Scott Crary's 2004 *Kill Your Idols* (on No Wave music and more recent New York alternative rock), Angélique Bosio's 2007 *Llik Your Idols* (which, while more focused on the later Cinema of Transgression, nevertheless also engages with No Wave music) and Celine Danhier's 2010 *Blank City* (which deals especially with No Wave film). In all of these retrospective reconstructions, the Lower East Side features prominently as a singular and intense environment in which the availability of low-rent spaces, like warehouses and former industrial buildings, are seen to have facilitated a plethora of creative activities and most notably blurred the boundaries between them. Thus artists would form bands, musicians make films, classical composers engage with punk rock.

All are seen to perform to a type of artistic micro-society, usually numbered as limited to around one thousand people.

This chapter will engage with two different bodies of cinematic documentation of this spatiotemporal environment. First, attention is turned to the No Wave films produced as an intimate part of the scene, as in the work of James Nares, Beth and Scott B., Vivienne Dick, and others who formed the No Wave or No Cinema movement, and whose works were made at the time, usually on Super 8, and often featured performers from No Wave bands or related art practices. (It must be borne in mind that few of these films were intended as documentaries and yet many of them have come to function as extremely valuable documents in which both musical performances and more often performers played key roles, even if within a fictional or experimental rather than documentary construct.) Secondly, attention is turned to the work that consists of the already mentioned documentaries, particularly *Kill Your Idols* and *Blank City*, which construct documentary narratives about what was happening in New York at that particular time, combining archival footage with interviews, voice-overs, and material filmed in contemporary New York. Unlike the first group of films, which were a living movement in relation to their surrounding environment and other creative practices, these documentaries epitomize the condition of "retromania," as diagnosed by Simon Reynolds,[4] in their attempts to delineate an idealized underground past that can only be engaged with nostalgically. Significantly, while No Wave music featured prominently in Reynolds' earlier account of post-punk, precisely as a refusal of the past and insistence on creating new forms of "anti-music,"[5] within a few years the post-No Wave scene had become decidedly "retro." This was not only because its key club, the Mudd Club, was staging funerals for dead rock stars like Jim Morrison and Sid Vicious,[6] but also in the adoption of a series of retro musical styles, from swamp rock and roll to lounge jazz, which was in stark contrast to No Wave's rejection of any musical legacies. For Reynolds this pointed to the ambivalence or even an interchangeability between the avant-garde and the "retro-garde" in that both attempt to escape from the present, whether by chasing future or past mirages: "This shared quest for an elsewhere/elsewhen explains why some people could jump so easily between avant and retro modes, or even operate in both zones simultaneously."[7] Reynolds has in mind musicians like Arto Lindsay who could play both in the uncompromisingly atonal DNA and the retro Lounge Lizards (a group which also featured No Wave filmmaker and performer John Lurie), or the way that Lydia Lunch's abrasive primitivism would soon morph into a series of retro styles from swamp rock to cabaret.

This chapter argues that a tension remains between these retrospective music documentaries and the archival material they incorporate, that is capable of destabilizing their nostalgic retro narrativization in favour of a different, non-linear and archaeological relation with the past that they present. This dynamic raises questions about the relations between music documentaries and documentation, since the resistance of these now archaeological visual materials to merely becoming documentation, in favor of coming to constitute a parallel mode of expression to the No Wave music scene, undermines or troubles their use as simple documents in a retrospective account of New York No Wave.

No Wave Cinema: Between Music and Film

While the early 1980s New York No Wave scene is typically understood in relation to music, recent commentaries on No Wave cinema have gone some way to readdress this balance. In any case, given that it was not uncommon at this time for an artist to form a band, a classical or No Wave musician to make or appear in a film, or a filmmaker to present art works, the dividing lines between these practices were highly fluid. While most of the No Wave films were made with technically unsophisticated equipment, usually Sync Sound Super 8 film, both the imagery and the soundscapes of these films played a crucial role in their embodiment of specific zones of the New York City cityscape. In fact, according to an apocryphal legend, No Wave cinema owes its beginnings to local petty crime, since it started when the "grey market" dealer "Freddy the Fence . . . acquired a case of new Super 8 Sound cameras. When members of the neighbourhood's . . . punk music and arts scene got wind of this, they leapt at the opportunity . . . and the result was a nearly five year boom in underground filmmaking on the Lower East Side."[8] While these films have generally been subject to critical neglect, the recent acquisition of some of the key works by the Whitney museum, as well as recent retrospectives such as at the Oberhausen Film Festival and the Vienna Film Museum, show signs of an overdue re-evaluation, perhaps spurred on by the concomitant resurgence of interest in No Wave music.

No Wave films, which were more likely to have been screened at rock clubs and bars than at film theaters or even alternative film exhibition spaces like the Anthology Film Archives, are highly expressive of a post-punk primitivism and were highly critical of the prevailing avant-garde orthodoxies of their time. Just as groups like Teenage Jesus and the Jerks, The Contortions, Mars, and DNA were trying to reinvent the very lexicon of popular music through raw, primitive, and discordant styles, something similar could be said of No Wave films in relation to the reigning orthodoxies of the avant-garde, such as structuralist film. Nevertheless, one surprising aspect of No Wave films was their engagement with both narrative and popular culture, two elements rejected by most of the previous generation of experimental filmmakers, as evident in the work of filmmakers like Michael Snow. As J. Hoberman put it in what remains one of the best accounts of No Wave film:

> Rejecting the academic formalism that has characterised the 1970s film avant-garde, as well as the gallery-art of video, the Super 8 new wave

represents a partial return to the rawer values of the underground of the 1960s (Jack Smith, Ron Rice, the Kuchar brothers, early Warhol). Like its precursor, the new underground's technically pragmatic films enact libidinal fantasies, parody mass cultural forms, glorify a marginal lifestyle, and exhibit varying degrees of social content.[9]

While No Wave cinema often presented itself as a total break with the past, Hoberman is correct to emphasize the continuities with some aspects of underground film, of which early Warhol and Jack Smith are possibly the most important exemplars. Even if No Wave film was not welcomed in established avant-garde venues, or supported by the main funding bodies, this does not mean it received no support at all. Some No Wave cinema was supported by Collaborative Projects or Colab, a small New York multi-disciplinary arts organization that funded several of the key early No Wave films and briefly also provided a screening venue in St Marks Square, the New Cinema. However, many of the films received little or no support from Colab or any other organization and instead the filmmakers found whatever ways they could to make films on a minimum budget.

Perhaps the most important connection between No Wave film and music was simply in their collaboration. While some musicians, like John Lurie of The Lounge Lizards, both made and appeared in films, more commonly No Wave performers like Lydia Lunch, Ikue Mori, and Pat Place appeared as key performers in the films, as did artists and other members of other New York subcultural scenes. As one of the filmmakers Eric Mitchell put it, "They were grabbing guitars, and we were grabbing cameras."[10] Despite the disconnect from structuralist film, some of the earlier generation, like Jonas Mekas, appreciated the punk attitude of these filmmakers.

No Wave filmmakers found a brief screening venue, in a small storefront on St. Marks Square, but this only lasted for about six months. Otherwise, apart from some collaborations with local public access TV, especially via shows like Glenn O'Brien and Chris Stein's infamous *TV Party*, the films were largely shown at unconventional venues. Nevertheless, this small amount of exposure was enough to crystallize an East Village scene that, however marginal, still made a significant impact on underground film culture. The Cinema of Transgression that emerged a few years later around figures like Nick Zedd and Richard Kern can be seen as a direct result of the practice and aesthetics of No Wave film, especially in the use of cheap sync sound and narrative, even if the No Wave desire for independence from existing formats was to be replaced by a fascination for generic and cult cinema, especially horror, in the Cinema of Transgression. While some critics such as Christian Höller like to make strong distinctions between No Wave cinema and the Cinema of Transgression,[11] clearly the use of primitive equipment for ambitious, often narrative-driven projects, as well as the central role played by post-punk music and performers, was a common characteristic. There was also an overlapping range of both directors and performers to the extent that sometimes the distinction between the two movements only comes down to the year of production. Nevertheless, it is still possible to differentiate a more political sensibility in No Wave, as opposed to the pure desire for transgressive extremity in the Cinema of Transgression: both movements were fascinated by violence and power, but these fascinations took different forms, as did their films. Finally filmmakers from both movements looked back to and sometimes referenced some avant-garde New York film traditions, such as that associated with Warhol's factory or the work of Jack Smith, as reinvented in a contemporary post-punk context. By 1980 some of the No Wave filmmakers became more ambitious, with several of the filmmakers such as Eric Mitchell, Amos Poe, Beth B., and Bette Gordon, all releasing 16mm feature films without, however, gaining major recognition as filmmakers. An exception to this rule was Jim Jarmusch who, while not strictly part of the No Wave scene, was closely related to it. Jarmusch would shortly attain art-house canonization. While Jarmusch was more of a New York University film school dropout than a truly underground filmmaker, his first films (especially *Permanent Vacation* and *Stranger than Paradise*, of 1980 and 1984 respectively) are nevertheless expressive of No Wave aesthetics, and performers in his films like John Lurie and Eric Mitchell also emerged directly out of No Wave. Jarmusch was also directly inspired by role models like Amos Poe who did not hesitate to make ambitious feature films on virtually non-existent budgets.

As for the films themselves, while their aesthetics and quality varies, several common themes or tendencies could be said to characterize them as closely related documents of their time and place. Apart from the engagement with the New York punk and No Wave scenes, there are thematics of role playing, the exploration of remote and disreputable corners of the city, often associated with the porn industry or hustling, and the exploration of power relations and sexuality, frequently in combination. Some early or proto-No Wave films were largely focused on the No Wave music scene itself, whether in a relatively conventional document like *Punking Out* (Maggi Carson, Juliusz Kossakowski, and Ric Shore, 1978) or more experimental offerings like Michael McClard's *Alien Portrait* (1979) in which the heads of band members of Teenage Jesus and the Jerks are shown in extreme slow motion over a live concert soundtrack. Prior to this, it was really Amos Poe who set the scene for this kind of no-budget filmmaking between cinema and punk, especially with his 1976 films *Unmade Beds*, a Warhol and Jean-Luc Godard-inspired fiction featuring Debbie Harry and what was perhaps the first punk documentary, *The Blank Generation* (Ivan Král and Amos Poe, 1976). Other No Wave films were more subversively sexually oriented, as with Tina L'Hotsky's *Barbie* (1977), for example, in which she casts herself in slow motion and a blond wig as a life-size Barbie doll. While the feminist statement of this film seems clear, it apparently escaped the filmmaker, who referred to it at the time of its production as an act of instinctual self-exploitation. One of the most remarkable No Wave films, if only for its ambition relative to means, was John Lurie's epic Super 8 "sci fi povera" film *Men in Orbit* (1979). Here two men (Lurie and Mitchell) simply pass the time for forty-five minutes in the living room of an apartment decked out as a spaceship (with cheap special effects and lots of tin foil), pretending they are in space while actually tripping on LSD. This epic delirium was only perhaps surpassed by James Nares' feature film, *Rome '78* (1978), in which a group of bohemian New Yorkers recreated the story of Julius Caesar and Caligula by performing largely improvised and often anachronistic dialog in front of whatever pillars, columns, or any other Romanesque architecture that could be found in New York City. One group scene in a circular room in a private apartment could only be filmed by the ruse of pretending to view the apartment for rental, and then sneaking back in at night via a window that had been left open for this very purpose. Whatever the fictional constructs employed in these films, they function as much and usually more as documents of contemporary New York artistic subcultures, documenting not only performers from No Wave bands but their larger-than-life artistic personae that would be repeated and developed across multiple filmic and musical performances.

One of the most important female filmmakers of this film scene was Vivienne Dick, whose first two films were directly connected to the No Wave music scene. In *She Had Her Gun All Ready* (1978) a complacent Pat Place, from the No Wave band The Contortions, is stalked by a malevolent Lydia Lunch, culminating in a confrontation on the Cyclone ride at Coney Island. In this and other No Wave films, musical performers are not so much acting as given free rein to extend their personas within a filmic context, including their typical gestures, clothing, and behaviour. This was even more apparent in

Figure 7.1 Debbie Harry in *The Blank Generation* (Ivan Král and Amos Poe, 1976).

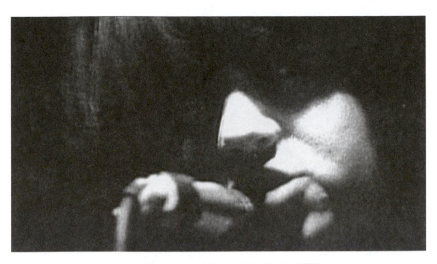

Figure 7.2 Lydia Lunch in *Alien Portrait* (Michael McClard, 1978).

Figure 7.3 Eric Mitchell and John Lurie in *Men in Orbit* (John Lurie, 1979).

Dick's first film, *Guérillère Talks* (1978), in which she profiles a number of strong female figures including Lunch and Place, in three-minute unedited sequences (that is, the length of Super 8 film reels). Such shots are the direct heirs of Andy Warhol's screen tests. Despite the title, the women in the film are not necessarily talking, or at least not in the manner one might expect. Pat Place considers hammering nails in various locations of her apartment, including her own head, and then reads a letter in which her parents advise her not to sell her Beatles records or take prescription tranquillizers. Her only

Figure 7.4 Rome '78 (James Nares, 1978).

Figure 7.5 Pat Place in *Guérillère Talks* (Vivienne Dick, 1978).

comment is "It's a different world." Ikue Mori, from the seminal No Wave group DNA, poses on a rooftop and what little she says is in Japanese, although she seems to prefer to take pictures. Lydia Lunch delivers a deadpan and angry monologue from the perspective of an urban child, forced to play with discarded junk in a burnt-out wasteland, while hanging off a fire escape. Her monologue finishes well before the film reel, leaving a minute or so for contemplating the destroyed environment in which it took place. Ikue Mori also features in another sequence of an impromptu No Wave music performance or rehearsal,

Figure 7.6 Lydia Lunch in *Guérillère Talks* (Vivienne Dick, 1978).

BLACK BOX
BETH B & SCOTT B

Figure 7.7 Lydia Lunch and Bob Mason in *Black Box* (Beth and Scott B., 1979).

where the use of fireworks is reminiscent of Kenneth Anger's films. As with all these screen tests the sound is as important as the image, if not more so, and the eccentric framings, unmotivated zooms, and unpredictable camera movements can be seen as part of a synaesthetic process of audiovisual disorientation. In both these films the documentation of performers, performances and places, like rooftops, junkyards, or amusement parks, takes on both documentary and poetic qualities that amount to the expression of a No Wave feminine aesthetic.

Figure 7.8 *Empty Suitcases* (Bette Gordon, 1980).

Figure 7.9 *Variety* (Bette Gordon, 1983).

Perhaps the most impressive of any of the No Wave films were those films made by Beth and Scott B., in which soundscapes and musical performers also play a key role. *G-Man* (1978) uses the transcripts of actual interviews to depict the life of a member of the anti-terrorist bomb squad, played by the artist and well-known East Village personality Bill Rice. Rice's performance is a key element of this film and provides a *noir*-ish take on the current state of New York City as permanently prone to terrorist assault. At the end of the film this powerful agent of order is shown submitting to a dominatrix, hence combining public and private power relations, and law enforcement and perversion, in a manner that must have seemed much more subversive then than it does now, its Foucauldian presentation of ambivalent power relations notwithstanding. What is most striking about the film is the economy of its taut narrative, whose clarity of articulation, montage, and use of sound are continually arresting. The notorious *Black Box* (1978) is even more technically accomplished, in its presentation of a young man pulled off the street to be tortured by an unnamed paramilitary organization within a "black box" device (apparently being deployed at the time by the US military in Central America). Within the box, the man is assaulted by both light and painful noise and Lydia Lunch plays the torturess, enthusiastically dishing out what appears to be an extremely painful and entirely unmotivated punishment. Beyond the film's clear political dimensions, it also stands out for its formal aspects: the second part of the film consists of an abstract noise and light show whose original soundtrack, inspired by the more discordant No Wave bands and featuring No Wave musicians, is as remarkable as its visuals. As Beth B. has pointed out, this film was largely shown in rock venues and was especially designed for this environment in which its projection, at loud volume, had a powerful and visceral impact, even to the extent that the venue itself was understood to have momentarily transformed into the black box, casting the audience as its victims.[12]

Other No Wave films function much more explicitly as almost ethnographic documents of a lost urban world in their depictions of specific New York cityscapes and their related erotic practices. Franco Marinai's *Blue Pleasure* (1981), for example, focuses on the facades of strip clubs around the then seedy Times Square, and incorporates scratched and otherwise reprocessed adult films, calling up a lost world of sexual desperation and promises of erotic fulfilment. Tessa Hughes-Freeland, a filmmaker who would also play a role in the cinema of transgression, provides in her film *Baby Doll* (1982) an intimate portrait of the lives and voices of Times Square strippers, while Bradley Eros's *Mutable Fire!* (1984) poetically reprocesses found footage, especially of adult films. In a related but distinct vein, Ivan Galleti's *Pompei New York Part 1: Pier Caresses* (1982) explores the then gay cruising area of the New York piers, whose graffiti and crumbling erotic frescoes constitute a modern Pompei (and which is now an equally lost world due to urban redevelopment). All these films in different ways explore a similar terrain of desire and exploitation and function as documents of the now-covered-over world of derelict New York and its sexual subcultures which, while only indirectly related to the No Wave music scene, nevertheless give a vivid portrait of its surrounding urban decay.

Kill/Llik Your Idols: From Documents to Documentaries

How have these generally unintentional documentations of No Wave film been incorporated in, or in some cases excluded from, contemporary documentaries dealing with the various facets of No Wave? *Kill Your Idols*, named after a song by Sonic Youth, establishes a pattern that is repeated in many of the documentaries in various ways: namely, No Wave is both identified as the core of what the film is about, but nevertheless passed over fairly quickly. Twenty minutes into the film, members of Sonic Youth and Swans go from discussing No Wave to their own post-No Wave musical ventures, and soon interview subjects as interesting as Glen Branca and Arto Lindsay are being asked about their reactions to The Strokes which, while not entirely uninteresting, hardly seems the best use of their time. Despite a promisingly poetic beginning to *Kill Your Idols*, in which a quote from Marina Tsetaeva overlies a black surrounded image of the Manhattan skyline, the film soon resorts to a fairly standard use of talking heads, interspersed with more or less appropriate audiovisual illustration in the form of music, stills, and later video. This begins with the Martin Rev interview, followed by the Suicide track "Mister Ray" that accompanies the title sequence. While the range of archival material used ranges from TV footage to underground film, none of these sources is acknowledged, and all the emphasis is placed on the musical history which begins with the contrast between Suicide and the New York Dolls. This contrast is followed by a fast-forwarding of time, by means of series of years superimposed in front of contemporaneous musical performances, until "1977." Here the viewer is introduced to Lydia Lunch, speaking in an uncredited film source, and so the film effectively skips early New York punk to arrive at the beginnings of No Wave. But even this apparent respect for chronology is immediately undermined. While the viewer is being informed about Lunch's arrival in New York City, scenes from the much later Nick Zedd film *The Wild World of Lydia Lunch* (1983) are seen, followed by an interview with those queuing for a Dead Boys gig (footage probably originating from the earlier *The Blank Generation*). Following this sequence concert footage of a more strictly No Wave provenance is seen, while a red title announces that this is Teenage Jesus and the Jerks, but not exactly when or where. This concert footage segues into the contemporary interview with Lunch, again announced with a title, which is soon overlaid with more Cinema of Transgression footage, this time courtesy of Richard Kern. This description is only made in order to bring out the way that the specificity of No Wave is elided in the film, partially in relation to the music but almost completely in relation to the archival filmic material that is used. By the time of the interview with Glenn Branca there is a barrage of visual material, cinematic and video, color and black and white, the only common feature being that it provides some documentation of No Wave bands. Even when this is synced to the musical soundtrack the moment rarely lasts for long and is subordinated to the stream of memories evoked by the talking heads, memories corresponding to the tropes identified above of cheap rent, wild energies, and intersecting creative practices. Lunch, Jim Sclavunos, Arto Lindsay, and Glen

Branca all emphazise both the amusicality and innovation of No Wave bands, their non-relation to tradition, even relative to punk, and the creation of a music that sounded like nothing else. However, after a very short period in which this noise is presented for itself, the noise soon becomes the subject of a double retrospective construction as members of Sonic Youth Thurston Moore and Lee Ranaldo discuss the influence of such noise not only on their own music but on groups as geographically dispersed as Germany's Einstürzende Neubauten and Japan's Boredoms. The accompanying footage at this point becomes even more atemporal, with gig footage from the 1990s illustrating accounts of the beginnings of Sonic Youth and other post-No Wave groups. This in turn gives way quickly to interviews with contemporary groups like The Yeah Yeah Yeahs and Gogol Bordello, whose music is only inscribed with difficulty in this historical account of New York noise. Not only is there a disconnect between these much more conventional rock bands and the inventive and uncompromising noise that preceded them, but their presentation, via the garish color of digital video, intensifies these differences by presenting a New York that looks and sounds like a different universe. This is only emphasized by a section followed by a brief experimental sequence with the title "Legacy" in which the various contemporary bands have clearly been asked to reflect on No Wave era music. Their banal answers about how "wild" or "small" or "existential" these bands were belies a lack of connection in which No Wave has already become a kind of compulsory legacy, one that is less remembered than quoted in a second- or third-hand manner, no doubt from some of the retrospective sources cited above. The fact that the documentary loses almost all its momentum at this point, despite the continuation of interviews with subjects like Lunch, Branca, and Moore, only reinforces the sense of a passage from memory and its representation to pure simulation. In this No Wave becomes a doubly absent object of nostalgia that the contemporary New York bands can only invoke in the vaguest of manners. Such a dislocation is made even more surreal by the questioning of the likes of Lindsay and Branca about the modish phenomenon of The Strokes, as mentioned above. Nevertheless the beginnings of the documentary does evoke at least the musical aspects of No Wave, paradoxically as much via the "noise" of its multiple visual sources as by its musical performances and recollections. And in a section entitled "Memory as Commerce" a unified chorus of the older and younger generations both speak of the victory of corporate capitalism over innovative subcultural creativity, but without, however, much in the way of reflexivity of the participation of either the contemporary bands or the film in this commerce of memory.

In Angelique Bosio's *Llik Your Idols* these No Wave musical origins are once again evoked, in order to tell the story of the Cinema of Transgression, through an even more total elision of its immediate forebears in No Wave cinema. The opening title sequence says it all:

New York. The Lower East Side. A new scene emerges that radically breaks with the past. No Wave turns the musical codes upside down. Young filmmakers perpetrate Super 8 films in a similar vein. In 1985 Nick Zedd baptises the movement as "the cinema of transgression."

In this genealogy, despite the asynchronicity of No Wave music and the Cinema of Transgression, they are presented as parallels while No Wave film disappears entirely. A different yet overlapping sequence of talking heads to the previous film, includes, in addition to Thurston Moore and Lydia Lunch, filmmakers Nick Zedd and Richard Kern, as well as the researcher Jack Sergeant and performance artists like Joe Coleman. They generally present the Cinema of Transgression as a creation *ex nihilo*, or a direct reaction to the cultural atmosphere of Reaganite America, rather than a continuation of an already existing underground culture. To be fair, Sergeant has elsewhere at least briefly acknowledged (in his book *Deathtripping*)[13] the influence of No Wave filmmakers like Beth and Scott B. on the Cinema of Transgression. But in the film even the accounts of Lydia Lunch seem to subsume any cultural predecessors into the extremity of the Cinema of Transgression as the direct reaction to an oppressively conformist society, as if everything began with Nick Zedd's *They Eat Scum* (1979), despite references to New York punk and No Wave music. Even No Wave music is allowed an engagement some 30 minutes into the film, and then for only a few minutes, as Jack Sergeant inaccurately assimilates the atonal music of DNA with the punk pop of The Ramones, claiming that both were just playing speeded-up Chuck Berry riffs. Perhaps such elisions and distortions are understandable in a film dealing with a later generation of musicians and filmmakers, and yet the absence of No Wave films distorts and exaggerates the originality of the Cinema of Transgression, and plays down its depoliticization of the sexuality and violence that had equally been a feature of No Wave film.

The more recent *Blank City*, directed by Céline Dahnier, finally places No Wave film and its filmmakers like Eric Mitchell, James Nares, Beth and Scott B., and Amos Poe firmly at the center of attention. This time the No Wave footage is clearly identified, and the often hilarious tales of its production, ranging from the use of John Lurie's bedsheets as makeshift togas, to the shooting of entire feature films without any script and virtually without any money, but just the desire to do so and the rich performative resources of the Lower East Side creative community. This film undeniably delivers a more complete picture of not only No Wave film but also its engagement with other creative practices like music, performance, and contemporary art. However, there are still some reductive retrospective tendencies at work that detract from this portrait of New York circa 1980. The first is the inscription of No Wave films in the development of American independent cinema, by means of an emphasis on such interview subjects as Jim Jarmusch and Steve Buscemi. While it is certainly true that these and other figures of independent

US cinema (such as Susan Seidelman and Lizzie Borden) owed their beginnings to the effervescence of No Wave cinema, their subsequent career trajectories are in marked contrast to those of their No Wave forerunners, and point to a fairly opportunistic use of the underground as a career springboard. To claim that No Wave was the birthplace or even invigoration of independent cinema at once says too much (in that independent film resulted from many other, mostly more mainstream sources) and too little (since No Wave film was largely about something other than a different kind of entertainment cinema, and was instead an experimental and confrontational practice, by no means aiming for future mainstream success). Again the coupling of No Wave with quite distinct film scenes from the Cinema of Transgression, to bigger budget hip-hop-oriented films like *Wildstyle* (Charlie Ahearn, 1983) detracts from the focus on No Wave film, as does the blurring of musical styles from punk to No Wave to later noise bands and hip-hop—a trope which this film shares with *Kill Your Idols*. Nevertheless *Blank City* does provide the most comprehensive and at the same time least nostalgic entry point into No Wave of the three documentaries discussed here, precisely by giving greater emphasis and respect to the expressivity of No Wave film as a rich visual discourse specific to its era, rather than reducing No Wave to mere documentation, or excluding No Wave altogether.

Conclusion

The experimental and ephemeral documenting of the No Wave scene in the No Wave films problematizes the more conventional recent documentaries, which are often saturated with nostalgia and formally incapable of being adequate to their subject matter. This generates various distortions and exaggerations, and leads to a retromanic fabulation of an absent No Wave past. Nevertheless the persistence of these archival filmic materials and amusical performances within these films, especially *Kill Your Idols* and *Blank City*, troubles both the talking heads narration of these films' discourses and their attempts to inscribe No Wave music and film within more mainstream histories. However redolent with nostalgia these films might be, there is something atemporal and unassimilable about No Wave, as expressed via both its sonic and visual inscriptions that these documentaries incorporate, and that resists chronological ordering. It would seem that an archaeological rather than a chronological, nostalgic approach to No Wave musical and cinematic invention remains possible. As Glen Branca says in *Kill Your Idols*, if No Wave has been subject to so much attention it is only because "there was something there." This can be identified as an insistent "now" of No Wave refusal, as embodied in the word "no," a kernel of which still undermines the seeming complicity of its key personae in its nostalgic documentary narrativization.

Notes

1 This chapter is based on research that was facilitated by attending the *No Wave 1976–1984* retrospective at the 56th Oberhausen International Short Film Festival (April 29–May 4, 2010) and at the Austrian Filmmuseum, Vienna (May–June 2010). Special thanks go to Christian Höller who curated both retrospectives, and to Sabine Niewalda.

2 See Marc Masters, *No Wave* (Black Dog: London, 2007); Marvin J. Taylor (ed.), *The Downtown Book: The New York Art Scene 1974–1984*, foreword by Lynn Gumpert (Princeton and London: Princeton UP, 2006); Byron Coley and Thurston Moore, *No Wave: Post-Punk Underground, New York, 1976–1980*, foreword by Lydia Lunch (New York: Harry N. Abrams, Inc., 2008); Karen Tate (ed.), *New York Noise with Photographs by Paula Court* (London: Soul Jazz Records, 2007), and Clayton Patterson (ed.), *Captured: A Film/Video History of the Lower East Side* (New York: Seven Stories Press, 2005).

3 See *Downtown 81* (Edo Bertoglio, 1981) and *Basquiat* (Julian Schnabel, 1996) respectively, although a number of documentaries have been made concerning the artist.

4 See Simon Reynolds, *Retromania: Pop Culture's Addiction to its own Past* (London: Faber and Faber, 2011).

5 Simon Reynolds, *Rip It Up and Start Again: Postpunk 1978–1984* (London: Penguin, 2005), 139–157.

6 Ibid., 267.

7 Ibid., 263.

8 Harris Smith, "No New Cinema: Punk and No Wave Underground Film, 1976–1984," in Patterson, *Captured*, 173.

9 J. Hoberman and Jonathan Rosenbaum, *Midnight Movies* (New York: Da Capo Press, 1991), 283. The section dealing with No Wave film is largely a reprise of Hoberman's earlier *Village Voice* article, "No Wavelength: The Para-Punk Underground," originally published in May 1979.

10 Eric Mitchell cited in Masters, *No Wave*, 139.

11 See Christian Höller, "No Wave 1976–1984," in *Oberhausen International Film Festival Catalogue: 29th of April to 4th of May 2010* (Oberhausen: Oberhausen Short Film Festival, 2010).

12 See Masters, *No Wave*, 158. According to Beth B., when projected at loud volumes in rock clubs, "the film became a box within a box."

13 Jack Sargeant, *Deathtripping: The Extreme Underground* (New York: Soft Skull Press, 2008).

Chapter 8

The Anxiety of Authenticity

Post-punk Film in the 2000s

Erich Hertz

Mid-way through Eric Idle's mockumentary *The Rutles* (Eric Idle and Gary Weis, 1978), he visits the banks of the Mississippi in order to investigate the Black origins of British rock and roll. Here, he finds Blind Lemon Pye and, while filming out on one of the docks in the Mississippi, discovers how Pye learned to play: "everything I learned, I learned from The Rutles . . . Until I heard The Rutles, then I decided, that's my type of music." The reason the joke works is because Idle stages a certain anxiety at the heart of British rock history films that trace their influence to the American South in order to acknowledge the authentic place where the music originates, only to flip the authenticity on its head. Even though Pye is the right age and from the right geographical location, he didn't discover the music he really liked until he heard the British version. This anxiety is central to talking about rock since Elvis: that this is not where this music really came from. The anxiety of authenticity haunts many varieties of feature and documentary films about music, but perhaps none more so than those about punk and post-punk where reactions against the inauthentic grand swaggering of arena rock bands were the grounding force. A punk band by its very nature had to be claiming a more genuine space and reacting more stridently to the forces of the music industry. Punks and post-punks could not be international or transnational phenomena like their disconnected forebears; instead, they needed to be rooted in, and products of, a specific environment in a specific historical moment. The recent spate of films about post-punk in the last decade often tethers their subjects to their cities to establish and stage this authenticity.

What is additionally compelling about these films in the last decade is the timing of their appearance. While the fall of Britpop precipitated or was caused by numerous factors, one was the resurgence of the post-punk sound of bands like Franz Ferdinand, Editors, Liars, Interpol, etc., precisely when Britpop had become the arena juggernaut that the original post-punks reacted against. Simon Reynolds also maintains that this explosion of rock documentaries in the last decade is tied to a recent drive to catalog moments in musical history: "Today is the era of the archivist, the curator, the documentarian: experts at sifting through the detritus left by rock's surge years, that period when people made history rather than chronicled it, lived it in real time rather than watched it long after the fact."[1] That is, as Reynolds would articulate more fully in *Retromania: Pop Culture's Addiction to Its Own Past*, there is a historical sense in which the movement and development of rock have turned in on themselves. All of the major "progressions" of each decade now seem to have stopped and it seems that nothing "new" is being generated anymore. The only maneuver left is to sift through the pieces and either mimic or create something out of the detritus. Therefore, the last decade has seen this explosion of exploring those moments that once were, precisely when it seems like musical "progress" has come to a standstill.[2] More, though, mainstream pop music around the world had seen a resurgence of performers who no longer write their own music. While some small contributions may be made by the artists in question, it is largely accepted (without compunction) that someone like Britney Spears (one of the largest music figures during the 2000s) does not compose her own material and is largely an artificial construction of a large cohort of composers and marketers. Even though artists like her weren't the only ones on the airwaves or being downloaded during the last decade, they certainly dominated the music world. Ideologically, then, the return to these moments of authenticity from the post-punk period are particularly important during a moment in music history when any claims to authenticity have been ceded.[3] The documentaries themselves serve a similar function to punk's own rejection of the self-conscious artificiality of glam rock and the self-aggrandizement of "classic" rock. However, even though the documentaries jockey themselves to align their subjects with a more authentic form of music, they nonetheless construct this position of authenticity nostalgically precisely at the moment when it seems to have been lost.

Julian Temple's *Filth and the Fury* from 2000 carefully constructs an era and a place for the emergence of The Sex Pistols. He rightfully focuses on the sanitation strike and includes clips of John Lydon talking about the mounds of garbage around London; Temple and Lydon make the quick link between the sound and the look of The Sex Pistols and the "filth" of the period. The gesture is a predominant one in documentaries of punk and post-punk bands. The most obvious effects are to draw class lines; however, those very class lines become the claims to a certain legitimacy in punk lineage. The spate of feature and documentary films focused on Joy Division in the last decade also share this particular attention to the decrepit state of England. Michael Winterbottom's *24 Hour Party People* (2002), Anton Corbijn's *Control* (2007), and Grant Gee's documentary on Joy Division (2007) all canvas their films with either a post-war crumble or welfare state concrete. The effect, again, is to link not only the band with their geographical space, but also to make implicit the authenticity of the musicians' pain or anger: only out of wretched circumstances can genuine music come. (This is made especially clear in John Dower's *Live Forever* (2003) in which the drama between Oasis and Blur is charted and the class conflicts made transparent. The major thrust is depicting

Damon Albarn and Blur as middle-class boys from Essex and London who couldn't possibly have anything real to say because they don't come from a legitimate place of real pain and struggle.) More, from the films about Joy Division to Eve Woods' *Made in Sheffield* (2004), post-punk films not only stage the dramatic shift in power politics in the music industry away from London, but they also link the music's authenticity to the fate of the cities themselves.

Aligning Joy Division with the post-industrial space of Manchester was a major part of their aesthetic from the beginning.[4] As Simon Reynolds notes in *Rip It Up and Start Again* (2005), many bands from the North of England took inspiration from J. G. Ballard's explorations of urban geography in novels such as *High Rise, Concrete Island*, and *Crash*.[5] Ian Curtis, in specific, took the tone and exact titles (like "Atrocity Exhibition") from Ballard's work and Joy Division themselves were keen to pose near decrepit buildings or the tenements that represented the worst of concrete social planning. (Given that one of the original photographers of these sessions was Anton Corbijn, we should not be surprised to see it as recurring imagery in his recent feature film *Control* (2007)).[6] Tony Wilson, one of the founders of Factory Records and one of Joy Division's earliest promoters, was especially intent on tying the music of the time to the social fortunes of Manchester itself.[7] As Wilson relays in the documentary on the early history of Factory Records, *Shadowplayers* (2007), the label was not named for Andy Warhol's Factory, but rather invented by Factory co-founder Alan Erasmus when he and Wilson passed yet another sign in Manchester for "Factory Closed." The idea was to begin a new space of, as it were, "Factory Open." And the idea wasn't just clever, but also signals not only Tony Wilson's vision for the era, but the predominant themes about films on Joy Division as well: that the music itself would transform the city, that the music and the city were intertwined. This recurring case being made for post-punk is particularly striking when considering other films about rock or pop. For just one example, the recent film on The Pixies, *Loudquietloud* (Cantor and Galkin, 2006), never makes any references to Boston and how coming out of Boston might have shaped them. And, perhaps more importantly, especially because of what post-punk was reacting to, this is *not* the sylvan Robert Plant leaving the countryside and his family, or Jimmy Page being drawn away from lake-side meditation to take the limo through the bustling streets of NYC in *Led Zeppelin: The Song Remains the Same* (Peter Cliftont and Joe Massot, 1976). Here, the non-diegetic sounds of NYC street life and the frighteningly large cavalcade of limos and police are replaced by the kind of English folk music that Page had turned to around this period. The code is transparent: Led Zeppelin are bringing their Englishness into the stage that confirms them as international superstars. If anything, documentaries of the mid-to-late 1970s try to emphasize having gotten out of England as the true marker of success.

However, even from the very title of, say, Eve Woods' *Made in Sheffield* (2005) we are to understand that post-punk matters precisely because it is a product of its place and history. This is partly to do with what post-punk represented: a shift from the centralized music industry in London to the rise of independent labels in the Northern cities. In a particularly rueful and comic moment in *Made in Sheffield*, the band The Extras recount relocating to London out of Sheffield in order to make it big, only to pass all the journalists leaving London to cover the Sheffield scene they just left. It seemed like the best career move that any English band could make, but they miscalculated; this is the moment that independent labels took off in the Northern cities and the music industry became invested in bands from the "outside." Partly out of civic pride and also out of a sense that this "outsiderness" could mark a certain authenticity, many post-punk groups thrived outside of the London scene. *Made in Sheffield*, then, is keen to ground the music in the city itself: members of The Human League, ABC, Heaven 17, and Cabaret Voltaire are all invited to describe precisely how the late industrial fortunes affected everything down to the level of how they looked at music. At one point Ian Craig Marsh of The Human League, and later Heaven 17, claims: "you'd go to sleep at night and there was, like, the sound of the, like, dropped forges [. . .] which was like having, like, a metronome, like a heartbeat for the whole city." Or, as Richard H. Kirk of Cabaret Voltaire related to Simon Reynolds: "you looked down into the valley and all you could see was blackened buildings. At night in bed you could hear the big drop forges crunching away."[8] The point here is not just that these artists came out of Sheffield and that Sheffield had a formative influence on them, but that the very sounds of the city itself are what was first, what was foundational to the creation of this sound. While electronic music had been experimented with in other areas of the world and, for that matter, in avant-garde classical music, there is an essential link to this particular kind of noise and these particular kinds of beat. Without the city of Sheffield, this sound, this music, would not exist. The effect, as I will also claim for similar films about Joy Division, is to make the city the foundation or the original creator of the sound, that the music that is ultimately made is just an expression of the city itself.

The first film to feature a depiction of Joy Division was *24 Hour Party People* in 2002, a paean to Tony Wilson and Factory Records. But it is also, of course, a story about Manchester. After depicting several apocryphal moments in Joy Division's history we finally reach the moment of recording the music in the studio. After comically reconstructing the scene of studio genius Martin Hannett disassembling and reassembling the drum kit on the roof of the studio, the band hops into a car to hear the finished product on the car stereo. In terms of the film's aims, it situates the revelation of the Hannett-engineered Joy Division sound in the context of the city itself. As the band listens, the street lights and the urban geography of Manchester infuse the scene. The sound switches momentarily from the diegetic car stereo to the non-diegetic when the film cuts to the sky line of Manchester. The music, as most of the world first heard it, is not unveiled in the studio where it probably could have been heard better, but rather as an expression of the exterior itself. Hannett's producing in the studio had made Joy Division's music distant and isolated in a manner that reflected Curtis's lyrics. Even though most members of the band were dissatisfied with what Hannett had done to their sound, the film makes no mention of this. Indeed, in the film, the actor playing Bernie Sumner chimes in during the listening session in the car: "it's great." It is more important that the music be the best expression of the Factory Records sound and how that sound came to represent Manchester than it is a representation of the band. Indeed, in *Shadowplayers* Tony Wilson claims that it mattered little what any band thought they wanted to sound like; they often didn't know what their release would reflect until weeks after Hannett was done manipulating it. In *24 Hour Party People* we are given a depiction of Joy Division as immediately recognizing Hannet's, via Tony Wilson's, genius.

Half-way through *24 Hour Party People* after Ian Curtis's suicide and the end of Joy Division, Steve Coogan, who portrays Tony Wilson, directly addresses the camera and claims that music history operates like a "double helix," when one kind of music is ascendant and another descendant. This is the film's segue into Factory Records' fraught relationship with The Happy Mondays. In the final analysis, there is an abyss of difference between Joy Division and The Happy Mondays, but the film intertwines them because: 1) the film is concerned with Factory Record's history, but 2) it wants to make a grand claim for how both performers, regardless of how different they are, weren't that directly interested in money (Shaun Ryder's need for drugs notwithstanding). Indeed, Tony Wilson is placed in this same category when it is revealed by the end that he cannot sell out the record label because, in fact, he doesn't own anything. Here, we get the depiction of the most authentic of artistic maneuvers: Joy Division, The Happy Mondays, and even Tony Wilson himself did it because of the love of artistic expression.

What's striking, though, is that this doesn't quite square with how the film and Grant Gee's documentary on Joy Division want to link this vision to Manchester itself. An early scene in *24 Hour Party People* recreates that world-changing moment of June 4, 1976 when The Sex Pistols played in Manchester.[9] The now-famous roster of the forty-odd people who actually attended the show included Tony Wilson and three of the guys who went on to form Joy Division. Again, Steve Coogan as Tony Wilson directly addresses the camera to point out everyone in that audience who would go on to do something in the Manchester scene.[10] When he gets to the guys from Joy Division, he, of course, mentions that they will go on to form Joy Division, but then notes, "later, they will become New Order." The film then jumpcuts to relatively recent footage of New Order playing to one of the largest crowds possible in an outdoor arena. And they aren't just playing any song: they are playing

"World in Motion" that was written for the 1990 World Cup: a sort of national anthem for a national sport that was their only number 1 song in the UK. They have risen from three guys in the back of The Sex Pistols concert to become national icons that can fill stadiums. This rise to mega-stardom is noteworthy given the stark realities of the beginning of the film and the almost certain knowledge that viewers have about Ian Curtis's suicide. The narrative frontloads the release of tension by reminding us of that impending stardom, but at the odd cost of placing a premium on the international popularity and marketability of the band precisely when the film is so concerned with authentic Mancunian roots.

This same tension is worked throughout Grant Gee's documentary that begins, first, with an aerial view of Manchester, then a series of three voice-overs. The first, not made known to us from the beginning, but apparent on repeat viewings, is a recording of Ian Curtis under hypnosis with Bernie Sumner encouraging him to explore previous lives. The maneuver is an ingenious one; its first iteration out of context is an eerie opening over the views of Manchester, but when it becomes apparent that this is a recording of Curtis's exploration of possible past lives, we enter a realm in which there is a historical gulf. Gee himself is attempting this very thing: to excavate a past which is no longer with us, but contains remnants in our present. Ian Curtis and his historical moment are no longer available to us, but Gee's documentary is a document of an attempt to unearth this past. This idea is rendered throughout the film as we constantly visit places that are no longer in Manchester. Gee visits the sites of these important absences and numbers them as "Things That Aren't There." The second voice-over is the 1910 prayer "For Our City" by Walter Rauschenbusch: "Oh God, grant us a vision of our city, fair as she might be: a city of justice where none shall prey on others: a city of plenty, where vice and poverty shall cease to fester: a city of brotherhood, where all success shall be founded on service, and honour shall be given to nobleness alone; a city of peace, where order shall not rest on force, but on the love of all for the city, the great mother of common life and weal." As its establishing maneuver, the film associates the arrival of Joy Division as the answering of the prayer of a city. And, finally, the opening sequence ends with a framing quote by Tony Wilson: "I don't see this as the story of a pop group, I see this as the story of a city that once upon a time was shiny and bold and revolutionary, and then suddenly, thirty odd years later, is shiny and revolutionary all over again. And at the heart of this transformation is a bunch of groups, and one group in particular." We then get a series of 1s and 0s, like a digital code, that eventually morphs into the words "JOY DIVISION" as a title placed over aerial views of Manchester in order to emphasize their unity. Here, the film frames Manchester as the first item of importance to come into view and then, literally, visualizes Joy Division emerging out of the spaces. It is, of course, the case that Joy Division was formed out of Manchester, but, like *Made in Sheffield*, the emphasis here is placed on the city itself. Indeed, the framing quote from Wilson that Gee leads with makes Joy Division in some ways secondary to Manchester in their own story. Importantly, it is striking to note that the remaining members of Joy Division only talk about Manchester when clearly prompted by the interviewer to describe what it was like. Gee splices in newsreel footage of Manchester being bombed in WWII, collapsed buildings, and the eventual conversion of row houses into concrete monoliths. In other words, the greater narrative of tying Joy Division's aesthetic to Manchester itself is largely a product of Grant Gee's direction and his following of ideas from Tony Wilson.

This drive to link Joy Division to post-industrial Manchester, despite their own reservations about it, is best exemplified in the scene when Joy Division makes their first appearance on Tony Wilson's Granada television show *What's On*. During their performance of "Shadowplay" graphics of highways and concrete urban housing were displayed over them. As Chris Ott relays:

> Static, negative footage of monotonous highway traffic and industrial cityscapes played behind them on a blue screen. The group were aghast: the utterly pedestrian subject matter of these *World in Action* documentary reels reminded them of the "production value" synthesizers with which John Anderson had ruined their RCA session. Sure, Joy Division had just performed on television, but they were soon to reissue *An Ideal for Living* and were concerned about the impact these cheap effects might have on their image.[11]

This scene is especially important in all three films about Joy Division: *24 Hour Party People*, *Control*, and *Joy Division* all feature this moment as Joy Division getting their big break. After verbally accosting Tony Wilson, Ian had finally secured a spot for the band on Wilson's show and, here, Wilson introduces them in the context of "everything from The Beatles to The Buzzcocks." In terms of all three films' narrative structure it is treated as the moment that marks their arrival as a band that has finally broken through to a larger audience. And it's here that they are introduced to the world as intricately linked to Manchester's urban spaces—the imagery itself even dominates over the band in some of the shots.

Here, too, we find not a band that is deeply troubled by Martin Hannett's production of *Unknown Pleasures*. In *Joy Division*, Peter Hook claims that he wanted to sound more like they did when they played live, but this line is noticeably moved to later in the film's staging away from the brilliance of Martin Hannett's production. Instead, we get Factory co-founder Peter Saville suggesting that "it might be heresy," but that he believes that "Hannett suggested a way to understand Joy Division." It's a great insight that holds a lot of truth, but is far from heretical when it is the predominate story foisted upon us through films of the last decade. In fact, it's practically canonical.[12]

And why Joy Division is so important is not only chalked up to Martin Hannett. The documentary deftly pulls together many people who were involved in creating the product that is Joy Division, from the aforementioned Tony Wilson of Factory Records, to the photographers who encouraged them to pose in front of those decrepit buildings and concrete tunnels, to Peter Saville, the artistic director of Factory who designed the look of their albums. In other words, without directly stating it, the film catalogs the way that Joy Division were a construction as carefully honed as many other rock bands. And that is why it is quite intriguing to hear Peter Saville claim at the end of the documentary that Joy Division are "one of the truest stories of pop; there are very few true stories in a business-dominated pop culture." This sense of "trueness" is the clear claim for Joy Division's authenticity and credibility. But, in what sense are they "true" or authentic? Many claims about Joy Division's authenticity rest on the tragedy of Ian Curtis's suicide. That is, when you listen to that depressing and moody sound, those introverted and isolated lyrics, you know that Curtis must have meant those feelings because he acted on them; he was not faking.

However, this is not all that Saville or Gee intends, because Saville's quote is prefaced by the following titles on the screen: New Order "became one of the most successful and influential groups of the 80s and 90s. And sold more than 20 million records." Much like *24 Hour Party People*, we have the markers of commercial success loaded into claims of authenticity precisely at the moment when such claims would seem counterintuitive. Again, aren't bands "true" to the extent that they produce their art in spite of commercial success? Indeed, in the documentary, we are told "they *had* to be up there [performing music]." So, their authenticity isn't predicated on the "trueness" of the dedication to their art. It is, instead, the frame upon which the entire documentary rests. A final quote by Tony Wilson restates and frames the objectives that begin the film: "the revolution [Joy Division] started . . . has resulted in this modern city, in what was the original modern city again becoming a modern city." This quote leads to scenes of new commercial development and the sun coming out over Manchester. The documentary's aesthetic framing, from somewhat gloomy overviews of the city at the beginning of the film, and a prayer of hope for the city, to its new-day sun-coming-out imagery at the end, makes clear and reflects upon Tony Wilson's claims: what's important about Joy Division is that they are a product of Manchester. Their authenticity is grounded in the fact that music comes directly out of this historical moment and this geographic location. And the fact of New Order's later commercial success mirrors Manchester's fortunes and validates a specifically Mancunian art form as a national and international art form.

This returns us to the scene from *The Rutles* and that comic exploration of the anxiety of authenticity. In these post-punk films the constant return to and grounding in the city and history is a gesture toward ameliorating this anxiety by housing the music in a very specific British context. In many instances, the music seems to "come out of nowhere." This very British punk moment "changed everything." After seeing The Sex Pistols tour the North of England, not many bands wanted to sound like them, but many decided they could do anything. There's something historically sound in these claims, but the recapitulation of that narrative is an attempt to reset music history on British soil. Post-punk bands *have* to be from their respective cities; in fact, the city comes first, because to be authentically post-punk means to make a claim for British music that stages the credibility and trueness of homegrown art that has sprung from the Zeus head of The Sex Pistols.

Notes

1 Simon Reynolds, "Tombstone Blues: The Music Documentary Boom" *Sight and Sound* (May 2007), 34.
2 See Simon Reynolds, *Retromania: Pop Culture's Addiction to Its Own Past* (London: Faber and Faber, 2011). Reynolds's argument is more nuanced than this insofar as he questions whether or not "progress" is something that should be attained in the first place. In other words, as he claims that "nothing new" has occurred in the last decade, he nonetheless does not state that this is not necessarily a bad thing, merely the way things are.
3 See Hugh Barker and Yuval Taylor's *Faking It: The Quest for Authenticity in Popular Music* (New York and London: W.W. Norton, 2007). They unpack the fundamental paradoxes of post-punk's relationship to authenticity in the chapter on Public Image Ltd ("Public Image: Punk's Paradoxes of Authenticity," 263–296).
4 See Contantine Verevis, "Disorder: *Joy Division*," *Studies in Documentary Film 2*, No. 3 (2008), 233–246. Verevis also finds strong connections between the way Joy Division are treated and its links to the city. While Verivis makes some great connections between the way Gee makes Manchester central to his documentary on Joy Division, he is mostly concerned with the way that connects to punk's history and its association with Situationist theory about the city.
5 Simon Reynolds, *Rip It Up and Start Again: Postpunk 1978–1984* (Faber and Faber: London, 2005), xxiv–xxv.
6 Richard Witts points out that such aesthetic strategies were not just a way to align Manchester groups to a crumbling post-industrialism, but that they were also untrue. That, while there were certainly sections of Greater Manchester suffering from urban blight, there were also many thoroughly modern buildings erected in Manchester's post-war history, leading Witts to proclaim: "contrary to the view promoted in the Factory story, the image that Manchester presented to the world was not of a derelict city but of a comprehensively modern one—that had got it wrong." See Richard Witts, "Building Up a Band: Music for a Second City" in Michael Goddard and Benjamin Halligan (eds.), *Mark E. Smith and The Fall: Art, Music and Politics* (Surrey: Ashgate, 2010), 25.
7 See also Nick Middles' account of this narrative in *From Joy Division to New Order: The True Story of Anthony H Wilson and Factory Records* (London: Virgin Books, 2002).
8 Reynolds, *Rip It Up and Start Again*, 150.
9 See David Nolan, *I Swear I Was There: The Gig That Changed the World* (London: Independent Must Press, 2006).

10 See Dave Haslam, *Manchester, England: The Story of the Pop Cult City* (London: Fourth Estate, 1999), 109–111.
11 Chris Ott, *Unknown Pleasures* (New York: Continuum, 2004), 43–44.
12 Paul Morley is especially astute about unpacking the various problems with making a narrative about Joy Division with Tony Wilson and Martin Hannett as the forces behind the scenes. In a particularly illuminating piece reflecting on viewing the making of *24 Hour Party People*, Morley describes a myriad of different threads that could have made just as much sense. See his *Joy Division: Piece by Piece, Writing about Joy Division 1977–2007* (London: Plexus, 2008), 289–302.

Chapter 9

"Every Tongue Brings in a Several Tale"

The Filth and the Fury's Counterhistorical Transgressions

Ailsa Grant Ferguson

> My conscience hath a thousand several tongues
> And every tongue brings in a several tale
> And every tale condemns me for a villain.
>
> (*Richard III*, V.iii.194)[1]

The Filth and the Fury (2000), Julien Temple's feature-length documentary on the seminal British punk band, the Sex Pistols, begins by setting the scene for the birth of the band: the winter of 1976. Dustbin men were on strike, unemployment was at a record high and racial tensions gave rise to rioting in the streets. "England was in a state of social upheaval ... total social chaos," says a reflective John Lydon (AKA lead singer Johnny Rotten) on the film's voice-over. Archive footage pans the cold streets of London, the uncollected rubbish bags, ironically, covered with picturesque snow. Steve Jones (lead guitarist) describes the setting with brutal negativity: "it was cold and miserable ... If you weren't born into money, you may as well kiss your fucking life goodbye." Suddenly, this barren, postindustrial landscape is interrupted by a regal Shakespearean figure in the form of Olivier's hunched, mischievous Richard III: "Now is the winter of our discontent/Made glorious summer by this sun of York." We are then thrust back into the 1970s, as a child surveys the bleak view from his run-down housing estate balcony.

Julien Temple had been associated with The Sex Pistols during their active years and was the director of *The Great Rock 'n' Roll Swindle* (1980), a mannered and surreal film that mocked the media version of the Pistols' reign. The film was the brainchild of self-styled Svengali and Pistols manager, Malcolm McLaren. *The Filth and the Fury* presents a completely opposing vision of the Pistols, with Lydon now the most dominant voice. *Filth* can be read as competing with other films that may color some audience members' perception of the Pistols story, not least Lech Kowalski's 1980 documentary *D.O.A.*, and Alex Cox's much more well-known fictionalization, *Sid and Nancy* (1986). *Filth* represents, in a bricolagic but not surrealistic mode, the formation, fame, and speedy decline of The Sex Pistols. Exclusively focused on this short historical period and discrete subject, the film combines a diverse range of sources and voices. Narration is shared between multiple voices (most frequently those of band members) and a story is pieced together via a combination of contemporary footage with purpose-made late-1990s interviews with the band's surviving members, John Lydon, Paul Cook, Steve Jones, and, minimally, original bass player Glen Matlock. However, in addition to these more conventional documentary storytelling techniques, *Filth* is simultaneously constructed as a bricolage of visual and audio clips from the 1970s period of the film as well as other influential postwar media culture, most consistently, it is infiltrated throughout by Olivier's 1955 film of Shakespeare's *Richard III*, which provides characterization and plot markers in a contrived chaos of contradictory accounts and eclectic imagery.

Mixing conventional documentary film genre signifiers (such as narrative voice-over) with transgressive imagery (such as presenting images of a blow-up bondage mask almost every time Malcolm McLaren's voice is heard), *Filth* destabilizes any audience's expectations of a "non-fiction" film. *Filth*'s bricolage of disparate elements consists of what Temple refers to as "scattershot use of archive" footage,[2] interspersed with new interviews. The result is problematic for standard theoretical framings of documentary film; *Filth* transgresses, flouts, and even parodies established documentary forms. Indeed, this film could be more aptly termed a "counterhistorical" rather than historical documentary. Counterhistory has been defined as:

> An account of the past which consciously rearranges known and/or hitherto unknown events in an explanatory pattern which counters a previously accepted pattern or patterns. Counterhistories are ideologically or politically motivated: they attempt to usurp "standard" views of the past in order to replace them with an interpretative rearrangement of processes and events which illustrates or justifies a (normally oppositional) set of principles or theories.[3]

Filth's relationship to history and facticity can clearly be understood as presenting such a "counterhistory": counter to McLaren's story (in interviews and *The Great Rock 'n' Roll Swindle*, both sampled in *Filth*) and counter to the hegemonic media presentation of the Pistols in the late 1970s (also presented, selectively, via many television current affairs program clips and images of newspaper headlines, including the eponymous headline proclaiming the band as "The Filth and the Fury"). The film's contrived flouting of documentary convention and style can by placed in two interrelated strands: its transgression of conventional documentary modes and its mischievous use of Olivier's iconic film version of Shakespeare's *Richard III* to subvert the convention of narrative parallelism.

While *Filth* superficially appears to follow the "rockumentary" format popular in the 1970s and 1980s, the film is rather a pastiche than a true example of the form. *Filth* both formally and structurally deviates from the conventions of this style, a style which itself has been parodied so often that it becomes hard to take seriously.[4] We could try to categorize *Filth* as an example of the "rhetorical form" for which Bordwell and Thompson have provided a taxonomy:

> First, "rhetorical form" addresses the viewer openly, trying to move him or her to a new intellectual conviction, to a new emotional attitude, or to an action . . . Second, the subject of the film is not usually an issue of scientific truth but a matter of opinion . . . The filmmaker tries to make his or her position seem the most plausible by presenting different types of arguments and evidence . . . Third . . . If the conclusion cannot be proved beyond question, the filmmaker often appeals to our emotions, rather than presenting only factual evidence. And fourth, the film often attempts to persuade the viewer to make a choice that will have an effect on his or her everyday life.[5]

Indeed, *Filth* could be aligned with many of these features, such as "appeal[ing] to our emotions" by revealing Lydon's grief over the death of bass player Sid Vicious, whose youth and tragic loss is highlighted while his alleged crime is sidelined, in opposition to his accepted place in popular cultural legend. The film's overt demonization of Malcolm McLaren, too, presents a clearly partisan argument. The film also "present[s] different types of arguments and evidence." Yet, despite *Filth*'s rhetorical tone, the plethora of opposing viewpoints transgresses and even parodies the persuasive purpose of rhetorical documentary-making. Narrators disagree, images clash and, while the audience may feel the pressure to be persuaded, the anarchic mix of viewpoints makes it difficult to extrapolate a clear rhetorical line of argument. Moreover, the belatedness of the twenty-first-century audience means their newly formed (if conflicting and confused) opinions of the Pistols and the punk movement may have little relevance to their "everyday life." However, this conflict and confusion of opinions could in itself be read as persuasive, in the sense that it reinforces the punk notion of chaos as a force of change: a trickster film with trickster protagonists.

One means by which to clarify *Filth*'s transgressions is to return to the foundations of documentary film theory. Bill Nichols's six standard "modes" of documentary film have become central theoretical devices in the task of unpicking the documentary form's problematic "non-fiction" status. Nichols remains one of the foremost theoreticians on "non-fiction" or documentary film and his taxonomy of "modes" continues to provide a basis around which much critical discussion on documentary is centered. Nichols's six modes are:

- Poetic
- Expository

- Observational
- Participatory
- Reflexive
- Performative.[6]

While the possibility of a single film combining more than one mode is not directly overruled, Nichols nevertheless tends to explain each mode in terms of its difference from the others, implying mutual exclusivity. And yet *Filth* transgresses every one of these modes. If the modes are viewed as more dynamic and flexible than Nichols originally proposed, they remain invaluable tools for understanding *Filth* as this example of late postmodern documentary.

During the late twentieth century, the delinearization and unstable temporality of narrative was understood as central to postmodern texts. While these tropes became apparent in fiction writing, and fiction film, the documentary film contains a narrative that is arguably most resistant to postmodern conventions. The documentary often remains fairly close to the realist modes (as defined by Nichols) that had applied to the documentary form during its development across the twentieth century. This may be because the documentary film by the 1960s had become much more commonly found on television than at the cinema. The populist imperatives of television conspire to offer comparatively less freedom and space to avant-garde and experimental concerns than cinema, which maintains an "art house" component, exerting influence on its mainstream. *Filth* stays close to some documentary and feature film conventions; especially notable is its reliance on basic temporal realism. However, the film draws attention to its own inaccuracy with a quintessentially postmodern self-reflexivity, particularly in respect of juxtaposing completely contradictory accounts, both of which are announced as factual. Moreover, *Filth* is entirely formed of highly diverse bricolage and intertextual references that firmly associate it not only with punk style but also with a broader postmodern sensibility. Therefore, rather than following a more conventional claim to a singular "true" history, as characteristic of the conventions of documentary, it becomes telling a counterhistory that is *Filth*'s agenda.

It becomes much easier to unpick the film's transgressive approach to the genre through the application of each of Nichols's "modes" of documentary. The "poetic mode" is key to *Filth*'s bricolagic style, both rhythmically and creatively forming image and sound fragments into a "poetic" form, as Nichols defines it:

> The poetic mode sacrifices the conventions of continuity editing and the sense of a very specific location in time and place that follows from it to explore associations and patterns that involve temporal rhythms and spatial juxtapositions.[7]

In *Filth*, a punk aesthetic is recreated by the creative juxtaposition of images of hegemonic and counterhegemonic styles and the cultures of the era, and the film is absolutely centered on a particular temporal and geographical location. However, the film's use of repetitive imagery, such as the band's infamous spitting into the audience or the repetitive use of Olivier's *Richard III* and "sacrifice [of] the conventions of continuity editing" in favor of "rhythms and . . . juxtapositions" are nevertheless clearly influenced by "poetic" documentary form. *Filth* appropriates a literally "poetic" Shakespearean element via fragmented language (such as in the repetition of Richard's self-disgusted phrase "deform'd, unfinish'd," I.i.20). This deconstructs a powerful symbol of cultural capital, Shakespeare—and potentially Olivier himself. Such an audacious fragmentation could be read as drawing the audience's attention to the abandonment of historical "continuity" in favor of aesthetic or poetic rhetoric, but in a self-consciously counterhegemonic way: deconstructing, rather than "worshiping," both Shakespeare and the dramatic and cinematic star value of Sir Laurence Olivier.

In addition to this contradictory poetic/antipoetic use of *Richard III*, a compartmentalization of *Filth* as purely "poetic" is prevented by its preoccupation with history and specific "truths." Lydon's opening voice-over states, "what you've seen in any documentary on any band before or since is how great and wonderful everything is. It's not the truth of it." This statement immediately asserts *Filth*'s conventional "documentary" purpose by comparing its verity (favorably) with other unnamed films in the non-fiction genre. This opening statement identifies generic "rockumentaries" as *untrue*, while establishing the "truth" of *Filth*. Lydon's voice is the first we hear, leading the audience to expect a "voice-of-authority" commentary (also known as "voice of God"), a key feature of Nichols's "expository mode" which, he writes, "assembles fragments of the historical world into a more rhetorical or argumentative frame than an aesthetic or poetic one . . . addressing the viewer directly, with titles or voices that propose a perspective, advance an argument, or recount history."[8] Certainly *Filth*'s bricolage is made up of the assemblage of "fragments of the historical world." However, fragments of other "projected worlds" and appropriations of quasi-truths, such as advertisements, augment the mix and confuse the viewer's perception and definition of an "historical world."[9] *Filth*, moreover, both exploits and subverts the voice-of-authority commentary convention in several ways. Most obviously, the commentary is ensemble-derived, comprising the voices of all living former members of the band, thus dividing the "authority" between different voices. This division in itself is not unusual in documentary styles. However, the voice-of-authority technique is further subverted by these different voices frequently being juxtaposed to disagree with each other, which parodies "expository" documentaries' pursuit of pertaining to represent "historical fact" and even challenges the very notion of singular truth.

Several of *Filth*'s comic moments illustrate this parodic approach to convention. For example, Steve Jones and Paul Cook (the drummer), both back-lit so as to appear in silhouette, speak of their first meetings with Nancy Spungen, a groupie who became Sid Vicious's girlfriend and of whose infamous, violent murder he was accused. First, Jones states clearly that he "hated" her from the very start, then a direct cut takes us to Cook explaining that the first time he saw Nancy was when he caught Jones having sex with her in a toilet. "I didn't like her," he states, categorically. There is then a further cut directly to Lydon who, speaking partly in silhouette and partly over unflattering archive footage of Nancy, explains, "Nancy was a hooker . . . and I actually introduced her to Sid. Shame on me." Following the other two band members' denial of responsibility and the dubious claims that they disliked Spungen from the start (and despite an implicit agreement with Jones and Cook's misogynistic categorization of a very young girl, Nancy, simply as a "hooker"-object), Lydon's apparent honesty is highlighted, portraying him as the voice to be trusted in the film. Yet this, too, is an open manipulation. This moment draws attention to the unreliability of "witness" testimonies, stylistically reflected in the silhouette shot, reminiscent of witness identity protection on television news programs. These associations imply the eyewitness candor of these speakers, casting the Pistols as witnesses to some unnamed crime, or conjure associations of shame and criminality, all adding to *Filth*'s sensationalism. Furthermore, all these extracts from interviews are short and out of context, and the editing of Lydon's voice, even within this short clip, is audible: no attempt is made to hide the director's manipulation of "truth" and, moreover, the very plurality of such a "truth."

Alongside the effects of ensemble narration, there is subversion, too, in the discourse the various narrators employ. Frequent expletives, insults, and recriminations flout expectations of the ostensibly objective role of the historical commentator. Lydon's opening "speech" sets a scene of resistance to expectations and norms, both social and creative. He says that "being in a band" is:

> horrible . . . it's enjoyable to a small degree but if you know what you're doing it for then you'll tolerate all that because the work, at the end of the day, is what matters.

So far, the audience is being presented with a conventionally acceptable commentary, in which the "work" can be assumed to be the music produced. Then the tone changes: Lydon suddenly spits out his plosives, returning to a hallmark aspect of his "Johnny Rotten" persona (and, indeed, Olivier's performance voice), as he defines that "work": "we managed to offend all the people we were fucking fed up with." Having employed a convention (the opening voice-over), the expectations it establishes are aroused in the audience. It is in such instances that the subversion has an impact since the "shock" produced by the transgression of these conventions involves the audience itself in the resistant moment. Exploiting genre convention is the ideal vehicle, then, for counterhegemonic messages: the audience is already dialogically involved in the text due to the way in which this audience recognizes and mounts expectations of textual codes and artifacts.

Returning to the notion of *Filth* as exemplifying postmodern documentary, the intertextuality so central to postmodern texts assumes a varying degree of interactivity in the audience, and varied understanding of meaning, dependent upon the individual spectator's knowledge and experience. *Filth*'s target audience is a potentially rather limited one. There is a heritage element, a nostalgic attraction, to the film, which would be likely to draw an audience of early middle age in 2000, who would have been the Pistols' rough contemporaries. However, the resurgence of the popularity of punk, in the early years of emo and new wave punk in the later half of the 1990s, following the punk ethos and aesthetic of the grunge era earlier in that decade, meant that *Filth*'s audience would also be likely to have included members of a similar age to that of The Sex Pistols during their active years. Perhaps an awareness of this younger audience offers one reason why the ex-Pistols, interviewed in the late 1990s, only ever appear as silhouettes, their middle-aged faces never emerging to break the spell of the fervent youth *Filth* portrays. Due to this potential for demographic duality in the special-interest audience of the film, the intertextual references can have wildly different effects. Put simply, the nostalgic audience sees nostalgia while the young audience is influenced anew by the Pistols and may enjoy the intertextual references as "retro" curiosities.

The potential gulf between two intended audiences (two generations, in fact, watching a film largely about generational disharmony) adds to the dynamic use of "shock" reversals in *Filth* itself (such as the opening "speech" examined above) that have historically functioned as subversive entertainment and expression, from the carnival to "culture jamming." It is not surprising then, that *Filth*'s transgressions of documentary styles are wider still. As well as subverting conventions of narrative voice, *Filth*'s structure and presentation make the film both a composite and a transgression of other documentary modes. The "observational mode," which "emphasizes a direct engagement with the everyday life of subjects as observed by an unobtrusive camera,"[10] is, then, the least relevant mode for *Filth*. However, the film does include some stylistically "observational footage," notably the filming of comings and goings in Vivienne Westwood and Malcolm McLaren's shop, SEX, on the King's Road in Chelsea. Yet, by combining the voice-over with the "observational" imagery, Nichols's compartmentalization is challenged. Indeed, questions of temporality emerge, since Nichols makes no mention of this issue: the "expository mode" is described as recording "history," yet the "observational" documentary is described as contemporary to its subject. In *Filth*, while much of the "observational" footage had been previously unreleased (and so had remained unseen), it was over twenty years old by *Filth*'s premier in 2000.

The complex result of *Filth*'s bricolage is highlighted when comparing the film's style to Nichols's definition of the "participatory mode," particularly in terms of the film's elaborate juxtaposition of interviews and archive. The "participatory documentary":

> emphasizes the interaction between filmmaker and subject. Filming takes place by means of interviews or other forms of even more direct involvement . . . [and is often] coupled with archival footage to examine historical issues.[11]

So the relevance of such a "participatory mode" to *Filth*'s style is clear since the film's principal narrative is generally told through interviews in various forms: voice-over speeches, sound bites, archive interviews (both by the director and from 1970s television sources) and those new interviews carried out by Temple "face to face" but presented in silhouette on screen. The effect is uncomfortable and creates a pastiche of the manipulative nature of editing interviews by splicing short phrases, sentences, and even single words together from different sources.

Filth's editing problematizes the question of objectivity (which is already difficult to define and quantify in any documentary and especially so for those in the "participatory mode") by leaving in, on two occasions, interviewees' references to "Julien." The first of these instances is taken from archive footage of an interview with Sid Vicious in a London park; Vicious remarks "we could've played abroad . . . couldn't we, Julien?" while complaining about McLaren's management of the band, so establishing "Julien" as on the side of the Pistols *against* McLaren. Later, Lydon talks to Temple about Sid's death, referring to unnamed enemies: "They just turned it into making money" and, moments later, "I will hate them forever for doing that. You can't get more evil than that, can you, Julien?" This whole section of interview is highly significant for the audience since Temple has continued to film while Lydon appears to break down in tears as he describes his anguish at Vicious's death. This moment is central to the film's structure as it shatters the illusion of the nihilistic, unemotional Rotten and replaces it with the human Lydon. The formal significance of this incident lies in Temple's overt manipulation of the interview footage; his deliberate inclusion of his own first name would appear to posit the interview style within Nichols's "participatory mode." However, the moment is also "reflexive" in "call[ing] attention to the assumptions and conventions that govern documentary filmmaking [and so] increas[ing] our awareness of the constructedness of the film's representation of reality."[12]

The silhouette shot of Lydon interferes with the potential for intimacy or realism. This technique draws attention to the interview as a definitively "filmed" event as opposed to attempting to give the audience any impression of a "conversation" between filmmaker and subject. Such an overtly impersonal shot seems to be in binary opposition to its subject matter. The decision not to edit out the word "Julien" and the fairly long-take are also explicitly incongruous in a film in which most interviews are edited into a series of disconnected sound bites. Thus the audience's attention is drawn to the manipulations available to the filmmaker throughout a text's production, which in turn posits the film not as objective "truth" but as a product of subjective viewpoints. This blurs *Filth* into the realms of what Nichols terms "performative" documentary that, he writes, "emphasizes the subjective or expressive aspect of the filmmaker's own engagement with the subject and an audience's responsiveness to this engagement."[13] This moment also contains a further layer of meaning to those who are already aware of the public story of the band. One of the major points of contention between Lydon and McLaren had been Temple's *The Great Rock 'n' Roll Swindle*, which was ostensibly an avant-garde portrayal of the Pistols playing "themselves" (without Lydon's direct participation) in a surreal counter-reality documentary of the band's "story." Lydon came to despise the film and publicly discredited it, calling it simply "rubbish."[14] It is puzzling, therefore, to see the apparent trust between filmmaker (Temple) and subjects (Lydon, Cook, Jones, and, posthumously, Vicious) in *Filth*. The editing of Lydon's speech compounds this unsettling effect: "they just turned it into making money. Ha, ha, ha, ha, how hilarious for them." The interview is edited so that "they" here remains undefined; perhaps Lydon refers to McLaren and Westwood (who produced t-shirts and other memorabilia of Vicious's demise), other members of the band, the press, or even the public (us). The only certainty established is that Temple is firmly positioning himself and this film as united with Lydon, because here Lydon speaks to "Julien" about "they" the enemy, inferring that he and Temple are "we."

The question of "them" (the hegemonic ideology, McLaren and his allies, any enemy, in fact, of the Pistols *qua* Lydon) versus "us" (Julien Temple, Lydon, and, perhaps, a sympathetic audience) is central to the narrative dynamic in *Filth*. The film's frequent use of a Shakespearean character functions within this dichotomy in contradictory ways at different points in the film: sometimes, Shakespeare/Richard/Olivier explicitly represents "us"; at other times, equally explicitly, "them." Unpicking this complex appropriation provides a means by which to examine the carnivalesque reversals of "them" and "us" in *Filth*.

Infamously "historically" unsound, Shakespeare's *Richard III* is a play that might appear to be a particularly incongruous appropriation for a documentary film, a genre and form inextricably linked to concepts of "truth" and "history."[15] Though *Filth* uses only tiny fragments of Shakespeare's text, *Richard III* is embedded via Olivier's film, in *Filth*, both diegetically *and* non-diegetically, as well as structurally and thematically. Most obviously, the figure of Shakespeare's Richard (as embodied in another cultural icon, Olivier) coheres

Filth's narrative in every major plot development, with parallel clips being included at moments. When Johnny Rotten joins the band, the image of Rotten is interposed with Olivier as the hunch-backed Richard. When "God Save the Queen" is released, Richard is seen as gleeful. And when the band self-destructs, Richard is killed.

If an audience's desire for realism, by way of tangible causality, is the key to creating a conventionally satisfying narrative, then in a documentary one could assume that this desire is easily satisfied given the "reality" of the subject. And yet the other aspects of narrative that an audience desires most are likely to be resolution and structure: a beginning, middle, and end to the "story," which may be harder for a feature documentary to deliver. Many documentaries avoid the challenge of actual resolution by merely shedding some "new light"[16] on their subjects, just as *Filth* openly claims to do. However, the recoding of *Richard III* in *Filth* also supports the narrative by superimposing a parallel "reality" that has been ready-fashioned into a plot.

The study of documentary has a tendency to place the genre within methodologies of presenting historicity and facticity ("documentary" photography and, more literally, documentary evidence), despite acknowledging the dangers of transposing narrative expectations and limitations onto a section of an infinite sequence of "real" events. Just as an early modern history play (as we define Shakespeare and his contemporaries' dramatic representations of historical events and figures) such as *Richard III* might present a politically manipulated, counterhistorical chronicle, *Filth* retells the past through a perspective of resistance or by taking an openly biased sociopolitical viewpoint. The counterhistorical value of *Richard III* becomes a means by which to tie *Filth*'s "history" to a tradition of (hi)storytelling and mockingly appropriates Shakespeare's much-contested cultural capital.

Filth is not just a chronicle of The Sex Pistols, but of the sociopolitical crisis in 1970s Britain when, Jon Savage observed, "the media was full of apocalyptic rhetoric."[17] While the Shakespearean label "Winter of Discontent" was not appropriated to describe Britain's social problems until the widespread strikes of 1978–1979,[18] the marriage of Shakespeare's phrase with the late 1970s in British popular imagination became firmly entrenched, frequently being recalled and re-used in response to any threat of strikes or social strife in the UK in the 1980s and 1990s. Shakespeare's manipulation of the events surrounding Richard III's short reign portrays, as does *Filth*, an age of social upheaval and strife. Appropriating this history play, *Richard III*, as "history," the film uses the play as a parallel "history" to its own. As such, the narrative of *Filth* is aligned not with Shakespeare's England but with the fictional landscape—or counterhistory—of medieval England, as portrayed in *Richard III* and re-imagined on film by Olivier. The upheaval portrayed in *Richard III* offers an easy parallel in *Filth*: it makes England's position in the 1970s seem all the more desperate by juxtaposing this position with a time in history known for its social and political chaos.

Indeed, the 1990s had just produced two relatively successful big screen Richards, Ian McKellan in Richard Loncraine's 1995 film of the play, and Al Pacino in his own video-diary-like documentary of a non-production, *Looking for Richard* (1996), both of which associate Richard with the gangster in some way: the former via a 1930s stylized setting and the latter via Al Pacino's seminal gangster roles that are inevitably attached to his star persona. These films of the mid-1990s will have produced a greater awareness of the play and its eponymous protagonist among Western (and perhaps international) audiences, while also affirming a notion of Richard's criminality via the gangster signifiers in both films. In addition, the flurry of Shakespeare films that had emerged after the surprising box office success that greeted Kenneth Branagh's *Henry V* in 1989 meant that Shakespeare was particularly associated during the 1990s with a nostalgia of heritage cinema, as with Branagh's *Much Ado About Nothing* (1993) and Trevor Nunn's *Twelfth Night* (1996). The setting of Baz Luhrmann's *Romeo + Juliet* (1996) challenged the "correctness" of British Shakespeare films and in its success set a precedent for greater mainstream acceptance of subcultural resituations of Shakespearean texts on film. In this particular period, then, *Filth*'s defiant, contradictory deconstruction of both Shakespeare and a luminary of Shakespearean film production, Olivier, becomes a weapon against the nostalgic mode of the British heritage film industry.

Placing *Filth*'s use of Shakespeare's and Olivier's *Richard III* as part of a broader use of Shakespeare in punk music, Adam Hansen sees *Filth*'s appropriation of Shakespeare's play as an offshoot of Lydon's self-fashioned persona, which he confesses is influenced by Richard's persona in both his autobiography[19] and his voice-overs in *Filth*. Yet to see *Filth*'s use of Shakespeare as tied purely to the Rotten persona is reductive. Hansen comments, on the temporal disjunction of the *Richard III* clips within *Filth*, that:

> Shakespeare is sufficiently disconnected and discrete from the decrepit period Rotten finds himself in to offer an opposition to that period. In other ways Shakespeare is close enough for Rotten to make productive connections with his work. To Rotten, Shakespeare's characters show a merciless but energizing disregard for moral niceties, and so reflect an earlier period where it was obvious those niceties were not universally maintained. This contrasts with the hypocritical, repressive and restrained state Rotten resists.[20]

This approach sees the use of a particular Shakespearean figure in *Filth* as representing a whole host of meanings in Shakespeare's entire body of work. Indeed, the only other Shakespearean figure to appear in the film is a brief clip of Olivier (again) as Hamlet. However Hansen's notion that *Filth* uses *Richard III* simply as a marker for Shakespearean characters who are understood to represent an anarchistic Arcadia where one can flout "moral niceties" is not entirely convincing. The play's relationship to the film is structural rather than personal, and the relationship of the historical periods presented is not just a matter of Shakespeare's England and Lydon's England. It is, rather, complicated by the visual presence of Olivier's 1950s medieval fantasy.

The temporal anarchy, achieved in the seemingly random injection of a medieval-cum-early modern (as imagined in the 1950s) figure, namely Olivier as Richard III, at frequent moments of *Filth*'s 1970s landscape, is an important element of the intertextual effect. Yet this chaotic approach to temporality is so quintessentially postmodern that it could be argued to be pastiche or posture. "One hallmark of postmodernism," writes Stephen M. Buhler, "is a detached playfulness with history: wry quotations of the past appear as isolated architectural elements, as re-contextualized figures in visual works, as characters haunted by lost (but tantalizingly 'present') connections with source-texts in narrative."[21] This view could brand *Filth*'s use of Shakespeare as a "hallmark of postmodernism"; in this sense the film's style works to place the film within the period that it portrays (indeed, a period when the postmodern, fragmentary style was *de rigueur*) rather than the *fin-de-Millennial* culture in which it was made. Semenza identifies *Filth*'s punk sensibility as "anti-history,"[22] and *Filth*'s "playfulness with history" is a feature of other punk texts which, in denying a "future" and denying or defying the "past," also sought to reclaim history.[23] Denying a hegemonically sanctioned retelling of history—and offering an alternative, marginalized voice to retell the past and potential futures—is an act of rebellion in itself. In these terms, *Filth*'s appropriation of *Richard III* is a part of that rebellion. The film's narrative strategy uses what can only be termed a meta-history (a "history of a history") in order to highlight the dynamic and protean nature of the past's so-called "truths." *Filth* focuses on a historical–fictional character, Richard III, who himself embodies both "fact" and "fiction." As Garber argues:

> It is the historian's job to discover the facts, and thus to dispel mystery, fantasy, undecidability. With this decidedly "professional", male, and hegemonic view of the use and abuse of history-writing [. . .] we may begin our consideration of a dramatic character who is self-described as both deformed and defeatured, himself compact of fact *and* fiction: "Cheated of feature . . . deformed, unfinished . . . scarce half made up."[24]

Filth makes a direct attack on the hegemonic ownership of "history" by appropriating Shakespeare's "compact of fact and fiction" in *Richard III*. Pauline Kiernan sees Shakespeare's use of anachronism as having "the effect of instilling an acute awareness that his present will become our past."[25] *Filth*'s reverse anachronism inserts several pasts (of 1950s "Medieval" on film, of fictionalized Medieval in the play, and of Shakespeare's own early modern context) within another, more recent, past (that of the 1970s), and newer interviews (of the 1990s).

Filth's temporal manipulations subvert and mock the imposition of hegemonic "histories" onto the punk movement's—and specifically the Pistols'—"story." Because chaos, contradiction, and carnivalesque mockery are all features of this process, it is problematic to try to categorize the process taking place. Carl R. Plantinga describes "historical narrative" films as telling "stories" through a "projected world . . . a model of the actual world,"[26] and *how* this is done is explained as a particular "discourse":

> The nonfiction film text is a physical entity—a string of projected images and amplified sounds, discourse is abstract—a formal arrangement. The discourse is the means by which the projected world or story events are communicated; its principal strategies, at the most abstract level, are selection, order, emphasis, and voice.[27]

In the case of *Filth*, Shakespeare's play forms a part of this "discourse," thus repositioning this mechanism as tangible rather than abstract, in the sense that the "selection, order, emphasis, and voice" in which *Filth*'s "story" is told becomes partly that of another, semi-fictional, text. The process is thus diverted and the result is further removed from "reality." Using Plantinga's model, *Filth* can be mapped: it translates its "actual world" (The Sex Pistols' short career) into a "projected world" (*Filth*) but detours via another "projected world" (Olivier's *Richard III*) and, subtextually, Shakespeare's "stage world" (*Richard III*), both of which in turn project a medieval "actual world." *Filth*'s temporal anarchy, aided by the use of Shakespeare's clearly historically inaccurate "projection," both exposes and parodies the complex mechanisms behind "non-fiction" film representation. The intertextual tangles that make it, in fact, impossible to categorize postmodern documentary's "discourse" and form are here laid bare.

Bordwell and Thompson identify parallelism's usefulness in constructing satisfying documentary narratives in that it "allows the film to become richer and more complex than it might have been had it concentrated on only one protagonist,"[28] seen to be exemplified in the documentary *Hoop Dreams* (Steve James, 1994). In *Filth* the paralleled protagonists (Rotten and Richard), and the "rise and fall" plot, deploy this technique. Bordwell and Thompson assert that, "our recognition of parallelism provides part of our pleasure in watching a film, much as the echo of rhymes contributes to the power of poetry."[29] In *Filth* we find both "pleasures" in one text: the literal "poetry" of Shakespeare is repeated and looped to make it obsessively present while the pleasing rhythms and comfortably convincing parallels contribute to a satisfying narrative. Moreover the completeness of Shakespeare's narrative resolution (Richard's defeat and death) lends finality to *Filth*'s narrative where otherwise it would be dominated by the messy, unresolved elements of its source events, such as the enduring mystery surrounding Nancy Spungen's violent death.

Yet in *Filth*, parallelism, like Nichols's modes, is subverted: the audience is teased with the possibility of a withholding of narrative satisfaction on Temple's part, and their expectations transgressed. By adopting this common narrative strategy, the audience is primed to expect the parallel to continue throughout the text and, in a way, it does. Richard does indeed continue to be paralleled with Rotten and the Pistols in general. This is not surprising, given Richard's place in Western cultural awareness, as both a symbol of lawlessness, self-gratification, and short-lived, brutal power and, conversely, due to his perception as a trickster and a showman, the ultimate magnetic personality. However, *Filth*'s deconstruction of *Richard III* and paralleling of Richard and Rotten (and to some extent the Pistols) is problematized by a series of opposing parallels. Richard is also paralleled with the monarchy, the hegemony, those enemies of the Pistols that the audience, inclined to sympathize with the subjects, should surely distrust. In this way, the parallel-protagonist gambit, a common feature in documentary film, is subverted to challenge the false neatness of documentaries' imposed parallels. So when *Richard III*'s narrative is transposed onto *Filth*, the audience's expectations of the familiar play are exploited to enable a carnivalesque set of transgressions and redirections to confuse, entertain, and challenge their approach not only to *Filth* and its subjects but to the whole notion of portraying a "history" as a neatly formalized narrative.

Throughout *Filth* expectations of documentary modes are subverted and transgressed, reflecting the mischievously counterhegemonic position of the subjects themselves. At the end of the film the modes climactically collide. Following interview footage of Lydon, *Filth* draws to a close with a montage of images and sounds, many of which are repeated from earlier in the film. A multitude of live performances are spliced together over a soundtrack of the song "No Fun," interrupted by sound bites from band members and McLaren. Images flash momentarily onto the screen: the bondage mask, Vicious as a junkie, the Pistols mucking around on stage. The last voice-over rests, unsurprisingly, with Lydon (thus bookending the film with his voice); he ends the film by saying, simply, "The Sex Pistols ended at exactly the right time for all the wrong reasons. But the wrong reasons were continued and people continued to perpetrate lies about a reality." These words return to the assertion at the beginning of *Filth* that there are extant and public lies to be rejected, and truths to be presented. Yet the majority of the film draws attention to the fluidity of the concept of any final "truth."

After these final words by the 2000 Lydon, *Filth* again makes use of *Richard III* (the king writhes on the ground in his famous death scene). Yet here the footage is played at high speed and wordless (Richard's famous last words *before* this death scene, "My kingdom for a horse," are conspicuously absent), thus "cheating" the audience of their expected ending. The speeding up of Olivier's particularly extended portrayal of Richard's demise reflexively draws attention to filmed media's power to manipulate image and sound. It portrays

Richard and the Pistols' shared humiliation by transforming a painful death scene into slapstick comedy. The montage (and the film) is completed with a clip from the Pistol's final performance that ended, after just one song, with Rotten's now famous final quip: "Ever get the feeling you've been cheated?"

The construction of any dramatic narrative based on historical events definitively differs from a fictional narrative; this narrative has the constraints of following (or appearing to follow) verifiable "real" events. In order to engage the audience with a story with which they may already be familiar, a common gambit is to simply insert the "new" into the old: the "previously unseen footage" that lends the "authenticity" that the audience desires. However, a historical plot also has the advantage of another sort of collective familiarity: nostalgia. Watching *Filth* it is easy to become immersed in the rebellion on the screen, but it is a rebellion against the society of another century—a century no longer our own. We know the ending. Perhaps it is in this narrative predictability that we find one of the possible motivations behind the presence of the Shakespearean in the film: nostalgia. Yet it is not a nostalgia for a lost society that we yearn for here, but for a time when we could still rebel: there was still something new that could be done.

For all its subversions, transgressions, and mischievous manipulations, is *The Filth and the Fury*, in the end, a progressive example of the music documentary, or seminal to the canon of music documentaries? What this film represents, in its style and its form, is an attempt to capture on film the bricolage, the anarchy, and the fun of punk. Yet it is ironic that it is only via technologies unavailable to the rebels of the 1970s that this quick-fire, scattershot style can be so fully achieved. A last gesture towards the visceral rebellion of the early days of punk may, in *Filth*, ironically become a herald of the coming communicative strategies of the new media of the new century. By the beginning of the twenty-first century the virtually exclusive use of digital editing, even down to the homemade montages found on YouTube, clearly demonstrates how obsolete the painstaking physical process of film editing has become. Yet *Filth*, by upturning or usurping the previously held demarcations of documentary forms and rejecting every attempt to compartmentalize documentary, legitimizes instead the power of retelling—and epitomizes the plurality of counterhistories.

Notes

1 This and all subsequent citations from the play are taken from Anthony Hammond (ed.), *The Arden Shakespeare: Richard III* (London and New York: Routledge, 1981 edition).

2 Temple makes this comment on the voice-over commentary of the UK DVD release (from FilmFour) of *The Filth and the Fury*.

3 Jeremy Hawthorne, *A Concise Glossary of Contemporary Literary Theory* (London and New York: Arnold, 1997), 36.

4 See, for example, the "Bad News Tour" episode of the UK television series *The Comic Strip Presents . . .* (Sandy Johnson, 1983) and *This is Spinal Tap* (Rob Reiner, 1984).

5 David Bordwell and Kristin Thompson, *Film Art: An Introduction* (New York: McGraw-Hill, 2008), 348–349. Current documentary filmmakers known for their employment of such a "rhetorical form" could be said to include Nick Broomfield, Michael Moore, and Morgan Spurlock.
6 Ibid., 100–105.
7 Bill Nichols, *Introduction to Documentary* (Bloomington, Illinois: Indiana University Press, 2001), 102.
8 Ibid.,105.
9 I borrow these terms from Carl R. Plantinga, *Rhetoric and Representation in Nonfiction Film* (Cambridge: Cambridge University Press, 1997), 85.
10 Nichols, *Introduction to Documentary*, 34.
11 Ibid.
12 Ibid.
13 Ibid.
14 Lydon, quoted in John Lydon with Keith Zimmerman and Kent Zimmerman, *Rotten: No Irish, No Blacks, No Dogs* (New York: Picador, 1994), 278.
15 *Richard III* was appropriated in one other feature documentary of the 1990s, and as also forming a fundamental element of narrative, structure, and themes. Preceding *Filth*'s release by four years, *Looking for Richard* (Al Pacino, 1996) portrays the piecing-together of an enactment of the play, where the process alone survives without product: the finished production was never performed.
16 Bordwell and Thompson, *Film Art*, 74.
17 Jon Savage, *England's Dreaming: Sex Pistols and Punk Rock* (London: Faber and Faber, 1991), 108.
18 The phrase was and is still generally used to describe the winter of 1978/1979 and was allegedly first adopted by Robin Chater as a headline in an issue of Incomes Data Report in 1977, and then in the newspapers the *London Evening Standard* and the *Sun* in late 1978.
19 In *Rotten: No Irish, No Blacks, No Dogs*, Lydon refers to his deliberate and conscious appropriation of Richard III as a character in his performances; Lydon *et al.*, *Rotten*, 54.
20 Adam Hansen, *Shakespeare and Popular Music* (New York: Continuum, 2010), 105.
21 Stephen M. Buhler, "Camp *Richard III* and the Burdens of (Stage/Film) History," in Mark Thornton Burnett and Ramona Wray (eds.), *Shakespeare, Film, Fin de Siècle* (Basingstoke: Macmillan/New York: St Martin's Press, 2000), 40–57.
22 Gregory M. Colón Semenza, "God save the Queene: Sex Pistols, Shakespeare, and Punk (Anti)History," in Gregory M. Colón Semenza (ed.), *The English Renaissance in Popular Culture: An Age for All Time* (New York: Palgrave MacMillan), 143–166.
23 This is most notably the theme in Derek Jarman's punk cult classic, *Jubilee* (1978), in which "narrator" Amyl Nitrate (played by punk muse Jordon) justifies her adaptation and appropriation of existing historical narratives in her own written history book: "But history still fascinates me; it's so intangible! You can weave facts any way you like. Good guys can swap places with bad guys. You might think Richard III of England was bad, but you'd be wrong."
24 Marjorie Garber, *Shakespeare's Ghost Writers: Literature as Uncanny Causality* (London: Methuen, 1987), 30. Italics in original.
25 Pauline Kiernan, *Shakespeare's Theory of Drama* (Cambridge: Cambridge University Press, 1996), 134–135.
26 Plantinga, *Rhetoric and Representation*, 85.
27 Ibid.
28 Bordwell and Thompson, *Film Art*, 76.
29 Ibid., 67.

Part IV

"Mockumentaries" and "Rockumentaries"

Chapter 10

The Circus is in Town

Rock Mockumentaries and the Carnivalesque

Jeffrey Roessner

Interviewer: Are you a mod or a rocker?
Ringo Starr: No, I'm a mocker.

A Hard Day's Night (1964)

In terms of its appeal, rock music is a curiously divided genre. Originating in black rhythm and blues and finding its hip-swiveling avatar in Elvis Presley, rock from the beginning reveled in sex, vulgarity, and subversion. Indeed, as it offers a sonic middle finger to the staid, work-a-day world of parents, responsibility, and rules, the music has been accused of inciting riots, rampant fornication, illicit drug use, and general mayhem. At the same time, however, rock appeals to the long-standing romantic narrative of the isolated, suffering poet who offers soul-bearing art for our deep pleasure and catharsis. And in fact, it's this latter, more easily domesticated version of rock—especially sixties rock—that we find foregrounded in many documentaries, from D. A. Pennebaker's *Don't Look Back* (1967)[1] through contemporary retrospectives such as Murray Lerner's *Amazing Journey: The Story of the Who* (2007). In their attempt to take us behind the music, these films elide the anarchic impulse of rock and roll by elevating it to the status of art and celebrating the genius of the tortured artists who create it.

Because of their implicitly mythic narrative structure, such earnest documentaries have spawned a subgenre of parodies. Over the past decade, films lampooning the style and narrative tropes of the documentary form in general have received an increasing amount of scholarly attention, and rightly so. Cynthia J. Miller's recent list of mockumentaries includes nearly 240 films, from the infamous *The Swiss Spaghetti Harvest* in 1957 up to *All You Need Is Brains*, a 2009 film about the The Zombeatles, a hybrid rock band living in a zombie universe.[2] The critical assessment of mockumentaries has largely focused on their challenge to the truth claims of documentaries, and explored the staging of reality in the films. In terms of mockumentaries specifically about rock music, *This is Spinal Tap* (Reiner, 1984) and the over-the-top machismo of heavy metal have been thoroughly critiqued from the point of view of gender studies.[3] So here I would like to leave aside the questions of documentary realism and the issue of gender to explore a different cultural question: why do we need rock mockumentaries at all? Why would rock music, a cultural form long associated with deviance and defiance, attract parody? As an initial response to these questions, this chapter suggests that rock mockumentaries—including *The Rutles: All You Need is Cash* (Idle and Weis, 1978)—lampoon the notion of high art and satirize the image of the solitary, suffering genius in an attempt to recuperate the carnivalesque heart of the music.

Mocking the Mockers

In the critical literature, mockumentaries make for decidedly serious academic business. The first full-length treatment of the subgenre, *Faking It*, by Jane Roscoe and Craig Hight, explores the "reflexive stance" as the defining trait of mock-documentaries, which appropriate and subvert the codes of "factual discourse" underpinning the documentary tradition.[4] The authors ultimately provide a hierarchy of mockumentaries, with three increasingly sophisticated and challenging levels: degree one films are simple parody, degree two represents critiques and hoaxes, and degree three offers deconstruction. *The Rutles* and *This is Spinal Tap* are degree one, of course, while *David Holzman's Diary* (McBride, 1967) and *Man Bites Dog* (Belvaux, Bonzel, and Poelvoorde, 1992) represent degree three. In essence, the films about rock bands are unchallenging entertainment, naturally, while the film about a film crew implicated in murder committed by its serial-killer subject is subversive and substantively deconstructs the documentary form. Similarly, Alexandra Juhasz and Jesse Lerner, in *F is for Phony: Fake Documentaries and Truth's Undoing*, note that although they "enjoy a good laugh as much as anyone does," the essays in the volume "focus on the more serious uses of the fake documentary . . . that most self-consciously and directly engage with history, identity, and truth."[5] In short, the editors acknowledge that they "neglect more mainstream film (*The Blair Witch Project* and *Spinal Tap*) in favor of more independent or underground fare."[6]

Curiously, theorists of the mockumentary form have little illuminating to say about mockery. They present parody as simple, unchallenging, and popular, and in this way, many film theorists embrace a high modernist penchant for difficulty and formal complexity: from this perspective, pop culture is not worth much serious attention. Such a neglect of the principal element of mockery—laughter—calls to mind Mikhail Bakhtin's work on the history of the medieval carnival in *Rabelais and His World*. Bakhtin notes that laughter, as the central element of the carnivalesque tradition, is "the least scrutinized form of the people's creation" and was "accorded the least place of all in the vast literature devoted to myth, to folk lyrics, and to epics."[7] Looking at Roscoe and Hight's hierarchy, we see that not much has changed in terms of genre distinctions: dark, tragic, and dour self-reflexivity are seen as more subversive in their effects on the audience than parodic forms. If we want to understand the importance of laughter in rock mockumentaries, then, we should begin at the intersection of rock music and Bakhtin's notion of the carnivalesque.

In a persuasive essay drawing on Bakhtin's work, Paul Kohl offers an account of sixties rock music as a modern manifestation of the carnival.[8] He argues that often in contemporary culture, the grotesque elements of the carnival are seen as freak shows, and thus work to reinforce ideals of normalcy by holding the *other* up for derision. Kohl suggests that such an approach ignores Bakhtin's insistence on the positive and regenerative qualities of the carnival. Indeed, Bahktin explains the critical or subversive potential of the carnival as "temporary liberation from the prevailing truth and from the established order; it marked the suspensions of all hierarchical rank, privileges, norms, and prohibitions."[9] But he also explores the duality at the heart of parodic forms: "Degradation digs a bodily grave for a new birth" and has "not only a destructive, negative aspect, but also a regenerating one . . . It is always conceiving."[10] For Kohl, one arena of contemporary culture in which we see the recovery of such positive values is rock and roll. Albums by The Beatles, Frank Zappa, Captain Beefheart, and The Velvet Underground not only degrade high-held concepts and suspend the rules governing everyday life, but also level hierarchies and affirm the centrality of the body—especially through emphasis on the rhythmic pulse of the music and the ecstatic, visceral response it encouraged in fans.

Although Kohl offers a compelling reading of rock as an intrusion of the carnival into contemporary life, I suggest that the very existence of mockumentaries complicates his analysis. Foregrounding the fact that the meaning of style is not stable or secure or universal, parodic films indicate the extent to which the meaning of rock has changed as the music has been absorbed into mainstream culture. Kohl's blind spot here is apparent as he references both *Sgt. Pepper's Lonely Hearts Club Band* and Frank Zappa's parody of it, *We're Only in it for the Money*, a juxtaposition which leads us to some critical questions: Why would the carnival make fun of the carnival? Why do the clowns turn their mockery on each other? It seems that rock and roll does represent the carnivalesque—in certain venues, at specific times, as heard by particular people. In other words, the meaning of rock and roll resolutely depends upon context and audience. *Sgt. Pepper* played out of an apartment window in 1967 means something different from *Sgt. Pepper* heard at a party today, which is different from its analysis as one of the hundred best albums of the sixties, which is perhaps different still from the album dissected in a documentary. Of course, the meanings produced in these contexts can be mutually reinforcing, deeply personal, or utterly contradictory. In this instance, Zappa's parody of *Sgt. Pepper* seems inspired by the album's very quick assimilation as art-object, and as the expression of the collective genius of

The Beatles (and of course, Zappa's antipathy for the hippies who saw the album as a countercultural identity badge). A similar reading applies to many classic rock documentaries: they uphold the music for both its historical importance and for its artistry—and produce narratives that, intentionally or not, underscore the seriousness of the genre and subdue its radical, threatening impulses. Consequently, such documentaries invite a return to the subversiveness associated with early rock and roll, and create a space for the emergence of mockery.

He's an Artist and He Don't Look Back

In the case of rock documentaries, we find a serious, historically grounded medium training its lens on a highly suspect form of popular culture, one that was disparaged not only because of its status as ephemeral entertainment, but because it aroused cultural anxieties surrounding taboo subjects such as race, sex, delinquency, and violence.[11] Films ostensibly documenting rock culture need to be read against this crisis of legitimacy. In essence, the documentary must substantiate not only its own value, but also the cultural worth of its subject. The desire to turn rock and roll into a respected cultural form is thus overdetermined, arising from the seriousness of the documentary form and the necessity of elevating the status of the music and musicians depicted. Focusing the camera on a subject must mean that the subject is worthy of being preserved on film, but the justification also works the other way, as film confers legitimacy on its subject.

In his essay on D. A. Pennebaker's documentary of Bob Dylan's 1965 tour of the UK, *Don't Look Back*, Keith Beattie takes issue with the claim that rockumentaries domesticate their subjects in a quest to establish legitimacy. He argues that films such as *Don't Look Back*, *Woodstock* (Wadleigh, 1970), and *The Last Waltz* (Scorsese, 1978) disrupt the high seriousness of documentary form: they focus on visual "spectatorial pleasure," and erase the distinction between the on-stage and back-stage as the musician-actors perform for the audience in concert and for the camera lens afterwards, behind the curtain.[12] In this way, rockumentaries subvert the essential aims of direct cinema, as they highlight the constructed nature of the truth being presented. Beattie here makes a persuasive claim about the performative elements in the films. But of course, filmmakers do not simply impose seriousness onto the music and musicians. Rock musicians have proven themselves to be fully invested in developing their reputation as artists and promoting themselves and their work. Consequently, the legitimacy narrative in documentaries often overrides or at the very least remains in distinct tension with the anarchic impulses of the music.

In his analysis, Beattie ignores how the documentary tradition has informed audience expectations, even for rock films. Most obviously, if rockumentaries were radically subversive of documentary form and did not invest in a serious tone, we would have little use for the films that mock them. As Cynthia Miller argues in relation to mockumentaries, "In order for the 'truth' to be subverted, parodied, or otherwise taken out to play, audiences must first believe that a format exists for reliably delivering that truth. While audiences of films, television, and new media are increasingly aware that documentary truth is 'relative' truth—authenticity that begs interrogation—that truth still functions to lend a degree of ontological stability to audiences' beliefs, experiences, and identities."[13] I would argue, then, that it is mockumentaries, not rockumentaries, that take the truth out to play and radically challenge ontological stability. When documentaries analyze, explain, or lend gravity to the carnival, it is no longer a carnival, but something else, something cerebral, something outside time, something much more difficult to dance to.

In particular, D. A. Pennebaker's *Don't Look Back* provides striking examples of the twinned impulses to display the carnival while elevating the status of the artist. Shot in the style of direct cinema, *Don't Look Back* captures Bob Dylan at a critical moment in his career—essentially on his last "folk" tour, but having already released his first album venturing into electric rock and roll, *Bringing It All Back Home*. The film shows that Dylan can still have casual interaction with his fans, as he talks with them and signs autographs, but also clearly exposes the growing claustrophobia of his fame and the mythology constructed around him. Shot with no voice-overs or directorial comment, the film purports to offer an objective lens on Dylan's experience both in concert and behind the scenes, in jostled hand-held shots of Dylan and entourage in hotel rooms, trains, and cars, as they deal with the grind of traveling and performing.

Direct cinema works in part because of the illusion that it creates of exposing the "real" artist at work. In *Don't Look Back*, this reality-effect is particularly heightened in one scene during which Dylan talks to keyboardist Alan Price about being fired from The Animals. After Price's pained comments, Dylan offers a rare acknowledgement of the camera by glancing at it as if to scold the filmmaker for recording the scene. The viewer is also treated to voyeuristic moments in other scenes as manager Albert Grossman argues with hotel staff, and an intoxicated Dylan rants about poets "like Brendan Behan." Such moments offer the delight of looking behind the scenes, which often conceal the elements of their construction, the editing, and the fact that the "actors" are aware of the camera and clearly in some sense performing for it. If we reconsider Dylan's look at the camera in this context, it works not only to confirm the "reality" of the scene, but also, oddly, to underscore the unreality of much of the film: by acknowledging the camera and expressing his sense of what is out of bounds, or too personal/real to be made public, Dylan exposes the constructed nature of the persona he and the film are collaborating to present.

How does this style relate to the carnivalesque? *Don't Look Back* entices viewers through its illusion of making the private public, of taking us behind

Figure 10.1 Hiding in plain sight: Bob Dylan's persona in *Don't Look Back*.

the scenes where all the adoring fans desperately want to be: in short, the film promises an intimate relationship with Dylan, though it ultimately complicates access to him because of his clearly performative character.[14] In so doing, the film offers a vision of the rock and roll tour as carnival for public consumption, but ultimately subsumes the carnival in a narrative of romantic genius. The film is rife with tropes of the solitary, brooding poet and his irresistible magnetism. We see scenes of folk singer Donovan performing for Dylan and courting his approval, the sycophantic Bob Neuwirth aping Dylan's hipster behavior at every turn, and Joan Baez mooning around Dylan, attempting to catch his fleeting attention. In this context, the most significant scene in the film may be the shots of Dylan in a hotel room typing while Joan Baez sings and others read or walk through the space. On a break from the chaos of touring, Dylan is a study of intent, inward focus as he types, restlessly bounces his legs, and makes a few off-hand comments to Baez. No matter how much the camera here lets us invade Dylan's private space, we cannot enter the intimate domain of his creativity, we cannot fathom the source of his insight, but only witness that somehow he transcends the rush of madness surrounding him to produce magnificent works of art.

Beyond documenting the incipient mythology of Dylan, *Don't Look Back* codifies and promotes that myth, conferring the imprimatur of documentary form on its subject, and becoming itself part of the unfolding drama underpinning Dylan's persona. Like countless documentaries that follow it, *Don't Look Back* represents a site of cultural production, through which codes of performance, dress, language, and a vision of the rock artist as *poète maudit* are disseminated. Consequently, this inflated, largely humorless image of rock performers becomes the primary target of mockumentaries.

The Act You've Known for All These Years:
The Faux Four

Given the aesthetic validation offered by many classic rock documentaries, it's no surprise that the first rock mockumentary took as its target the biggest, most mythologized band of them all: The Beatles. Arising out of a skit on *Saturday Night Live*, *The Rutles: All You Need is Cash* presents the faux documentary of four hapless Liverpool musicians whose legend will "last a lunchtime." Conceived and written by Monty Python alum Eric Idle, with music and lyrics supplied by Neil Innes, the film reflects painstaking attention to period details, including everything from vintage clothing (leather gear, collarless jackets, and psychedelic regalia) to stage sets from the Cavern, the Royal Command Performance, and Shea Stadium; dated film stock for the grainy black-and-white shots, video for early television performances, and vivid color stock for the late sixties promo films; and authentic instruments from the era, which also firmly anchor the film's original music to the sixties. To achieve such a striking degree of accuracy, Idle based much of the parody on exclusive access to archival Beatles footage provided by friend George Harrison—who was especially interested in "debunking the myth of The Beatles."[15] It's worth noting that *All You Need is Cash* was released three years before the first retrospective rockumentary of the band, *The Compleat Beatles* (Montgomery, 1982). Indeed, the documentary conventions and the attendant mythic narrative of artistic triumph were already so well-established and predictable that, in this instance, the parody *preceded* the original.

The Compleat Beatles exhibits the familiar conventions of documentary representational style. Opening with black-and-white stock footage of row houses, shipyards, and dock workers, the film both identifies the band as poets of place and emphasizes their mystical incarnation in the dismal post-war landscape: the first words intoned by narrator Malcolm McDowell are, in fact, "Liverpool, England . . . Nothing much ever came from Liverpool." *The Compleat Beatles* then unspools as a classic thesis-driven documentary, explicitly presenting the argument to be developed through archival footage, retrospective interviews with principal figures in the band's history, and analysis supplied by the voice-of-God narrator. The film's central claim is presented explicitly at the outset: "The Beatles: poets of a generation, heroes of an era. Like all poets and heroes, they both expressed and reflected the spirit of their time . . . They were determined and they were lucky . . . but most of all they were good—very, very good—crafting a unique style out of their musical heritage."

The film supports the narrative of astonishing artistic development with expert testimony: we're told that "William Mann went so far as to point out in *The London Times* the chains of pandiatonic clusters in 'This Boy' and the Aeolian cadence of 'Not a Second Time,' which he compared to Gustave Mahler's *Song of the Earth*." This celebration of artistic genius culminates, unsurprisingly, with *Sgt. Pepper's Lonely Hearts Club Band*, presented as The Beatles' masterpiece, which changed "attitudes, graphic design, fashion, and the recording industry itself." In *The Compleat Beatles*, Patti Smith's guitarist Lenny Kaye avers that "It was an artistic statement in a music that was never regarded as art before," while musicologist Wilfred Mellers goes so far as to claim that "Sgt. Pepper . . . is the most definitive event in pop's brief history. And it marked the turning point . . . when The Beatles stopped being ritual dance music and became music to be listened to." Note here the decisive shift away from the body: as The Beatles' music evolved to the point at which it could be taken seriously, you listened rather than danced. Mustering the collective opinion of journalists, musicians, and academics, the film presents The Beatles' artistic mastery as incontrovertible truth.

From its opening scenes, *The Rutles* assaults the mythologizing filmic strategies of *The Compleat Beatles*, particularly as the parody savages the documentary investment in location as "origin." In his attempt to pin down the legend of the "pre-fab four," the on-screen narrator, holding a microphone, begins with these words: "From these streets, very close to the Cavern Rutland, came the fabulous Rutland sound." In a long tracking shot as he strolls on a sidewalk, he explains that "We shall be asking many people who really knew them what they were really like." But as he speaks, the camera increasingly picks up speed, until he is chasing it in full out run. In a subsequent scene, he arrives breathlessly at a barren, debris-strewn field beside industrial buildings. Having finally caught the camera, he asks, "But where did the story start? The answer is right *here*. [He emphatically points to the ground.] For on this very spot Ron Nasty and Dirk McQuickly first bumped into each other." As he continues speaking, the camera begins to pan away, so that he is again forced to move to stay in frame: "At this precise point, uh, just a few feet back here, Ron Nasty invited Dirk to help him stand up . . . And here, well, a few feet back there, a musical legend was born." No magic or attendant aura imbues the originary point of this legend, particularly as the narrator stumbles over rocks and waste to follow the camera, which takes on an increasingly perverse, mercurial persona. Ultimately, the film takes the satire of place to even more ridiculous ends, as the narrator announces, "I'm actually standing outside the actual hotel in which the *Rutles* actually stayed in 1964. Actually, in this room here [he points to the hotel], and it was actually inside this actual room in which I actually spoke to the actual Paul Simon," and when the film relocates to "New Orleans to find out just how expensive it is to make these documentaries." Ultimately, in a reversal of the opening tracking shot, the narrator is hospitalized after being literally run over by the truck on which the camera is mounted.

Along with undermining documentary filmic conventions, *The Rutles* offers a direct assault on The Beatles' musical prowess, particularly by linking the appeal of the *Rutles* to a running gag about their trousers. The mother of

Rutle manager Leggy Mountbatten comments to the increasingly uncomfortable interviewer that her son was attracted to the boys not because of their music or personalities, which he hated, but because "Their trousers, they were very, um, tight. You could see quite clearly . . . everything. Outlines. Clear as day. Nothing left to the imagination." Among others, music publisher Dick Jaws also weighs in: "Well, I liked their trousers right away. I mean, I'd been in the garment trade and I knew a thing or two about inseams. And these were winners." Here we have a prime example of satire as diminishment, in which the band's success depends upon their clothing far more than on their talent or charm (two oft-repeated themes of *The Compleat Beatles*). But the scene also works as a revelation of desire and underscores the attractiveness of the performers' bodies. Leggy's mother reminds us not only of Brian Epstein's attraction to The Beatles and Lennon in particular, but also that The Beatles' leather gear carried a heavily sexualized meaning, particularly when read against the backdrop of their performances in Hamburg's notoriously licentious Reeperbahn.

Along with grounding the band's appeal in the body, the film wickedly spoofs the aesthetic value of the music itself and the pretensions of those who would take it seriously. Noting that the *Rutles* had begun "attracting respectable critical attention" and had been praised in *The London Times* as "The best since Schubert," the interviewer asks Sir Brian Morrison at the University of Oxford "just how good, musically, were The Rutles?" The stern-looking professor in full academic garb strides to the door and slams it in the face of the camera. Undeterred, the narrator follows up by asking the same question of Stanley J. Krammerhead III, Jr., "an occasional visiting professor of applied narcotics at the University of Please Yourself California." In this sequence, Krammerhead lounges beside a pool with a catatonic brunette sunbathing beside him. With long flowing hair and moustache, holding a cigarette as though it's a joint, he wears an unbuttoned yellow Hawaiian shirt, sunglasses, and a headband. Krammerhead begins his rapid-fire, incoherent litany:

> Musicologically and ethnically the Rutles were essentially empirical melangists of a rhythmically radical yet verbally passe and temporarily transcendent lyrical content while they were historically innovative melodic material transposed and transmogrified by the angst of the Rutland ethnic experience which elevated them from essentially alpha exponents of in essence merely beta potential harmonic material into the prime cultural exponents of Aeolian cadensic cosmic stanza form.

Pleased with himself, Krammerhead smiles, pushes a nostril closed, and sniffs as though doing a line of cocaine. The narrator wryly notes that in responding to the question, Krammerhead "didn't really tell us either." Krammerhead's phrase "Aeolian cadensic cosmic form," of course, directly spoofs *The London*

Times critic who praised the Aeolian cadence of "Not a Second Time." In its dissection of The Rutles, the film takes neither the Oxford professor nor the California hippie seriously, lampooning the notion that analysis, either straight or stoned, square or hip, could adequately explain the carnival.

In The Beatles, of course, it was John Lennon who personified the serious, uncompromising artist, and *The Rutles* holds him up for particular ridicule. In this parody, Lennon is depicted as Ron Nasty, with his acerbic wit and pointed comments rendered as a permanent sneer. Lennon's first book, *In His Own Write*, drew comparisons to Lewis Carroll and James Joyce. Here, Nasty's book is called *Out of Me Head*, and he's shown during the rooftop concert in *Let it Rot* sending a bent-over sound man off the top of the building with a kick to the posterior. The greatest mockery, though, is reserved for the depiction of Lennon's relationship with Yoko Ono. Here, Ono's stand-in is Chastity, a severe, cropped-haired woman in full Nazi regalia whose father had invented World War Two, and whom Nasty meets during her show at the "Pretentious Gallery." Their artistic ventures include not a bed-in, but a press conference in a bathtub complete with running shower that, according to Nasty, underscores their protest of society as nothing more than an "efficient sewage system."

The belittlement of The Beatles' aesthetic sensibility is underscored in the soundtrack, too. We hear lyrics ranging from insipid collages of the early

Figure 10.2 Promo shot for the Sgt. Rutter's album.

Figure 10.3 Rutle Ron Nasty and wife Chastity, whose father invented World War II.

material ("Hold my hand, yeah, yeah") to incisive parodies of the band's avant-garde pretentions. In the confessional vein of Lennon's "In My Life" or "Help!," one track opens with the evocative phrase, "I have always thought in the back of my mind" before concluding with "cheese and onions." The ridicule extends to Lennon's incipient political engagement in "Piggy in the Middle," which includes the immortal lines, "They say revolution's in the air/I'm dancing in my underwear/'cause I don't care." Paul McCartney's work also comes under fire: when Dirk marries, he ineptly stammers through a song, in tuneless falsetto, for his wife: "I love you . . . It's you I love . . . today is our wedding day for you always I will wait." He only finds his groove when he joyously lapses into pure rhythmic nonsense: "Dee de dee dee," etc. Parody finds its target both by deflating self-importance and inflating the inherent absurdities in The Beatles' lyric style.

All You Need is Cash offers a more complex and subtle relationship to the documentary tradition—and to the history of rock and roll—than it has been given credit for. The target is not simply The Beatles themselves, but the mythology that surrounded them and that they alternately promoted and assaulted (George Harrison, for example, has suggested that the movie freed him in some way). *The Rutles* also targets the solemn documentary and critical tradition that upholds the mythology. The movie challenges the realistic representational style and ridicules our epistephilic desire for knowledge about the band (after all, the only way you get the jokes is if you know far more than is necessary about The Beatles). The problem for film critics seems to be the twinned impulse of parody: laughter and mockery are rarely monologic, delivering clear and literal meaning. Instead, as Bakhtin claims in regard to the carnival, laughter is both destructive and generative. The myth needs to be challenged, the kings dethroned, the hierarchy overturned. But the parodic elements of the carnival also affirm and create. So we pay to see the *All You Need is Cash*, *This is Spinal Tap*, and many other parodies. And beyond that, we buy the soundtracks of original music and go to see the "fake" bands in concert.[16] Rock and roll documentaries need their uncanny doubles: mockumentaries remind us of the music's power, and that behind any domesticated narrative, we find a potentially transgressive force—one that is, in this case, unleashed through laughter.

Notes

1   The on-screen title of the film is actually *Dont Look Back* (no apostrophe).
2   Cynthia J. Miller, "Mocumentary Filmography," *Post Script* 28, No. 3 (Summer 2009), 134–143.
3   See Carl Plantinga, "Gender, Power, and a Cucumber: Satirizing Masculinity in *This is Spinal Tap*," in Barry Grant and Jeannette Sloniowski (eds.), *Documenting the Documentary: Close Readings of Documentary Film and Video* (Detroit: Wayne State UP, 1998), 318–332.
4   Jane Roscoe and Craig Hight, *Faking It: Mock-Documentary and the Subversion of Factuality* (Manchester: Manchester University Press, 2001), 4.
5   Alexandra Juhasz and Jesse Lerner (eds.), *F is for Phony: Fake Documentary and Truth's Undoing* (Minneapolis: University of Minnesota Press, 2006), 5.
6   Ibid., 21.
7   Mikhail Bakhtin, *Rabelais and His World*, trans. Helene Iswolsky (Bloomington, Indiana: Indiana University Press, 1984), 4.
8   Paul Kohl, "Looking Through a Glass Onion: Rock and Roll as a Modern Manifestation of Carnival," *Journal of Popular Culture* 27, No. 1 (1993), 143–161.
9   Bakhtin, *Rabelais and His World*, 10.
10 Ibid., 21.
11 Glenn Altschuler, *All Shook Up: How Rock 'N' Roll Changed America* (Oxford: Oxford University Press, 2003), 107–108.
12 Keith Beattie, "It's Not Only Rock and Roll: 'Rockumentary', Direct Cinema, and Performative Display," *Australasian Journal of American Studies* 24, No. 2 (December 2005), 23, 25–27.
13 Cynthia Miller, "Introduction: At Play in the Fields of Truth," *Post Script* 28, No. 3 (Summer 2009), 3.
14 Beattie, "It's Not Only Rock and Roll," 29.
15 Clark Collis, "Long Live Mock!" *Entertainment Weekly* (December 7, 2007). http://www.ew.com/ew/article/0,,20164903,00.html (accessed March 2012).
16 Ibid.

Chapter 11

Visualizing Live Albums

Progressive Rock and the British Concert Film in the 1970s

K. J. Donnelly

We tend to think of films as distinct aesthetic objects. A group of British films of the 1970s makes more sense when approached from the perspective of the music industry rather than the film industry. Music formats of the time were translated onto celluloid: concept albums led to rock operas and live albums became concert documentaries or "rockumentaries." While from both a critical and industrial perspective, British cinema of the 1970s generally was fairly poor, from a music point of view, British popular music of the decade was unproblematically outstanding. Live concert films emerge at a specific moment in British cinema in the late 1960s and early 1970s due to film and music events. Whilst the success and acclaim heaped upon American rock documentaries had doubtless been the inspiration, the buoyant status of British rock music and the shortcomings of the film industry in Britain produced something quite specific.

At the turn of the 1970s, the term "crisis" was used in relation to the British film industry.[1] The evacuation of US funding which had bankrolled British films for a few bumper years led to a more frugal industry in the UK. However, the production of feature films starring pop music and musicians remained something of a constant into the seventies, culminating in Ken Russell's *Tommy* (1975), an extremely expensive adaptation of The Who's rock opera album. Rockumentaries or "rock documentaries" had emerged in the previous decade. The first was the Canadian production *Lonely Boy* (Wolf Koenig and Roman Kroitor, 1962) about Paul Anka.[2] It seems that in its first years, the rock documentary was essentially North American, with such notable films as the British-shot but American-registered *Don't Look Back* (D. A. Pennebaker, 1967) about Bob Dylan, *Monterey Pop* (Pennebaker, 1968), *Woodstock* (Michael Wadleigh, 1970), and *Gimme Shelter* (the Maysles brothers and Charlotte Zwerin, 1970). These were event-based films and included much besides the on-stage performance.

As the 1970s dawned, the British film industry had a significant downturn in production and budgets; concurrently, there was a massive boom in worldwide record sales.[3] It was therefore no surprise that the 1970s saw a large-scale move to use pop and rock music in films, where it offered new aesthetic possibilities for filmmaking as much as access to youth audiences. It should perhaps have come as no surprise that British cinema should exploit British musical success. In terms of popular music, Britain had been the center of attention since the mid-sixties and the massive international success of The Beatles. Dramatic developments had happened to British music in less than a decade: from the "Beat Boom" of the mid-sixties, through late sixties psychedelia and the counter culture, to the "glam rock" and progressive rock of the early 1970s. In contrast with the film industry there was a lot of money around; in fact, more than there had been in the sixties. For example, Elton John earned more than The Beatles at their peak.[4] The release of live albums as a phenomenon ran for about a decade, from a heyday at the end of the 1960s to a virtual disappearance by the early 1980s. Rock concert films largely correspond with the same period. Against a backdrop of rising recording costs, live albums clearly made good business. The most basic were cheap to record, with outputs being taken from the concert's mixing desk, and the package having a character similar to a "greatest hits" LP. Also, they exhibit important characteristics of "progressive" rock of the time, those of musicianship and authenticity, both of which are particularly evident in a live setting. Such music was also particularly suited to film, as it projected the showmanship and ambition of these musicians.

Progressive Rock

Progressive rock defies simple definition, and perhaps was more a tendency or a vague marketing category for music than anything more solid. It was also a banner of aspiration, for musicians and consumers who wanted to aim beyond the simplicities of pop and rock. Initially it was a *British*—in fact, overwhelmingly English—phenomenon, and remained dominated by British groups.[5] It emerged from late 1960s psychedelia, and was influenced by jazz-rock fusion and art music experimentation (including electronic music). Its general characteristics are that musical compositions are longer and much more ambitious and sophisticated than in pop, with elaborate arrangements (rather than simple alternating verse–chorus structures). There were extended instrumental sections which allowed musicians to show off their virtuosity, and often complex, conceptual, or fantasy-inspired lyrics. Album-oriented—sometimes ambitious "concept" albums—rather than singles, progressive rock was geared towards career longevity, was interested in technological innovation and retained a "serious" demeanour (some might say self-important).

Progressive rock groups include perhaps most notably Pink Floyd, King Crimson, Genesis, Emerson, Lake and Palmer, Yes, Gentle Giant, Van der Graaf Generator, Camel, Soft Machine, and many more who might cross categories. All those listed are British. Their work has tended to be described as "sophisticated," "self-indulgent," and even "pretentious." Since the late 1970s, progressive rock was regularly demonized,[6] until recently when it has come in for something of a reappraisal. Recent notable books on the subject include Edward Macan, *Rocking the Classics: English Progressive Rock and the Counterculture*, Paul Hegarty and Martin Halliwell, *Beyond and Before: Progressive Rock Since the 1960s*, and Kevin Holm-Hudson's edited collection *Progressive Rock Reconsidered*.[7] In July of 2007, *Classic Rock* magazine published a progressive rock special issue with a DVD of interviews with Yes attached to the cover. Current musicians such as Porcupine Tree have openly espoused progressive rock, while the King Crimson song *Moonchild* was covered by Doves and also appeared in the film *Buffalo 66* (Vincent Gallo, 1998).[8]

While music historians and analysts might have written about progressive rock in recent years, there has been little written about rock documentaries, and even less written about live concert films.[9] An isolated article by Adrian Wootton discusses key aspects of rock documentary (such as backstage and "setting up" components). Led Zeppelin produced one of the most prominent of British rock concert films, *The Song Remains the Same* (Peter Clifton and Joe Massot, 1976), and Wootton cites this as a "classic example" of films "being produced by the so-called dinosaur groups [which] were often pretentious, uninteresting and uncinematic."[10] Yet these films were for fans rather than general film audiences (or indeed film critics), and directly reflected their interests in the music involved. *The Song Remains the Same* is first and foremost a recording of a live concert, although it also includes fantasy sections which function as inserts while retaining the continuity of the live soundtrack recording. Such criticism misses the point. Wootton's comment—once we strip away the disdain—confirms that these films fail to "make sense" as "cinema."[11] These films make more sense as live albums with added images. Many of them are compounded by the simultaneous release of the soundtrack LP, which, arguably is the primary product. In terms of distribution, the discs far outweigh the films: that is where the real money is being made. Consequently, it is no surprise that the overwhelming majority of these films were produced by record labels rather than film companies. In fact, live films could be characterized simply as counterparts to live albums. However, we might make a working distinction between the more fulsome rock documentary and the more direct concert film:

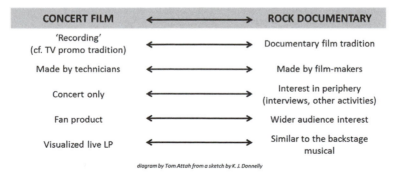

diagram by Tom Attah from a sketch by K. J. Donnelly

While this may not be a solid distinction, we might note that there are broad tendencies within this format. Rock documentaries/rockumentaries often appear like DVDs of concerts but with optional DVD extras cut into the film from time to time. An interesting example of this is *Born to Boogie* (Ringo Starr, 1972), which includes a selection of outtakes integrated in the film, most notably perhaps the "Some Like to Rock" section. However, the film is essentially a live concert recorded for posterity despite its inserts and bizarre paddings. *Born to Boogie* was an exception, focusing on Marc Bolan and his glam rock group T. Rex, whose audience was dominated by young teenagers. The concert films appeared particularly suited to progressive rock groups, and often were less concerned with cinematic variation than with "authentic" duplication of the exciting reality of performance and the veracity of high-level musicianship and serious endeavour.

Although there were many British-made short films and television programs,[12] significantly there were an astonishing number of feature films, most of which had fitful cinematic release for short runs (and sometimes only single screenings). However, they also had a shelf-life that ran for a few years, sometimes appearing as late-night attractions. Below is a list of all British concert and rock documentary films released in the 1970s:[13]

- *Let It Be* (Michael Lindsay-Hogg, 1970) [The Beatles]
- *Reggae* (Horace Ove, 1970) [a festival]
- *Supershow* (John Crome, 1970) [concert including Led Zeppelin]
- *Mad Dogs and Englishmen* (Pierre Adidge, 1971) [Joe Cocker]
- *Bird on a Wire* (Tony Palmer, 1972) [Leonard Cohen]
- *Born to Boogie* (Ringo Starr, 1972) [T. Rex]
- *Glastonbury Fayre* (Nicholas Roeg and Peter Neal, 1972) [a festival]
- *Pictures at an Exhibition* (Nicholas Ferguson, 1972) [Emerson, Lake and Palmer]
- *Glastonbury Fayre* (Peter Neal, 1973) [a festival]
- *The London Rock 'n' Roll Show* (Peter Clifton, 1973) [concert including Chuck Berry]
- *Yessongs* (Peter Neal, 1973) [Yes]
- *The Butterfly Ball* (Tony Klinger, 1976) [a stage show mixed with animations]
- *Pleasure at Her Majesties* (Roger Graef, 1976) [a concert event]
- *Genesis: On Stage* (Tony Maylam, 1976) [Genesis]
- *The Song Remains the Same* (Peter Clifton and Joe Massot, 1976) [Led Zeppelin]
- *Bob Marley and the Wailers Live* (Keef [Keith Macmillan], 1978) [Bob Marley]
- *The Punk Rock Movie* (Don Letts, 1978) [various groups]
- *The Secret Policeman's Ball* (Roger Graef, 1979) [a concert event]

Many of these films are obscure and not held in official film archives. Most remain in the more popular/commercial "archive" of television screenings in slots far away from prime time and on obscure stations. Many had limited video and DVD releases, and for years historians and collectors had to scour second-hand sources, although more recently such films have often become available as small-run DVDs from "microbreweries" (both legal and illegal), through internet filesharing, or perhaps even on YouTube. If the artist remains bankable, then the film will retain a higher distribution profile. Consequently, some films have disappeared without trace. A few isolated examples apart,[14] the British concert film had disappeared by the 1980s. Progressive rock went out of fashion and fewer live albums were released, while at the turn of the decade the music industry went into a sustained crisis.[15] There were fewer groups who wanted their onstage exploits expensively preserved for posterity and the advent of home video shifted live music films away from cinema release.

Concert Films

Emerson, Lake and Palmer were a "supergroup" formed by members of The Nice, King Crimson and Atomic Rooster. They released *Emerson, Lake and Palmer* (December 1970), *Tarkus* (June 1971), and then *Pictures at an Exhibition* (November 1971). The last had been recorded live in March of 1971 and was a dramatic rearrangement of Mussorgsky's *Pictures at an Exhibition*, a late-nineteenth-century concert hall piece originally for solo piano, but better known in its orchestral arrangement by Maurice Ravel. This was a loose "concept album" rather than a collection of unrelated songs. Mussorgsky's piece had been used in rehearsals at the time of their debut LP's release, and was recorded live at Newcastle City Hall. Distinct from the album, the corresponding film had been released in February of 1971, before the recording of the LP. It had been shot in December of 1970 at the Lyceum Theatre in London, at the time when their debut LP was on release. It was ninety-five minutes long although some versions in existence are as short as forty minutes (the VHS video is short, the Japanese Laserdisc is long).

Pictures at an Exhibition (Nicholas Ferguson, 1972) contains some startling visual effects, which are reminiscent of psychedelic light shows. These swirling patterns, which on occasions overlay the images of the group on stage, are an example of early Quantel video effects. Indeed, the film was shot wholly on video, and two cumbersome television cameras on dollies are fitfully visible in shot to "catch the action" of the live event, much like in televised sport. According to a *Melody Maker* article their use of video was due to the future arrival of video as a medium as well as its technological possibilities.[16] This is a production that has little to do with filmmaking in Britain and more connections to the television industry. It was filmed by the band's producer friend Lindsey Clennell, for "Visual and Musical Entertainments." The visual recording equipment was television standard and it was directed by television director Nicholas Ferguson. Drummer Carl Palmer commented on the film:

> There are lots of basic shots of the band . . . we had a lot of ideas about modern filming techniques which we wanted to see done, but instead . . . it was done as a straight film, like the early Beatles films . . . Because a friend of ours is doing it is the only reason we let him release it.[17]

So it seems that "progressive" music embraced a "regressive" film style. There was an air of uncertainty about the whole endeavour. According to Palmer, the group did not intend to release the live LP, as it was not their original material.[18] More significantly, perhaps, their regular engineer Eddie Offord was absent and the sound recording quality of the film was poor and hardly acceptable to the increasingly "hi-fi" demands of progressive rock audiences. The demand for a soundtrack album stimulated by the film led to a plan to record a coming live show, with the aim of achieving excellent sound, and indeed the LP apparently was used as a demonstration disc in some hi-fi shops.[19] *Pictures at an Exhibition*'s corresponding soundtrack LP, rather than existing as a supplement and advertisement for the film, was in fact the principal commodity itself.[20]

For British progressive rock groups, *Pictures at an Exhibition* set something of a precedent. Musicians wanted films to showcase their abilities and imaginations, but also there appears to have been an extra tier added to rock's product chain: the repeated normality of album and associated tour could include a feature-length film as part of rock groups' intermittent bursts of product. *Yessongs* (Peter Neal, 1973) was released at a time when Yes had become suitably successful. They had been featured on the front cover of *Melody Maker* for the first time in early 1972, had their first sell-out tour and had two albums go gold in terms of sales. The second of those, *Fragile* (released in January 1972), was the first with the "classic" line-up of Jon Anderson, Bill Bruford, Rick Wakeman, Steve Howe, and Chris Squire. It was also the first with a futuristic cover by artist Roger Dean, an aspect of the group's albums that became a continuous characteristic. This LP was followed by the more highly acclaimed *Close to the Edge*, released in September 1972.

The *Yessongs* album was a triple album with a sumptuous Roger Dean gatefold sleeve, and must have been a risk for Atlantic Records. Indeed, triple albums have remained a rarity.[21] It was recorded mostly in late 1972 at a selection of concerts and released on May 18, 1973, reaching number 7 in the UK album chart and number 12 in the USA. However, the film is not the same as the album. It was recorded at one event, the London Rainbow Theatre Christmas night concert in 1972. In fact, there is only one section of a song shared with the album and some songs appear that are absent from the triple LP. The film is a single event, while the album is a composite of different events, despite having the feeling of being a coherent single event.

Technological expediency means that it is easier to record sound at events (through the mixing desk), while film footage is much more difficult to secure. Sound also can be "sweetened" more easily through equalization and filtering, remixing, and in some cases even re-recording passages in the studio afterwards. The structure of the film, as in the case of the overwhelming majority of concert films, follows the structure of a concert. In this case the dynamic order of song presentation remains, while each member of the group is allowed an extended solo section.

According to the *Monthly Film Bulletin* review, there were no shots of the audience.[22] This is actually not true. There are few, however, with two appearing during the encore. This structural "reverse shot" to the fetishistic focus on the stage is often an important, although sometimes not regular, characteristic of the concert film. *Monthly Film Bulletin*'s statement shows that there was an *expectation* to see the audience. Indeed, *Pictures at the Exhibition* shows the audience a few times. They are sitting down, thoughtfully and do not add any sense of dynamism to the proceedings.[23] These moments when the camera turns onto the audience are something like a supplementary rockumentary "DVD extra," but function more clearly as a guarantee of the veracity of the concert as an event.

Yessongs includes some visual distortion effects like *Pictures at an Exhibition*, but contains more sustained passages of animation, retaining a sense of desire for visual variation despite the likelihood that film audiences would prefer to see the group. The aim perhaps is to make it seem more of a "film" than simply a "recording" of the group in action. Significantly, *Yessongs* was released in a Quadraphonic version. Much has been made of Ken Russell's *Tommy* (1975) as the first film released in a Quad version, but despite being recorded two years earlier, *Yessongs* was released at about the same time. Such impressive stereo would have done justice to the group's intricate progressive rock, and a *Melody Maker* article just before the film was shot noted that musicians were less interested in Quadraphonic than were hi-fi companies.[24] Indeed, Quadraphonic's development into multi-speaker systems for cinemas has been a lasting bequeathment of the music industry to the film industry.

Similarly, Led Zeppelin's *The Song Remains the Same* (1976) had a release in four-track stereo, in this case with the music on the magnetic strip of the film print rather than synching up a magnetic tape recording to a silent print. The album was billed as the "original soundtrack" and the record and film are closely related, although some parts of the double LP are different from the film. Footage was taken from a few nights at Madison Square Garden, New York, at the conclusion of Led Zeppelin's 1973 tour.[25] *The Song Remains the Same* is first and foremost a recording of a live concert, although, significantly, it contains fantasy sections which embellish the primacy of the performed music. These are bold and remove the focus from the productive origins of the music. For instance, Jimmy Page's sequence in *Dazed and Confused*, during an extended solo where he plays the guitar with a violin

178 K. J. Donnelly

bow, has images of the group on stage replaced by a short film depicting a shrouded figure climbing to the top of a mountain and swinging a sword that looks remarkably like the light sabres that appeared in *Star Wars* (George Lucas, 1977) the following year. For just over four minutes the music has remained constant while the images have become in effect non-diegetic, like an accompaniment to the soundtrack emanating from an elsewhere.

Despite rock music's appeal to authenticity and the self-proclaimed "honesty" of many bands during this period, *The Song Remains the Same* was dramatically "sweetened." The album is a composite not only of songs from different days mixed together with audience noises to sound like a continuous event, but individual tracks comprise edited-together sections of different performances.[26] Similarly, the images are an amalgam of shots from different performances. Furthermore, some shots are from a re-staging of Led Zeppelin's show at Shepperton Studios in London, where a facsimile of the Madison Square Garden stage was re-created to allow for more in the way of close-up shots. Bass and keyboard player John Paul Jones had cut his hair short after the original concerts and was forced to wear a wig at Shepperton to aid the illusion of continuity.

Genesis: In Concert (Tony Maylam, 1976) has no corresponding live album, although a year after its release a double live album, *Seconds Out*, was released. The film was shot during the 1976 tour at two concerts (Glasgow July 9 and Stafford July 10), while the group's album *Wind and Wuthering* was residing at number 1 in the album charts. The live album was recorded a year later during the 1977 tour (apart from one song recorded earlier with a different drummer), during a five-night stint at the Palais des sports in Paris (June 11–14). The film was on release at the same time that the live album was being recorded. *Genesis: In Concert* had its gala premiere in July 1977 with royalty (Princess Anne) present,[27] but it had no "official release" and distribution. It toured the country selectively on double-bill with another film directed by Tony Maylam, *White Rock* (1977). This was a documentary about the winter Olympics presented by James Coburn but sold through its musical soundtrack by Rick Wakeman, previously the keyboard player in Yes. Apart from being a straightforward record of the group on stage, *Genesis: In Concert* includes some non-diegetic inserts where the soundtrack remains the same (continues diegetically), while images "move" to somewhere else (thus becoming non-diegetic). For "I Know What I Like" the soundtrack is of the group performing live, while the images following roadies constructing the stage some time earlier, subsequently changing to showing the group performing towards the end of the song. Along similar lines, "The Cinema Show" includes an excerpt of an old silent comedy film about a rolling globe. Whilst the album was sweetened in studio it is clear that the film was not to any noticeable degree.

While these films tend to include little or nothing in the way of interviews and backstage insights into the musicians, they often include some form of visual interlude from the concert. Perhaps the most famous is from *The Song Remains the Same*, where each Led Zeppelin group member has a visual "solo" cut across the continuing soundtrack of the band's concert. Although not a British production, *Pink Floyd: Live at Pompeii* (Adrian Maben, 1972) has interlude sequences showcasing the ruins of Pompeii and Mount Vesuvius. Similarly, the image effects of *Pictures at an Exhibition* and *Yessongs* also amount to non-diegetic interventions. These facets make proceedings visually more varied and interesting, and appear to be a concession to a perceived need to compensate for the lack of "liveness" and the excitement of the actual concert event. This "interference" with the image track underlines the centrality and sense of integrity assigned to the concert sound recording, and the malleability of the "accompanying" images (reversing the commonly conceived relationship of film image and sound). When it came to film, progressive rock groups certainly lived up to their name in that they used innovative visual technology (videotape, quantel) and cinema sound (Quadraphonic). Only now can we see the impact that this musical impetus has had on more recent cinema, while the influence on music television might also convincingly be traced.

Conclusion

In terms of aesthetics, live concert films are seemingly more "music" than they are "film." They remain firmly minority interest films, often not pandering to a wider audience and lacking the aspiration to be "mainstream films" with a general release. Distribution could often be through "roadshowing"—making a succession of appearances at different locations rather like a rock band on tour. Exploiting late-night bills, double-bills and special showings, these were more an event than part of any regular visit to the cinema. As an example, in January of 1972 the celebrated Jimi Hendrix film *Jimi Plays Berkeley* (Peter Pilafian, 1971) was screened in the UK as a touring event, accompanied by two American groups that had some connection with him.[28] Whilst special films might be roadshown, this is far more like a musical group tour than conventional film distribution.

Distribution aside, who financed and produced these films? In the majority of cases it was not established film production companies. Britain did not have many and the audiovisual industry was changing, fuelled by companies conglomerating.[29] The 1970s saw the dramatic convergence of British film and music industries, most obviously in the music company EMI, who diversified into film production. This continued into the 1980s, where the further diversification of audiovisual companies was embodied by Richard Branson's Virgin, which had started as a record distributor, then producer, and later moved into film production, an airline and beyond. In a number of cases, film became used as a vehicle for the music. The most obvious case is the expensively made musical *Absolute Beginners* (Julien Temple, 1985), which was part of the increasing move towards films having simultaneous release with "synergetic" soundtracks.[30] Over a decade earlier things were already moving solidly in this direction: *Reggae* was produced by Bamboo Records, *Mad Dogs and Englishmen* was produced by A&M Records, and *Let It Be* and *Born to Boogie* were produced by Apple (the label owned and run by the Beatles). So, in terms of both aesthetics and production–consumption these films might be seen as more closely related to musical formats than to traditional film forms. Indeed, these films emanate directly from musical concerns of the time: while the "concept album" might be seen to have an equivalent in the rock opera, the live album is almost directly translated into the concert film. Their essential function is as a vehicle for the prime commodity: the music. The films are incidental, more like a tie-in, adjunct, or secondary product (like video games of films). Indeed, from an industrial point of view, it is highly surprising that the British film industry did not exploit British music more than it has, seeing as since the early 1960s Britain has been a world leader in popular music, punching well above its international weight. These films are more fruitfully approached from the point of view of music history than of film history, although their disappearance in the 1980s can be accounted for by both film and music determinants. Cinema has had a not inconsiderable influence on rock music, and perhaps live films have had a more tangible influence. It seems ironic that over the past twenty years, large concerts in stadia almost always involve large-screen live projection.[31] So audiences in effect end up watching a concert film at live events.

Notes

1   "A major crisis is undoubtedly developing in the industry, says Film Production Association president Clifford Barclay in a report on his recent visit to America. . . . [He] says the main purpose of his visit was to strengthen communications with the world's richest film market, [and] the main source of finance for British films . . ." Anon, "Barclay Warns: A Major Crisis Developing," *Kinematograph Weekly* 629, No. 3241 (1970), 3.

2   Barry Keith Grant, "The Classic Hollywood Musical and the 'Problem' of Rock 'n' Roll," *Journal of Popular Film and Television* 13, No. 4 (Winter 1986), 201.

3   Dave Harker, "Blood On the Tracks: Popular Music in the 1970s," in Bart Moore Gilbert (ed.), *The Arts in the Seventies: Cultural Closure?* (London: Routledge, 1994), 249.

4   Ibid., 244.

5   A significant determinant in the rise of British progressive rock was the outlet enabled by the new development of a universities circuit of concert venues in the wake of the proliferation of universities in the 1960s. This is clearly evident with reference to Genesis tour date lists in the early 1970s in Sid Smith and Alan Hewitt, *Opening the Musical Box: A Genesis Chronicle* (London: Firefly, 2000).

6   John Street sums up the "problems" of progressive rock: "In trying to transform popular music into electronic classical music, progressive music was, in fact, 'regressive'; it sought to establish aesthetic criteria and patterns of consumption which were both elitist and traditionalist." John Street, *Rebel Rock: the Politics of Popular Music* (Oxford: Blackwell, 1986), 101.

7 Edward Macan, *Rocking the Classics: English Progressive Rock and the Counterculture* (Oxford: Oxford University Press, 1997), Paul Hegarty and Martin Halliwell, *Beyond and Before: Progressive Rock Since the 1960s* (New York and London: Continuum, 2012) and Kevin Holm-Hudson (ed.), *Progressive Rock Reconsidered* (London: Routledge, 2002). Notable articles include John Covach, "Progressive Rock, *Close to the Edge* and the Boundaries of Style," in John Covach and Graham M. Boone (eds.), *Understanding Rock: Essays in Music Analysis* (Oxford: Oxford University Press, 1997).

8 Despite being demonized, progressive rock was also misconstrued: a decade ago British soap opera *EastEnders*'s story about a noisy neighbour had him playing King Crimson's *Red* as a form of exuberant noise that might have stood for punk rock or similar.

9 There are a handful of general reviews, such as Simon Reynolds', where he declares that rock documentaries are "Rarely inspired and often less than enthralling, they nevertheless have a curious quality of watchability. Low key verging on the ambient, they seem made for TV." Simon Reynolds, "Tombstone Blues: The Music Documentary Boom," *Sight and Sound* (May 2007), 32. This misses the fact that those of the 1970s were made for the big screen and, indeed, are highly impressive in a cinema rather than idly consumed on a TV in a home living room.

10 Adrian Wootton, "Looking Back, Dropping Out, Making Sense: A History of the Rock-Concert Movie," *Monthly Film Bulletin* 55, No. 659 (1988), 356.

11 Jonathan Demme's concert film of Talking Heads, *Stop Making Sense* (1984)—which Wootton lauds—ironically adds other layers of structure to the concert format (props, progressive development), precisely so that it "makes sense" as a film.

12 There were plenty of short films produced, for instance Van der Graaf Generator's *Godbluff Live in Charleroi* (1975), and Derek Jarman's film of Throbbing Gristle: *TG: Psychic Rally in Heaven* (1981). There were also contemporaneous television equivalents in the BBC's *In Concert* and *Rock Goes to College* programs.

13 Included in this list are feature-length films that were registered in the UK and secured a vaguely systematic cinema release.

14 There was diverse compilation *Urgh! A Music War* (1981), D. A. Pennebaker's late rock documentary about David Bowie's final Ziggy Stardust concert from 1973 in *Ziggy Stardust and the Spiders From Mars* (1982), *Culture Club—A Kiss Across the Ocean* (1984), and *The Cure in Orange* (1987).

15 Harker, "Blood On the Tracks," 253.

16 Keith Emerson noted that ELP had made a video of *Pictures at an Exhibition* to be ready for when video became more pervasive. "A Quad View of Quadraphonic Sound," *Melody Maker* (January 23, 1972), 34.

17 Carl Palmer, quoted in George Forrester, Martyn Hanson, and Frank Askew, *Emerson, Lake and Palmer: The Show that Never Ends* (London: Helter Skelter, 2001), 70.

18 Ibid., 69.

19 Ibid.,70–71.

20 *Pictures at an Exhibition* reached number 3, remaining on the chart for five weeks after entering on December 4, 1971.

21 Double and even triple albums were something of a characteristic of progressive rock and had certainly been a rarity before the 1970s. They allowed a space for longer songs and musical pieces and more elaborate and developed narrative concepts.

22 Review in *Monthly Film Bulletin* 43, No. 508 (May 1976), 111.

23 This contrasts with the exuberant audience in other concert films of the time such as *Born to Boogie*.

24 Leo Lyons (producer and ex-member of Ten Years After), studio manager at Wessex Studios, noted that rather than musicians, "The main pressure for [quad] is coming from the domestic hi-fi manufacturers." Edward Jones, "Studio Session: Why Rock is Fighting Quad," *Melody Maker* (May 24, 1975), 37.

25 Peter Clifton constructed and directed most of the film. Some had been shot by Joe Massot, and Led Zeppelin manager Peter Grant went to extreme and intimidatory efforts to secure this footage. Stephen Davis, *Hammer of the Gods: Led Zeppelin Unauthorized* (London: Pan, 1985), 269–270.

26 An extraordinarily detailed analysis of album and film is provided by Eddie Edwards, "The Garden Tapes." www.thegardentapes.co.uk/ (accessed May 8, 2011).

27 Smith and Hewitt, *Opening the Musical Box*, 49.

28 "Hendrix Film Tour," *Melody Maker* (January 8, 1972), 1.

29 Similarly, PolyGram had formed from the merger of Polydor Records and Phonogram Records in 1972 and was jointly owned by Phillips and Siemens. It ate up many more companies and moved rapidly into film production.

30 A process emblematized by successful record and film collaborations such as *Flashdance* (1983) and *Footloose* (1984).

31 Of course, this might mean that if the relay is recorded footage can be released later in some form.

Part V

New Directions in the Music Documentary

Chapter 12

"Moogie Wonderland"
Technology, Modernity, and the Music Documentary

Andrew Burke

While the conventional music documentary takes as its focus a performer, a group, a scene, or an event, Hans Fjellestad's *Moog* (2004) is structured around a piece of technology and the man who invented it. The Moog synthesizer revolutionized music-making in the 1960s and 1970s and its influence on a dizzying range of musical forms and genres continues today. Fjellestad's film is at once a portrait of the man behind the machine, Robert Moog, and an examination of the impact and legacy of the synthesizers that bear his name. The film examines how a whole history of contemporary music flows from the instruments Moog created. From the classical pastiches and bachelor pad exotica that defined the synth's early years, to their use in prog rock and disco throughout the tumultuous 1970s, to their rediscovery by electronic and experimental artists more recently, Moog synthesizers have been at the core of contemporary music for nearly fifty years. Fjellestad's film offers a different model for the music documentary, one that focuses not on the charisma of a musician, the energy of a scene, or the impact of an event, but on the musical possibilities opened up by technological innovation. *Moog* is about the man, but it is also about the "Moogie Wonderland" (to steal the title of a Moog-heavy Stereolab song) the modular synthesizer unlocks.[1] *Moog* maps this space of sonic play and experimentation, moving from the circuit boards and patch cords of the synth itself to the astral realms and galactic sounds the machine is best known for producing.

In strictly formal terms, *Moog* is a rather conventional documentary. Moog himself takes the lead role, narrating his own story in a series of interviews conducted on the front porch of his home in Asheville, North Carolina and as he travels around the world to give lectures, visit musicians, reminisce with former business colleagues, and attend concerts honoring him and his machines. These interviews are supplemented by archival footage from trade shows where early Moogs were met with a mixture of awe and bewilderment and from demonstration films meant to introduce the world to the sounds of the future. The film also visits the Moog factory in Asheville and has Moog walk the viewer through the construction and assembly of a synthesizer, as well as providing some basic lessons on how the machines work and the extraordinary range of sounds they can generate.[2] The film is, however, more than the sum of these modular parts. Moog emerges as a thoughtful man who far from conforming to any stereotype of the rational engineer uninterested in questions beyond technology, sees a spiritual dimension in electronically produced sounds and insists that "my instruments do retain some kind of memory of me." Similarly, the film invites a renewed understanding of the synthesizer itself. Too often reduced to a mere tangle of cords and wires lacking the rock authenticity of the electric guitar, the Moog is a fitting symbol for the late twentieth century and for the sonic adventurousness of both pop and experimental music. While its origins are grounded in the technology of World War Two and the postwar electronics boom, its development in the 1960s and 1970s coincides with aspirations for a better world and the effort to imagine what the future might look and sound like.[3] The Moog today functions as a privileged symbol of an analogue modernity that has passed. Part of what Fjellestad achieves in the film is a history of the Moog as a symbolic vehicle, charting its trajectory from an emergent technology to a residual object; from futuristic to anachronistic.

The film is not without precedent, even if the way it connects an instrument to its inventor is rather unusual. The most notable connection is to *Theremin: An Electronic Odyssey* (Steven M. Martin, 1994), which tells the story of Leon Theremin and the hands-free electronic instrument he invented in the late 1920s. Moog himself is interviewed in that film and pays tribute to Theremin as an influence on his thinking about sound and electronics. Beyond this direct precedent, there are a few other films which to varying degrees take up the role that instruments, electronics, and engineering have played in shaping the course of music history. In its survey of electronic dance music culture, Iara Lee's *Modulations* (1998) assesses the role synthesizers, drum machines, and samplers have played in its origins and development.[4] Similarly, *High Tech Soul: The Creation of Techno Culture* (Gary Bredow, 2006) looks at how artists such as Juan Atkins, Derrick May, and Kevin Saunderson pushed the technological limits of electronic instruments in order to produce a new kind of music. *Alchemists of Sound* (BBC Four, 2005), a documentary about the BBC Radiophonic Workshop, shares with *Moog* a desire to capture the spirit of sonic adventure that existed in the 1960s and 1970s and to detail how audio experimentation was linked to a kind of technical expertise distinct from traditional musical virtuosity. Finally, the Moog's symbolic importance as a machine that represents the enthusiasms of the modern finds some comparison in *Vox Pop: How Dartford Powered the British Beat Boom* (BBC Four, 2011). This short documentary tells the story of the company behind the iconic AC30 guitar amplifier that, much like the Moog, combines technical ingenuity and modern design in a manner that transformed the thing itself into a highly desirable and much fetishized object. None of these documentaries blend biography and object study quite in the way *Moog* does. Even *Theremin* differs from *Moog* in that Theremin's extraordinary life (born in Russia, he lived in the United States in the 1930s before abruptly returning to the USSR in 1938, either as part of a KGB kidnapping plot or to escape U.S. tax bills) takes center stage and because the Theremin, unlike the synthesizer, did not directly generate a whole array of new musical forms. What makes Moog unique is the way that subject and object combine, how the name Moog covers both man and machine.

Early in the film, whilst listening to Money Mark produce a series of alien sounds from a Minimoog, Moog jokes that "everybody knows that's what aliens sound like." Yet for all its ability to conjure up images of outer space, the Moog is a reassuringly material machine that has a very terrestrial history. Moog developed the core ideas for his first synthesizer while doing his PhD in engineering at Cornell University in upstate New York and opened his first factory in nearby Trumansburg in 1963. This small town setting, oddly enough, proved hospitable to Moog's endeavors at least in part because his methods derived as much from his background as a hobbyist as his professional training as an electrical engineer. As a consequence, the Moog factory seems to have functioned more along the lines of an artisanal country workshop than a corporate research and development department. This hands-on approach manifests itself in the material form of the synthesizers themselves. In the scenes in the Asheville factory (where Moog reopened his company in 2002 after losing ownership of the name and technology throughout most of the 1980s and 1990s), Fjellestad presents a montage of the Voyager model being assembled from its component parts; soundtracked of course by the familiar synthesized burps and gurgles of the Moog. The machine is a mixture of the synthetic and the organic. The internal electric circuits and connectors are housed in a lacquered walnut frame. The overall effect is retro-futurist, much like the televisions or high-fidelity systems developed in the same postwar period that domesticated new technology by presenting it as furniture. Yet, whereas these things now have adopted the glossy hi-tech sheen of characteristic technological postmodernity, many models of the Moog retain the wood finish which, along with their array of knobs and buttons, make them at once the symbols of a future past and an enduring residual technology that retains its subcultural cachet today.

To underscore this mixture of futurity and residuality, Fjellestad follows Moog from the factory to his home along the roads of rural North Carolina. Rather unexpectedly and somewhat amusingly, Moog drives a rusted-out Toyota Tercel five-door from the 1980s that features hand-painted flowers on its side. Once home, Moog gives the camera a tour of his organic garden and laments that his pet chickens have eaten most of his collard greens. While such a scene seems out of place in a documentary about music and technology, it provides Moog with an opportunity to speculate on the connections between the ecological and the electrical: "Growing things requires you to get in tune with nature. What this has to do with inventing, I'm not too sure. Somehow they all feel like the same thing to me. Both my wife and I have the view of our universe, of the environment we're in here, as a very complex ecosystem that has to be taken care of, just like a finely-tuned machine." The musical metaphor not only bridges the gap between the earthy and the electronic but also allows Moog to correct the most common misconception about the synthesizer. The term has a long and complicated history in the field of electronic music, but as Moog explains in the documentary, his company embraced the term for their modular instruments in their 1967 trade catalog. The synthesizer is named such not because the sounds it produces are synthetic or artificial but because they synthesize an array of sonic components in their production of a harmonic whole. Far from pointing toward some kind of merely imitative inauthentic simulation of the real, the very concept of the synthesizer contains within it ideas of integrated holistic plenitude. As such, this quiet scene provides the key to understanding Moog's sometimes seemingly far-out ideas about the coalescence of matter, energy, and identity. Both the synth and the soil channel and transform energy to produce something new.

Such was the expense of the early Moog modular synthesizers that few individuals could actually afford them. As a result many of them found a home in university music research labs or with music houses, where they were used primarily to produce future-sounding music and assorted weird noises for advertising. Moog juxtaposes the synthesizer's experimental and commercial history. Fjellestad shows a minute-long advertisement that seems more a promotional film for the Moog than a conventional commercial for its ostensible client, Schaefer Beer. The clip is even afforded the respect of a title, "Edd Kalehoff at the Moog Synthesizer," and features the rather funky looking Kalehoff at the controls of a Moog modular system, concerned as much with the knobs on the consoles as the keyboard itself. Surrounded by oscilloscopes measuring waveforms and the blinking lights of the voltage controllers, Kalehoff exemplifies a kind of hippie modernity and the clip makes visible the way in which technology mediated between commerce and the counterculture. At the very same time that the instrument was being embraced by commercial music houses, the Moog also found its place with experimental musicians and in concert halls. The film is largely silent on John Cage's 1960s Moog experiments and it mentions Wendy Carlos's hugely influential *Switched on Bach* LP only in passing, but it does examine the impact of Gershon Kingsley's *Moog Quartet*, which, when it was performed at Carnegie Hall on January 30, 1972, was the first electronic music to take that prestigious stage. In conversation with Kingsley, Moog learns the modules he first sold to him have now ended up in the Smithsonian Museum, which speaks not simply to the synthesizer's historical importance as a musical instrument, but also to its status as an object.

Indeed, Fjellestad's film lingers on the materiality and iconicity of the Moog, both in its early modular format and as the later, more easily portable Minimoog. This attention to design and product detail should perhaps not be surprising given that one of the producers of the film is Gary Hustwit, best known as the director of a trio of documentaries, *Helvetica* (2007), *Objectified* (2009), and *Urbanized* (2011), that look at design, objects, and everyday urban life. *Moog* anticipates these later works in the way that it dwells on the objectness of the Moog and examines how it is both the product of, and itself produces, historical shifts and transformations. As such, the film is a music documentary, albeit an unusual one, but also forms part of a movement that documents, preserves, and celebrates modern design history. Hustwit's films are probably the most notable cinematic examples of this new genre, but books such as Sophie Lovell's on Braun's in-house designer, *Dieter Rams: As Little Design as Possible*[5] and Jonny Trunk's *Own Label: Sainsbury's Design Studio 1962–1977*[6] also represent this desire to archive the modern. The Moog synthesizer brings together the two elements of this contemporary fascination with modern design. The object itself represents the complexity of postwar life and its emergent technologies, while the Moog Music trademark, with its distinctively minimal typeface (integrating a musical note) represents modernism's desire for uncluttered functional simplicity. The film plays on the iconicity of the logo, using the Moog font for its credit sequence and onscreen identifications, but also lingers on the synths themselves in their material objectness, understanding that their form and bulk now visually symbolize their historical significance.

Moog features a wealth of musicians whose work has been shaped by their use of the synthesizer, but the selection is by no means comprehensive and tends somewhat problematically toward progressive rock. There can be little dispute that Keith Emerson of prog supergroup Emerson, Lake and Palmer and Rick Wakeman of Yes both played a huge role in popularizing the Moog in the early 1970s, with their onstage theatricality complementing their musical virtuousity. Yet the film dedicates a great deal of its running time to them at the cost of neglecting other significant Moog users. Most strikingly perhaps, the film omits Kraftwerk, whose 1974 Moog-driven track "Autobahn" not only combines the pop and avant-garde possibilities of the Minimoog, but also inspires and inaugurates a diverse musical lineage that shares the coolly structured repetitions and warm pitch-shifted tonalities that Moog's machines made possible.

Likewise, as much as the film pays tribute to a community of mainstream rock fans who embraced the new sounds of the synthesizer, it glosses over other pop genres, and their corresponding social practices, that were more definitively shaped around electronic sounds. The film mentions Giorgio Moroder only in passing, yet the Moog's use in disco is paramount. As Peter Shapiro argues, "I Feel Love," the 1976 Donna Summer hit that Moroder wrote and produced, stands as a revolutionary experiment in the way that it connects the beat and the body, finding the erotic in the electronic:

> Motion, escape and fantasy had all been ascribed to the synthesizer before 'I Feel Love', but never corporeal pleasure or sexual gratification. With

Summer's mock-operatic fake-orgasm vocals set against an entirely synthesized background of syndrums, stereo-panned percussion effects and a Moog playing that galloping bassline from 'Do What You Wanna Do', 'I Feel Love' was a masterpiece of mechano-eroticism.[7]

While the vicissitudes of organizing interviews must certainly have shaped the scope and coverage of *Moog*, the documentary's subordination of disco is especially frustrating given how neatly the genre brings together some of the film's preoccupations, from the sense of community and communality that electronic music is capable of generating to the feelings of liberation once existing conventions and restrictions, whether they be social or musical, are left behind. The utopian energies and possibilities that the Moog represents are most powerfully audible in disco, and the machine itself was central to the way in which the genre sought to liberate the body as well as free the musician from the limits of conventional instrumentation and rock's fetishization of authenticity and virtuosity.

The film's engagement with funk and jazz is somewhat better, due to the presence of Bernie Worrell, the keyboardist from Parliament-Funkadelic who played the Minimoog to dazzling effect on songs such as "Mothership Connection (Star Child)" and "Give Up the Funk (Tear the Roof off that Sucker)." As Moog himself notes in the film, electronically produced sounds have long been associated with outer space. This association came to the fore for several funk and jazz artists in the 1970s who used the Moog and its otherworldly sounds to forge a connection between an Afrocentric past and an interstellar future. As Kodwo Eshun describes, Worrell's use of the Moog allowed Parliament to question the very stability of reality and recast contemporary political tensions into a liquid soundscape at once terrifying and latent with revolutionary possibilities:

On the 10.38 *Flashlight* 12 mix, former child prodigy and New England Conservatory-trained Bernie Worrell becomes the latest Afronaut to land on the Moog. Synthesizing the bass from the Moog turns the low end into gloops and squidges from giant Claes Oldenburg toothpaste. Worrell's mutant Moog is radioactive plasma [. . .] Moog becomes a slithering cephalopod tugging at your hips, dragging your neck into its boneless maw, sinking holes in your ears and sucking out the balance mechanism— thereby sliding solid ground from under you.[8]

The Moog was a key vehicle in the formulation of seventies sonic afro-futurism, with musicians such as Worrell and Sun Ra (who appears briefly in *Moog* in a clip of him at his Minimoog drawn from *Space is the Place* (John Coney, 1974)) using the synthesizer not simply to conjure up an intergalactic imaginary but to critique earth-bound realities. Fjellestad's documentary gestures toward this radical history and the Moog's key part in it, but does not adequately convey the importance of the synthesizer to these sonic experiments and social critiques. As such, the film underplays the crucial historical role black artists have played in the exploration of the new sound worlds made possible by electronic instruments, as well as the way in which black music has been at the forefront of domesticating these otherworldly sounds as part of everyday life in the production of new forms of pop music, from funk to disco to early hip-hop and electro.

While the film largely neglects the key role the Moog played in the explosion of seventies afro-futurism, it fares better in its examination and acknowledgment of the synthesizer's centrality to contemporary hip-hop, electronica, and turntablism. DJ Logic and Mix Master Mike speak to the integration of the Moog into forms of hip-hop more readily identified with scratching and sampling, pointing to the synthesizer's capacity to generate an array of sounds ranging from the percussive to the melodic. The film also tries to bridge the historical gap by having Luke Vibert, a contemporary electronica artist, join Gershon Kingsley on stage. While Kingsley demonstrates the range of the Moog by introducing all kinds of sonic manipulations to the basic melodies of "Frère Jacques" and "Three Blind Mice," Vibert adds beats and noises from his laptop. The sequence asserts continuity between old and new but also suggests a harmony as well, as the analogue blends and mixes with the digital, each producing sounds and textures the other cannot.

In the film, it is DJ Spooky (Paul D. Miller) who provides the most theoretical analysis of the synthesizer, its operating logic, and how its basic principles are reproduced in the practice of sampling. Moog explains to him that it was never his intention to create a machine that would simply imitate already existing instruments, but one that would create new sound worlds. As Moog puts it, the noises produced by his synthesizers "weren't meant to be fake anything. They were real synthesized sounds." Spooky argues that, just as the Moog synthesizes its sound from a number of component parts and processes, so does sampling in the way that it blends a number of sound sources to produce a new sonic combination. While the Moog channels and controls electricity in order to generate its noises and notes, sampling draws on the energy of already existing recordings to produce a soundscape synthesized out of its component parts. But perhaps more important than this effort to see the continuity between an older instrument and newer practices is Spooky's observation that the basic technology of the synthesizer can be put to a number of different uses, even imitative ones. While the documentary is silent about the electronic devices that followed in the wake of the Moog, Spooky's comment invites a comparison of the synthesizer to later electronic devices; namely the Roland TR-808 Rhythm Generator and the Roland TB-303 Bass Line. In both cases, these machines were meant to be imitative, reproducing the sound of actual instruments, however imperfect and artificial this sound turned out to be. But the real success of these machines came when artists, most of them producing new musical forms and genres such as house or techno, pushed them past imitation to generate new and unanticipated sounds. In doing so, they reached Moog's starting point and put his principles into practice: electronic instruments should innovate rather than imitate. Fjellestad's documentary does not fully recognize the impact of this, but Moog himself does, at least on a technical level, when he tells DJ Spooky that "once you had the envelope and if it were controlling pitches, it can control anything. It can make it louder or softer, it could make it brighter or darker; it could change the whole sound from one thing to another . . . that was one of the really important concepts behind the synthesizer." The synthesizer allows for the electronic manipulation of sound that forms the basis of much contemporary music, but more specifically fuelled the creation of a variety of genres, from early electronic through the flurry of forms that populated the 1980s and 1990s and into today.

Whatever the limitations and blindspots of Fjellestad's documentary in fully mapping out those artists whose work was made possible by Moog synthesizers and the electronic genres that emerge out of Moog's radical and open thinking about sound, the film's closing moments are both moving and powerful. After seeing Moog travel from Los Angeles to New York to Tokyo, the final shots show him back in rural North Carolina, standing on the banks of a river with a Theremin. The Theremin is a key precursor to the synthesizer. It is an electronic instrument developed in the first half of the twentieth century that, even more than the Moog, is inextricably associated with the name of its inventor, Leon Theremin. The Theremin is a device that does not require physical touch to produce sound. The player controls pitch and volume by moving his or her hands in relation to two antennae. It is a significant instrument for Moog, who built Theremins when still in high school, and credits the experience for catalyzing his interest in electronically produced sounds. He manufactured and sold Theremins throughout the 1960s to subsidize his early efforts to create the modular synthesizer.[9]

The sound of the Theremin is both eerie and ethereal and it has long been pressed into service on soundtracks for science fiction and horror films. But there is also something elegiac and mournful about the instrument, and it is these qualities that come out when Moog plays "Old Man River" at the film's conclusion. Moog died of a brain tumour in 2005, just a year after the film's release, and this certainly lends the scene a retrospective poignancy. But even without knowledge of the tragedy to come, the sequence is affecting because of the way that it condenses and concludes Moog's meditations on his life's work. In an interview that appears in the film just prior to this riverside performance, he suggests that "if the right channels, if the right connections are established, I don't see why a piece of matter, a piece of broken glass or an old record, can't make contact to this very high level of reality that has access to everything past and future." Moog very much sounds like Sun Ra here, connecting abject material reality to a cosmic sublime. He explains further that he feels a bond to the instruments he has designed and that he believes they preserve a memory of him in their very construction: "I know that when I am working on them I feel, not explicitly, I don't hear voices in my head or anything, but I have this feeling that I'm making a connection with them. And, you know, the circuit diagram, that is then converted into a circuit board, which then becomes part of an instrument, is something, is a record I made, so I guess, in that sense, is certainly a memory." The Moog, understood in this way, bears both the name and the imprint of its inventor, his memory wired into the very circuit boards that enables the machine to generate the sounds that define it.

Moog, as its very title suggests, is about both the man and his machines, with the proper name having long become synonymous with the synthesizers he invented. Yet, Moog's philosophy, of both sound and spirit, makes this synonymity all the more appropriate as the distinctive modernity of the synthesizer's sound is precisely what enables it to conjure up a sense of the sublime, of inner and outer space, and of pure energy. Fjellestad's Moog is a flawed documentary if it is taken solely as a cultural history of the instrument. There are simply too many elisions and missed connections for it to do full justice to Moog's impact and legacy. But understood as a documentary that blends biography and object history, it fares much better, not least because Moog's importance resides not simply in the machine and the sound worlds it opened up, but in the concept behind the synthesizer. The desire to produce new sonic territories through the creation of new sounds has utterly reshaped music, and Moog documents the connections between man, machine, modernity, and music.

Notes

1   Moog's preferred pronunciation of his name (to rhyme with "rogue") makes this an imperfect pun, yet the idea of a "Moogie Wonderland" highlights two important moments in the life of the Moog synthesizer. Stereolab's allusion to Earth, Wind and Fire's hit "Boogie Wonderland" from 1979 remembers the Minimoog's importance to disco, while their 1994 play on that title confirmed the Moog's return as a prized piece of gear for a new generation of alternative and experimental artists.

2   For a comprehensive biography of Robert A. Moog and the history of the Moog synthesizer, see Trevor Pinch and Frank Trocco, Analog Days: The Invention and Impact of the Moog Synthesizer (Cambridge, MA: Harvard UP, 2002).

3   Dave Tompkins' extraordinary How to Wreck a Nice Beach traces the history of the vocoder and links the development of electronic music in the latter half of the twentieth century to technological innovations from its first half accelerated by the urgency of World War II. Moog has a cameo in Tompkins' history since he drew on military electronics technology in his experiments with synthesized sound. For more see Dave Tompkins, How to Wreck a Nice Beach: The Vocoder from World War II to Hip-Hop: The Machine Speaks (New York: Melville House, 2011), 159–60.

4   For more on the role electronic instruments played in the development of electronic music see also the edited volume that accompanied the documentary: Peter Shapiro

(ed.), *Modulations: A History of Electronic Music: Throbbing Words on Sound* (London: Caipirinha, 1999).

5   Sophie Lovell, *Dieter Rams: As Little Design as Possible* (London: Phaidon, 2011).
6   Jonny Trunk, Emily King, Damon Murray, and Stephen Sorrell, *Own Label: Sainsbury's Design Studio 1962–1977* (London: Fuel, 2011).
7   Peter Shapiro, *Turn the Beat Around: The Secret History of Disco* (London: Faber, 2009), 101.
8   Kodwo Eshun, *More Brilliant than the Sun: Adventures in Sonic Fiction* (London: Quartet, 1998), 151.
9   Tompkins, *How to Wreck a Nice Beach*, 160.

Chapter 13

An Ethnographic Video Project for the Music Classroom

Christopher L. Ballengee

I have been teaching a course called "Introduction to World Music" at the University of Florida for some time. Both to mitigate difficulties in generating student engagement in such a diversely populated survey course and to emphasize a conceptual turn from studying music as a decontextualized object to studying music as the product of living, creative, and dynamic communities, I have incorporated an ethnographic fieldwork project into the course; students create ethnographic videos on local musical communities. In this chapter, I will discuss the world music survey course as an element of university level multicultural education, in the process situating my ethnographic filmmaking assignment, which I call the Fieldwork Video Project, as a learning activity that fulfills the goals of both multicultural mandates and objectives of the course. Next, I will describe the elements of the Fieldwork Video Project. Finally, I will conclude by suggesting that the Fieldwork Video Project is a valuable tool for students to understand the cultural and social forces that give rise to and maintain musical traditions, and that a sustained project of this kind can also greatly benefit the communities in which students work by creating an admittedly limited, but nonetheless profound, musical ethnography of place.

Multicultural Perspectives and the World Music Survey Course

Requirements mandating the teaching of multicultural perspectives in the United States began changing school curricula with the Civil Rights Movement in the 1960s. Today, multicultural perspectives are integral to the university experience, often with students required to earn a number of multicultural credits while completing obligatory courses for their major program of study. At the University of Florida, students are required to accrue a number of "diversity" and "international" credits in addition to humanities, math, science, and language skills credits, all of which are associated with a set of general education courses. Couched in a liberal arts tradition, these general education requirements are intended for "students [to] gain fresh perspectives, methods and tools for understanding the traditional and the newly discovered" so that students can "better understand [themselves], [their] neighbors, other cultures and times, and the principles governing the natural world and the universe."[1] Intro to World Music is one of a handful of general education courses at the University of Florida that fulfill three credits each of the humanities and international requirements, which equals thirty-three percent of students' required humanities credits and one hundred percent of students' required international credits (see Figure 13.1). Thus, my course is quite popular.

Part of virtually every program of study, survey courses are integral components of contemporary university education. Any survey course has as its goal the coverage of a broad range of material on a particular subject that aims for relevancy while avoiding over-complexity. Thus, survey courses generally offer students what the name implies: a bullet list of topics that form the foundation of a given discipline. Often intended for those early in their programs of study, these types of course generally feature large class sizes, extremely diverse enrollment, and provide for very little interaction between individual students and their instructors. This challenges instructors to retain student engagement while avoiding the tendency to teach to the lowest common denominator.

This is the context from which the world music survey emerges. Each section of my course has a capacity of one hundred students, a rather low number relative to many core courses, yet certainly enough to intimidate many students who would otherwise fully engage in class discussion. Therefore, class participation is largely limited to a handful of enthusiastic students while it must be consistently coerced from others who attempt to melt into the crowd.

My in-class lessons cover music fundamentals, development of critical listening skills, and basic rhythmic and melodic performance, all this embedded in exploration of fundamental ethnomusicological concepts. The comparison

Areas	Credits
Composition (C)	3
Humanities (H)	9
Mathematics (M)	6
Physical (P) and Biological (B) Sciences	9
Social and Behavioral Sciences (S)	9
Total Credit Requirements:	**36**
International (N) and Diversity (D) taken in conjunction with C, H, S, P, or B	3 each

Figure 13.1 The University of Florida's General Education requirements. Courtesy of the Board of Trustees of the University of Florida.

of music across cultures serves to maintain intellectual coherence in a world music survey. Identification of similarities and differences, not only in musical structure but also in function and place within social hierarchies, emerges as a way of drawing together seemingly disparate notions about music, especially as contrasted with students' own experiences. Thus, the primary goal of a world music survey, as I see it, is to prepare students to broadly, yet critically, examine music in and as culture. Having students actively participate as music makers and listeners is critical for achieving this goal. Patricia Shehan Campbell suggests that students learn by making music "as [they] are in a sense placed inside the music and its sonic structures."[2]

Yet, music consists of more than sonic structures. Rather, from composition, performance, and reception to dissemination, critical analysis, and beyond, the whole complex of activities surrounding music touches a multitude of people's lives along the way. Clearly the "study of [music's] connections to the past and the present [adds] depth to musical understanding while also allowing music to function in its natural way as an important piece in the study of the world and its people."[3] If the goal of a world music survey course is for students to understand music in and as culture, then the Fieldwork Video Project helps achieve this objective by teaching about the dynamics of global musical cultures by way of examining localized musical phenomena. With the Video Project as a capstone activity in the course, the world music survey indeed more specifically addresses the mandates of the University of Florida's General Education program as students come to understand music as a complex, human-centered process that informs connections across time and across the world.

The Fieldwork Video Project

In 1975, Margaret Mead flatly and somewhat pessimistically described anthropology as a "discipline of words":

> Much of the fieldwork that laid the basis of anthropology as a science was conducted under conditions of rapid change, where the fieldworker had to rely on the memory of the informants rather than upon observation of contemporary events. The informant had only words in which to describe the war dance that was no longer danced [and] the buffalo hunt after the buffalo had disappeared . . . Thus ethnographic enquiries came to depend upon words, and words and words, during the period that anthropology was maturing as a science.[4]

Mead goes on to advocate film as a means of more holistically capturing information that would inevitably be lost in even the best ethnographic writing. A pioneer of the subdiscipline of visual anthropology, John Collier echoes Mead, suggesting that the camera gives the anthropologist a "whole vision" of culture, working to capture information that the unaided eyes, ears, and memory would overlook.[5]

But the camera is not a miracle fieldworking tool. Clifford Geertz, among others, pointed out that ethnography is essentially an interpretive endeavor, one that involves much more than simply collecting data.[6] Rather, ethnographies, either in print, on film, or otherwise, are perhaps best considered a filtered product, containing information selectively given by informants, processed in the minds of ethnographers, and further edited for publication. Thus, the camera with its supposed "whole vision" still requires an ethnographer to point, shoot, and edit the information it records. I strongly emphasize this point to my students as they complete their work.

The Video Project indeed represents an exercise in ethnographic fieldwork, one in which students investigate musical communities within the city of Gainesville, Florida where the university is located. As described below, students choose a viable research topic, explicate planned methodology, use filming and editing as both a means of research and presentation of results, and reflect upon the process in a final written essay.

In the beginning, I envisioned the Video Project as a replacement for the traditional term paper. With one hundred students and no teaching assistants, I put students into workgroups of four each, thus reducing my workload to grading only twenty-five projects, with the Video Project representing forty percent of each student's final grade. Beyond this practical consideration, I also believed that video projects would be more meaningful for students than a standard research paper. If the assignment were more meaningful, I reasoned, then students would invest themselves in the project, more faithfully represent the people with whom they worked, and ultimately learn more through direct experience than they could from doing library research alone.

Further, I also wanted a project that would level the playing field in a course where students' musical knowledge varies greatly. Only a small percentage of enrolled students are music majors, most of whom feel they can rest on the laurels of their Western music education without truly engaging in the course material. By contrast, non-musicians are often intimidated by a lack of musical understanding, a source of great anxiety for many. Thus, the Fieldwork Video Project represents a meeting point where all can enter with a fresh perspective, in the process spurring creative thinking and productive collaboration.

The project includes four assignments with deadlines spaced throughout the term. A thorough written description of the entire project, complete with grading rubrics for each of the four assignments and sample videos from past semesters, is posted online for students to see from the first day of the semester.

Part One: Topic Exploration Assignment

The first part, the Topic Exploration Assignment, counts toward ten percent of the Video Project grade and is due within the first few weeks of the course.

For this assignment, I ask students to identify at least three possible topics and think about the viability of proceeding with each. I provide each workgroup with three copies of a questionnaire that asks students to consider a number of factors ranging from travel expenses and time commitments to community benefit and personal interest. These topic exploration question-naires are submitted to me for review and graded only in terms of completion.

This assignment is intended to have students realistically estimate how much of the group's resources will be expended in completing their work. My comments generally include rankings of each topic in terms of viability and inform students of any obstacles of which they may not be aware. Ultimately, however, the group decides how to proceed on its own. When I first began using the Video Project, I did not include the Topic Exploration Assignment. At that time, a small percentage of students tended to get themselves involved in projects that were unfocused, over-ambitious, presented few opportunities to observe rehearsals and performances, involved individuals (i.e. children, illegal immigrants, or the homeless) who made on-camera interviews ethically impossible, or were otherwise unviable in such a limited time frame. After implementing the Topic Exploration Assignment, students now fare better as I can help direct research in ways that present fewer stumbling blocks.

Part Two: Topic Proposal

The second assignment, which I call the Topic Proposal Assignment, is due about one week after the Topic Exploration Assignment has been returned and counts toward thirty percent of the Video Project grade. The Topic Proposal Assignment asks students to narrow their choices to one viable topic and to formally propose a plan to complete the project. In the proposal, students thoroughly explicate four criteria.

First, I ask for a general topic description in which students clearly describe the individual, group, or idea to be studied as well as what the group wants to find out about this subject. I encourage students to write simple questions for themselves to answer in prose form within the proposal.

Second, I ask students to justify the significance of their research. Students often consider this the most difficult portion of the assignment simply because they have never considered their own research important. Despite professors' mandates for original insights in university term papers, undergraduate students are generally trained not to be original as they write about the same old things that generations of students have written about before. For this project, however, students are asked to do original work with people who have never appeared before in any academic literature. This work will not change the world, but I feel that it is vitally important that students recognize the poten-tial they have to affect the community with their research. Sometimes their results will be trivial, and other times truly groundbreaking. But when all of these projects are collected over time, they each contribute to a sensitive and dynamic musical ethnography of Gainesville.

Third, I ask students to discuss their methodology. For the purposes of the Topic Proposal Assignment, I want students to tell me everything they will be doing in the process of completing their projects including library or internet searches, interviews, observances of rehearsals or performances, participation in music making, filming, audio recording, editing, and any other means of collecting and interpreting data. I additionally ask students to identify key individuals who have been contacted as research associates. I ask students to describe how they will access equipment and to name the specific model of camera and editing software to be used. As I review this information in student proposals, I can better guide students' work by identifying and mitigating potential methodological, ethical, or technological problems. Moreover, the plan laid out in this assignment serves as a quasi-contract between the students and me, investing them in the process by means of explicating their research activities and giving them a solid plan for proceeding with the work.

Finally, I ask students for important dates and a bibliography. By requiring a list of at least three dates for rehearsals, performances, or scheduled interviews in the proposal, I am ensured that students have a timeline to follow. I also require students to review print and electronic sources that will help inform their research and to provide these sources in a short bibliography attached to the proposal. Students are not expected to cite these sources anywhere within the video itself. Rather, the bibliography is intended for reference only.

Part Three: The Video

The video is the third assignment of the Video Project and counts toward forty percent of the Video Project grade. Art and ethnography are not mutually exclusive. As such, I encourage students to be creative in their work, especially given the constraints of time and resources. Filmic clichés, clever use of montage, animation, and other non-linear manipulations of audio and video are welcomed as means of conveying ideas, yet I do not penalize students for poor production quality unless this overly distracts from the work's coherence.

Most importantly, the video should demonstrate that students have conducted quality fieldwork by synthesizing footage from interviews, rehearsals, performances, personal reflection, or other sources as appropriate into a coherent ethnographic narrative informed by hands-on research. I limit the length of videos to ten minutes, thus pushing students to make important decisions that affect the clarity and purpose of their work. The video should also stay on topic, with all elements contributing to a clearly recognizable thesis that extends from the plan set out in the proposal. The most successful video projects feature a purposeful narrative that remains clear throughout, with every bit of information carefully selected to support this narrative, with any necessary background information well integrated into the flow of the video, and a concise ending providing a sense of conclusion.

In terms of preparation, I provide a few in-class tutorials on the practical aspects of using video cameras and editing software. Apart from screening a few good and bad examples of past student projects, I give little in the way of artistic instruction. Rather, I allow students to discover filmmaking on their own terms. Though I am certainly more a musician than a filmmaker, I am always available to give technological and conceptual advice. The video is due near the end of the semester during a two-week period of screenings in which groups critique each other's work.

Part Four: Project Summary

As a final step in completing the project, I ask each group to write a short Project Summary paper discussing their project, which counts toward ten percent of the Video Project grade. The paper should chronicle the complexities of planning for and completing the project with particular attention paid to the problems encountered and overcome during the fieldwork process. The paper should additionally reflect upon the success of the representation of the video's subjects, gauge the work's impact on the community, and describe lessons learned from engaging in the project and what students hope others will learn from viewing the project.

Assessment

Each of the project's constituent assignments is graded as objectively as possible. I have developed grading rubrics and sample assignments to accompany each part; thus students generally know what to expect from the outset. As such, students work within a set of guidelines that help define boundaries and clarify ambiguities. Rather than restrict creativity, these guidelines allow students to worry less about the shape of the overall assignment and concentrate more on the research process.

Some workgroups decide that members will work together through each step of the process while other groups delegate tasks to individuals according to strengths and interest. Whatever the division of labor, all students in each group receive the same Video Project grade. On the rare occasion when students report a group member not pulling his or her own weight, I intervene to solve problems. In extreme cases, I implement a peer grading scheme in which students within the group grade each other in terms of participation. This peer grade is then factored into each student's Video Project grade.

Problems and Considerations

When I first spoke with my colleagues about implementing this project, I encountered a mixture of enthusiasm and skepticism. My fellow world music instructors initially felt that the Video Project would be too much to administer and assess, much less troubleshoot, as students encountered problems. At least one colleague suggested that students at this level (mostly first- and second-year college students) are not mature enough to handle the sensitivity and subtleties of ethnographic fieldwork, even as basic as it is in this project, and further explained that my experiential emphasis was indeed inappropriate for such a course.

I have found, however, that most students are quite capable of doing simple ethnography and are more than able to perceptively critique their own work and that of their classmates, especially where representation is concerned. And an experiential approach to music study is, I think, exactly what we need more of. It is not easy to design, implement, and assess projects as I have described, but it is clearly worth the effort if students emerge having learned valuable lessons about the place of music in their own lives, their communities, and around the world.

Three other world music instructors at the University of Florida adopted slightly modified versions of my Fieldwork Video Project in their classes to much success. I have since also received much interest from the Music faculty at large, some of whom have expressed a need for developing a broadly interdisciplinary student project beyond the world music survey course that is integrative, cuts across university departments, and injects music into other interest and research areas. Russell Robinson, chair of the music education division in the University of Florida School of Music, notes that my Video Project indeed promotes "collaboration" and "multi-sensory and experiential learning." Upon observing video presentations in my class, Dr. Robinson offered his comments:

> This is one of the most innovative approaches to the teaching/learning process in music that I have experienced in my 28 years in higher education ... I experienced one [video] on the music of the sitar and one on "stepping" (a new term to me) ... They were truly outstanding ... The comments, engagement, and enthusiasm of the class were stimulating as well.[7]

Robinson's remarks pinpoint the primary advantages of the Video Project, namely that it intends to place students within the musical traditions they study as much as possible given the limitations of time and experience and that the resulting videos give shape to music of the present, music happening here and now in our own backyards, that we as aging, sheltered faculty tend to miss. There are, however, some drawbacks to assigning the project in a world music survey course. The most frustrating obstacles are of course technological. When I first began implementing the project, students had no university-administered access to video equipment other than basic editing software installed on campus computers. Rather, students came to their projects with a variety of old and new camcorders borrowed from friends and relatives.

Students often had hours of footage before discovering that their analog VHS or Hi-8 camcorders would not communicate so easily with modern computers. Even those with more compatible Mini-DV or hard-drive-based camcorders often found that they spent more time solving problems with their equipment than they did filming or editing.

I attempted to solve the camcorder problem by requesting departmental funds for dedicated equipment. This request unfortunately coincided with university-wide budget cuts and was thus expectedly denied. For some time, I had to depend on the resourcefulness of my students to find their own video equipment. Eventually, the University of Florida Libraries purchased a number of Flip Video cameras available for all university students to borrow for up to three days at a time. The availability of this equipment, the near ubiquity these days of point-and-shoot still cameras and mobile phones with video capabilities, and students' increasing comfort with digital video technology have greatly reduced the stress most students feel about camcorder access. I certainly care more that students are thinking about the issues than whether they are procuring the best technology for creating a technically perfect film.

Apart from access to equipment, many students also experience some anxiety as they come to understand the concept of the Fieldwork Video Project as a practical exercise in musical ethnography rather than a means of studying "world music" as an end unto itself. To a wide-eyed first-year student, for example, it may seem contradictory to spend so much time investigating local musical cultures while enrolled in a course that ostensibly asks them to consider musics beyond the local. As such, students often seek the exotic in an effort to fulfill their conception of the course objectives. Our local Hare Krishna congregation, a number of reggae bands, and the non-Western music ensembles offered through the School of Music have thus received an ample amount of coverage over the years. However, the majority of students who are truly engaged in the course and in the project recognize that all music at all times is worthy of ethnomusicological inquiry. I further emphasize this in class lectures and often steer projects away from studying "African music," for example, and toward studying the culture surrounding Pazeni Sauti, the University of Florida's Africa Choir whose membership is vastly non-African.

Though we must be aware of the potential representational pitfalls of any sort of ethnography, Jeff Todd Titon suggests that "representing people making music on film and video seems more real than representing them in books."[8] In other words, moving sounds and images replay the performative aspects of music and life in general in ways that written words cannot. This is surely not to say that written ethnographies do not have the potential for sensitive descriptions of musical phenomena. One must look no further than the volumes of ethnographic literature in the musicological canon to eliminate any shadow of a doubt. Rather, as this volume in part attempts to affirm, film and video have become particularly suited for documenting musical cultures precisely because of their "undeniable evocative power" to transform a jumble of light and sound into a convincing impression of real life.[9]

Conclusion: Creating a Musical Ethnography of Place

After some time working with these projects I came to realize something rather profound. In the beginning, I had simply wanted students to get out of the classroom, to experience what ethnography is and what ethno-musicologists do. What I had somehow failed to see until much later was that the aggregate of student projects over time in effect formed a musical ethnography of our city. Upon reviewing successive semesters' videos, I began to see connections among the individuals and groups depicted in the videos and among the students themselves. I indeed had my students embarking upon a long-term musical ethnography of place, one that emerges out of the individual musical communities described in my students' work.

The result of each project individually is a document of a particular musical culture within the city. In the course of a semester's worth of work, these individual soundscapes considered collectively form a snapshot of the musical happenings of our area at a given moment in time. In the first semester implementing the Video Project, for example, I received videos covering a wide range of material including a student-run Latin dance group, an independent music festival, and music at a local Baptist church among many others. Though the individuals within these studied groups may never meet, they all live and make music within the geographic bounds of the city as recorded over a finite timeframe. Each semester students again probe the musical depths thus creating a record of musical constancy and change in our city.

Some people continually crop up in student projects, thus suggesting connections between and among culture groups. During my first semester teaching at the University of Florida, Evan was a student of mine whose group studied the local bluegrass music scene. One semester later, Evan himself was featured in two student videos, one as a member of the band Umoja Orchestra and one as a member of the University-based Cuban rumba group Fundamento Rumbero. Two semesters later, he was yet again featured in a student video on music performed at a local restaurant. These videos to a certain degree document one individual's involvement in a number of intersecting musical micro-communities over the course of about one year. Though the documentation is clearly brief and certainly amateur, it nonetheless indicates the existence of a certain web of musicultural involvement within the city through time.

Further characterizing this web of activity, a number of landmarks tend to repeatedly appear in student projects as well. Spaces within the University of Florida Music Building tend to recur with expected frequency, as do regular public performance spaces including the University Auditorium and the Bo Diddley Plaza in downtown Gainesville. For residents of the city who are familiar with these everyday spaces, the landmarks' appearances in student videos help to contextualize the information on screen, and viewers who have no knowledge of these spaces will eventually recognize them after a time.

When taking a step back from the narrow focus of individual projects, a sense of space emerges that is not so much about being emplaced or being in place than it is about movement, constancy, and change within the musical space of the city. Any notion of continuity is tempered by the notion that the university community is by nature largely transient as students and faculty come and go, myself included.

In the end, the Fieldwork Video Project has become a means of making the study of music and musical culture more meaningful in the lives of my students. With each semester's projects, I am constantly delighted by the creativity, sensitivity, and seriousness with which my students go about their work. Furthermore, students often tell me that the Fieldwork Video Project is one of the most fun, most inspiring, yet most difficult tasks they have been asked to complete in college, a point of pride for me as a teacher. And not only do students give me good end-of-semester evaluations, but they also learn a lot about doing ethnography and about a community that is often deeply touched as students move within and among the people of our city.

Notes

1 "General Education Requirement," *University of Florida Undergraduate Catalog 2011–2012*. https://catalog.ufl.edu/ugrad/current/advising/info/general-education-requirement.aspx (accessed October 7, 2011).
2 Patricia Shehan Campbell, *Teaching Music Globally* (Oxford: Oxford University Press, 2004), 197.
3 Ibid., 216.
4 Margaret Mead, "Visual Anthropology in a Discipline of Words," in Paul Hockings (ed.), *Principles of Visual Anthropology* (Berlin: Mouton de Gruyter, 2003), 5.
5 John Collier, Jr., *Visual Anthropology: Photography as a Research Method* (New York: Holt, Rinehart and Winston, 1967), 2.
6 Clifford Geertz, *The Interpretation of Cultures* (New York: Basic Books, 1973).
7 Russell Robinson, email message to author, August 6, 2008.
8 Jeff Todd Titon, "Representation and Authority in Ethnographic Film/Video: Production," *Ethnomusicology* 36, No. 1 (1992), 90.
9 Ibid., 91.

Chapter 14

Mediating *The Agony and the Ecstasy of Phil Spector*

Documenting Monstrosity?

Mark Duffett and Jon Hackett

In February 2003 Lana Clarkson was found shot dead at point blank range inside Phil Spector's Los Angeles mansion. It appeared that just as she was about to leave, the former model and actress, who had been working as a hostess at a West Hollywood nightclub, had kissed the barrel of the famous Wall of Sound producer's loaded gun. Just over four years later, Spector's trial for Clarkson's murder in 2007 resulted in a hung jury. The infamously eccentric producer and his lawyers maintained that she had pulled the trigger herself, in effect accidentally committing suicide. Just over a year later, the BBC Arena series screened Vikram Jayanti's special feature-length documentary, *The Agony and the Ecstasy of Phil Spector* (2009). Based on a series of exclusive interviews with Spector, the documentary was primarily marketed as an analysis of one man's musical creativity. Yet it was also screened to coincide with the re-opening of Spector's judicial case and featured footage of his first trial. Within two years Spector was convicted in a retrial of shooting Clarkson dead. The central narrative of Spector's life story is well known: as the creator of a ground-breaking production style he made some of the most truly popular music of the 1960s, but the solipsistic producer soon entered into an extended period of personal and creative decline in which his eccentric behavior and self-imposed isolation became ever more pronounced.[1] As well as exploring the production and critical reception of the Arena project, this chapter will critically examine *The Agony and the Ecstasy of Phil Spector* as a media representation that carefully negotiated its subject's monstrous public image. Based on the unusual theme of a genius musician's perceived criminality, the documentary raises questions of agency, complicity, and mediation in the portrayal of its subject. The argument presented here is that filmmakers used the resources at their disposal, particularly the juxtaposition of different channels of communication, to make Spector's musical creations express his culpability as a killer.

Phil Tagg's recent discussion of "visible music" provides a point from which to analyze Phil Spector as a documentary subject. According to Tagg, "we are in a new stage of musical culture, in which audio-only/visible music has been replaced with audiovisual/invisible music" which means that "popular music studies needs to engage further with music and the moving image."[2] Tagg elaborates on this theme in his discussion of music heard in conjunction with moving images: "The vast majority of that music is invisible in the sense that we don't see anybody making (or even pretending to make) the sounds we actually hear."[3] Hence, for Tagg, invisible music is (generally) soundtrack music, whereas visible music is the harmonious sound visibly performed by musicians on screen. Tagg's distinction is an extremely useful tool to analyze the music documentary, but we can also extend the distinction to distinguish between visible and invisible *musicians*. Although visible musicians may not be seen all the time, their craft (for instance singing or playing guitar) is frequently constructed as an engaging spectacle. In contrast, while invisible musicians can be crucial in the making of musical sounds, we are not conditioned to see their craft as visually spectacular. As a producer whose innovations changed the face of American popular music, Spector is perhaps the ultimate invisible musician.[4] Tony Visconti, now a famous producer in his own right, recalled first seeing the "tycoon of teen" on television:

> The first time I heard the term "Producer" was in the '60s when a mad looking man on the Jack Paar TV show (one of the very first talk shows) audaciously proclaimed that he dictated the musical taste of teenagers in America. He was introduced as a record producer and his name was Phil Spector. I already loved his productions without really knowing that someone other than the artists and musicians were [*sic*] involved (I still melt when I hear "Walking In The Rain" by The Ronettes). It was Spector who brought this role to the public's attention, but most records of that time were still produced anonymously.[5]

Since the singles that he wrote and produced were already hits by this point, Spector's television appearances were less about marketing than taking credit for the music. His oft-repeated claim that he was making "little symphonies for the kids" emphasized an artistic and visionary dimension of his work, which was never just a case of documenting sound, and allied it to the idea that he resembled a classical conductor. When orchestral symphonies are performed, the conductor is of course *not* an invisible musician; he or she is instead a highly visible but inaudible figure whose musical contribution (interpreting the score, setting the tempo, orchestrating different players) is heard only through sound made by others. The analogy expressed Spector's need for attention, a need which would eventually lead him to fashion his visual image as a peculiar spectacle. The producer's increasingly unusual wigs were taken by music writer Nick Kent, amongst others, as signifiers of his eccentricity and social isolation:

> Cast your eyes along a gallery of photographs taken of the mega-producer/rock 'n' roll legend Phil Spector throughout the past forty years

and soon enough you'll find yourself entering a bizarre world of celebrity wig-wearing that would make even Elton John blush. Spector's mercurial rise as teen pop's very own Richard Wagner at the beginning of the sixties coincided with him also losing his hair at an equally dramatic speed. He correctly deduced that a balding pate would hinder his progress as omnipotent tycoon of teen and promptly filled several closets of his various residences with every style of hair he could get his hands on. The wigs were short haired and well groomed in the mid-1960s when he was riding the big waves of success with the Ronettes and Righteous Brothers, but after his "retirement" in 1966 they—like their owner—got stranger and stranger.[6]

Kent's discussion is worth further exploration as it reveals how Spector's visual style was perceived to signify his personality. The music critic explained that the images which came from Spector's 2005 *Vanity Fair* photo session indicated that "he demonstrated once again that he had no shame where rugs were concerned." The producer's "wizened tiny face [was] framed by a hideous-looking mullet wig that made him look like Mr Magoo reincarnated as a drowned rat." Kent continues, "As the new millennium started, he could sometimes be sighted sporting a ludicrous Louis XIV wig at A-list LA parties." He then updates the story by reporting Spector's first court case: "Perhaps recognizing that this would be one of his last moments as the spotlight kid, he chose his most bizarre wig to wear in court: a voluminous grey monstrosity that made him look like Mozart's senile grandfather."[7] In his theatrical wig-wearing, Spector is not perceived in the same way as, say, Lady Gaga. Rather than artistic self-statements his hair pieces are interpreted, in effect, as markers of shameless narcissism and increasing insanity. Even in a situation as serious as his trial for murder trial, the "egomaniac dandy," as one reviewer described him, thought he was simply in the public spotlight.[8] He could not understand that his humour was inappropriate. Strange, shameless, ludicrous, hideous and monstrous, Spector's wigs are not taken by Kent as benign indications of his individuality or good humour, but as visual markers of Spector's social transgression that indicate his abject status.

Kent's interpretation was hardly surprising; in the public eye Spector's association with the death of Lana Clarkson affirmed his monstrosity. The crime could be readily explained as the nadir of his descent into depression and madness. Commentators began to make sense of Spector's psychosis in terms of the suicide of his father when he was just a child and the further loss of his son on Christmas day in 1991. As Kent surmised, "[t]he anger created the mighty Wall of Sound but it also sowed the seeds for his downfall: he could never rise above it and his sound became increasingly tainted as a result."[9] According to another biographer, Dave Thompson, in the 2010 edition of *Wall of Pain*:

In the years since the police were called to his home in the Los Angeles suburb of Alhambra in February 2003, there to discover the lifeless body of actress Lana Clarkson, and even more so since a Los Angeles court sentenced him to spend the next two decades in prison, more articles on Phil Spector have been published and republished than appeared in the two decades before that, an astonishing deluge which, frankly, makes one wonder what there could possibly be left to talk about?[10]

Despite a crowded field of news stories, articles, and biographies, Spector had rarely given interviews. *The Agony and the Ecstasy of Phil Spector* was a joint venture between Vikram Jayanti's Vixpix film production company and the BBC Arena show. Jayanti's career moved from the academic world to professional documentary: back in the 1980s he had taught a graduate seminar in anthropological documentary at the University of Southern California's Center for Visual Anthropology and made a film called *In Her Own Time* (1985) about the fieldwork of cultural anthropologist Dr Barbara Meyerhoff. The Spector project was licensed to Argot Pictures, a documentary distributor which did a good job of getting the film theatrically released to over thirty film festivals and screenings across the USA. It was also nominated at the Sydney, St Louis, and Ficunam International Film Festivals and played for one week at American Cinematheque's Egyptian Theater in Hollywood.

Reviewers of the documentary made two main points. The first was that Jayanti seemed unfairly sympathetic to his subject. In the *Village Voice* film critic J. Hoberman explained, "Spector is a notorious credit hog—and Jayanti proves to be something of an enabler."[11] For *Boxoffice* magazine, John McCarthy saw the documentary as taking an uncritical approach to Spector and biasing interpretations of his case in his favour: "As for the trial excerpts, it's apparent Jayanti intends to raise doubts about whether Spector shot Clarkson at his LA-area mansion after a night of partying at The House of Blues, where she worked." He added that "Jayanti lobs ingratiating softballs that were either intended to allow Spector to reveal and hang or reveal and justify himself. Considering the hagiography that surrounds the interview, the latter must have been the case." McCarthy also explained, "While this film's grandiose title, a riff on the 1961 novel about Michelangelo, matches Phil Spector's exalted view of himself, most of its truth (and any irony) is undercut by director Vikram Jayanti's fawning approach.[12] McCarthy was not alone in his opinion. Other critics agreed that Jayanti came down strongly in Spector's defense.[13] One lamented, "Sometimes, even your staunchest defenders can't keep you from looking, well, nuts . . . We see lots of footage from the court proceedings, but, oddly, only *hear* testimony that bolsters the defense's contention that it was a suicide."[14] These accusations of bias suggested that Jayanti's actions were largely those of a music fan. As one reviewer put it:

In its thoughtful, frowny mode, the movie's unspoken undertone is, "No one likes a murderer." But even though Jayanti tries to give the whole enterprise a calm, classy veneer, there's always a degree of fannish devotion—a wide-eyed "This is Phil F-ing Spector we're talking about!" breathlessness—at work.[15]

The second point upon which most reviewers tended to agree was that despite Jayanti's approach, the documentary's human subject was himself both mesmerizing and irredeemably abject. As one explained, referring to Spector's comments about surrounding himself by bodyguards, "The agony, such as it is, lies in another of Spector's harsh truths: 'I can't be difficult [for you] if you can't get near me.' If this is the real Spector, chances are, you don't want to."[16] The *Washington Post* reported that the film "contains obscenity, crime scene photos and discussion of violent death."[17] A reviewer commented, "Spector may be a paranoid loon with blood on his hands, but he's also a fascinating, tragic case study in splendid isolation."[18]

The term monster can mean an inhumanly cruel or wicked person, but it can also reference a terrifying creature of the imagination. In that sense, Spector in his megalomaniac ramblings was, for Hoberman, a "monster of self-absorption."[19] However, for monstrosity to exist it has to be socially realized: documented and iterated time and again. As Chris Baldick noted in his discussion of the politics of monstrosity, in its traditional usage the term "monster" referenced a history of moral demonstration. It comes from Latin verb *monstrāre* which was the present active infinitive of the word *monstrō*, meaning to advise, show, point out or denounce. In other words, the process of moral demonstration (*monstrāre*) and its result (monster) are bound together: monsters "reveal visibly the results of vice, folly, and unreason, as a warning to erring humanity."[20] A monster serves as a demonstration of the perils of overstepping the bounds of the human and aspiring to the divine. Baldick's work reminds us that monstrosity is not so much a natural state as the result of a social process. If Spector killed Clarkson as the jury agreed, his *act* was undoubtedly monstrous, but as a famous producer he was inevitably more than a murderer. The question for Jayanti was how to present a character study that encompassed the full range of Spector's accomplishments without unduly seeming to humanize him. The Arena documentary therefore had to walk a line between being denied access to its subject and presenting him in a light which would alienate a wider audience who understood him through a monstrous crime. Jayanti could ignore neither the ecstasy nor the agony: he had to address both the Wall of Sound years and Clarkson's death. In subtle ways then, *The Agony and the Ecstasy of Phil Spector* had to *demonstrate* its subject's monstrosity as part of its dualistic narrative.

As film scholar Patricia Aufderheide has explained:

> documentaries are about real life; they are not real life. They are not even windows on real life. They are portraits of real life, using real life

as their raw material, constructed by artists and technicians who make myriad decisions about what story to tell to whom, and for what purpose.[21]

The interview material for the Spector documentary was culled from fifty hours of interviews made during the reclusive producer's first trial.[22] Asking questions such as "Your sense is that you are being hounded now, that this trial is about something else, right?" Jayanti uses his sycophantic role to draw Spector out as an aging and insecure star who is paranoid about his own legend. By turns the Wall of Sound producer compares his struggle to that of "great men" of art and science like Leonardo da Vinci, offers an ambitious yet inevitably biased critical appreciation of his contribution, and questions the creativity or cultural merit of other musicians from Tony Bennett to Brian Wilson. There is a sense in which in the interviews alone he has been given enough rope to hang himself, but the documentary presents much more than that. Its cultural work was noticed by reviewers like Michael O'Sullivan in the *Washington Post*:

> Every now and then Jayanti simply shows the actors in the courtroom drama in wordless slo-mo, accompanied by the ominous and bizarre telling of a bell. At one point, he zooms in on Spector's face, as the man sits on the interview couch in his pin-striped suit and red silk shirt, slowing the film down until Spector looks like a fish gasping for air. At those moments, Jayanti's subject comes across as even more of a freak than he already does, with his now infamous assortment of obvious wigs, and facial expressions that swing back and forth between affectless inscrutability and inappropriate laughter. Is all that really necessary?[23]

This active portrayal of Spector did not just extend to themes, camera work, and editing, however. Its construction did not go unnoticed by reviewers: Laura Clifford, for example, explained that "Jayanti's use of Spector's music as a gateway to understanding the man, and, potentially his crime, is thinking out[side] of the box . . . It's clear that Jayanti's trying to layer his film like Spector built up his studio tracks."[24] Writing for the *Detroit News*, Tom Long described the documentary as taking "a crazy quilt approach" that Jayanti skillfully weaved together.[25] Kevin Lally elaborated in the *Hollywood Reporter*:

> Spector might have recorded his legendary "Wall of Sound" hits in mono, but Jayanti takes an unusual multitracked approach: The songs often play out over silent, banal footage of the trial while florid comments about the recordings by critic Mick Brown crawl across the bottom of the screen.
>
> The documentary was indeed built up from four sources: footage of the interview, the songs, the court room and quotes from a biography by Mick Brown. Jayanti's *main* tool in the portrayal of Spector's monstrosity was not so much what came through each channel of communication,

but how those channels were linked together. As reviewer Stephanie Zacherek explained, "he can't just allow the lush grandness of the Wall of Sound speak for itself."[26]

In an essay on the attributed meanings of photographic images, Roland Barthes argued that written captions inevitably add new meanings to their referent images.[27] Since words and pictures are different semiotic systems, there is inevitable gap between them. The gap can be narrow (the image as illustration of the text) or wide (the text loading the image with unexpected meanings), but the words of a caption can never be the image that they represent, so they always have a connotative role. Barthes' work draws attention to the complex processes of communication involved when multiple streams of communication are presented simultaneously. Critic Ronnie Schieb explained in *Variety* that the Spector documentary was characterized by its juxtapositions:

> But the most original contribution to *The Agony and the Ecstasy of Phil Spector* is the quasi-Godardian juxtaposition of silent-running trial footage, complete with diagrams, videotapes, displays of bullet trajectories and blood spatters, with signature lush orchestrations of Spector's music, as one familiar tune after another, playing out in its entirety, trumpets his artistry. Effusive quotes by Mick Brown, enumerating each song's peculiar brilliancies, are displayed onscreen.[28]

Beyond the use of specific images, editing, and other streams of communication, it should also be noted that Jayanti's team made further critical decisions. For instance, two songs, one by The Righteous Brothers and the other by Tina Turner, were each played twice in the film, once as performance footage, the next time as a bed of soundtrack material to accompany courtroom scenes. To understand such strange choices, this section will present the results of a close reading.

A chronological summary of the documentary's content helps to expose a subtext that many of the reviewers seemed to miss: the juxtapositions are deliberately used to tell their own story of Spector's folly. An opening caption of *The Agony and the Ecstasy of Phil Spector* draws on viewers' romantic conceptions of musical creativity by using a quote from *The Word* magazine: "Spector's personal disaster stems from the same place as his musical brilliance." The film starts with Spector discussing his court case. Speaking about jury bias he explains, "We have a jury questionnaire that they filled out. Forty-five percent of them wrote down that they believed I was guilty. Twenty percent of them wrote down I was insane." As if to supply a visual vouchsafe for his insanity, the next shot, taken from CBS's *Inside Edition* (2007), shows the producer in a fright wig and Hawaiian shirt. Playing "He Hit Me (It Felt Like A Kiss)," the film then uses a Mick Brown quote: "With its over-heated production and melodramatic arrangement, 'He Hit Me' sounds kitsch, if one didn't suspect that Spector was in deadly earnest—the idea of love as sado-masochistic battle-zone." This is rather ironic insofar as Spector did not write The Crystals' 1962 hit: it was, rather, written by Gerry Goffin and Carole King. Goffin and King were inspired by Little Eva's explanation of her violent relationship. On the *Allmusic* website reviewer Dave Thompson sutures Spector into the song's legend:

> It was a brutal song, as any attempt to justify such violence must be, and Spector's arrangement only amplified its savagery, framing Barbara Alston's lone vocal amid a sea of caustic strings and funereal drums, while the backing vocals almost trilled their own belief that the boy had done nothing wrong. In more ironic hands (and a more understanding age), "He Hit Me" might have passed at least as satire. But Spector showed no sign of appreciating that, nor did he feel any need to. No less than the song's writers, he was not preaching, he was merely documenting.[29]

In other words, the Spector legend is so strong that Thompson reads the producer's misogynistic tendencies into the bombastic way that the song was arranged and recorded. It is as if Spector's psychosis was *audible* in the music he records and he had failed in a *moral* obligation to frame the lyrics in a way that would diffuse their perverse meaning. It is interesting here that "merely documenting" takes on such a sinister tone. As a news report of the crime explains, Clarkson was shot when she was about to leave Spector's mansion, so the documentary's soundtrack shifts to The Ronettes' 1963 single "Be My Baby." After the title sequence, we see footage from 1977 of Spector sitting in his darkened mansion and explaining his thoughts on loneliness as a state of mind. For the first time, the sound of a bell tolling ominously, a sound signifier taken from the start of John Lennon's painfully forlorn, Spector-produced hit "Mother" (1970) is introduced on the soundtrack. This jarring audible counterpoint to Spector's Wall of Sound music is used repeatedly on the film's soundtrack to signify the gravity of his situation, as if to ask for whom the bell tolls. Jayanti next uses the device when the roles of the courtroom professionals are outlined, then after Spector discusses who he could have been if he had not lost his father. A later sample is used over footage of court witnesses being called.

As the documentary moves forward, Spector discusses his place as a high-school loner who wanted to be accepted. Meanwhile we hear The Crystals' "He's A Rebel" from 1962, a song actually written by Gene Pitney, on the soundtrack. Soon, in one of the craftiest poetic juxtapositions that Jayanti creates, we hear another Spector production, the 1964 Dixie Cups' single "Chapel of Love," played over footage of the court room introducing Spector's history of misogynist violence. As guns are examined in the court room and we are shown images of metal gun barrels and bullets as evidence, Brown's caption explains that in the music, "[h]e had alchemized the base metal of his own pain, alienation and resentment into something fabulous, mythic and beautiful." Here, as if the connection were completely natural, the (musically) alchemized "base metal" is manifest in his firearms and weaponry. Next the Crystals' famously jaunty 1963 hit, "Da Doo Ron Ron," with its first verse recounting a romantic encounter, is played over footage of the court asking Spector to identify himself on CCTV meeting Lana Clarkson at the House of Blues nightclub in Los Angeles. In another characteristic juxtaposition, a famous Spector-penned and -produced top ten hit by the Crystals, "And Then He Kissed Me," is played as we see his former girlfriends and female acquaintances give evidence of his fetishes in court: "There was a gun pointing to my temple, actually touching my temple"; "He had a gun literally at my face, a pistol." A court official is heard saying to an expert witness, "If I put a gun into your mouth and shot you, where would you expect to find [the spray of blood] . . . Again, all sorts of splatter." The notion here of the gun blast as a kiss resonates not only with "He Hit Me (And It Felt Like A Kiss)" but also by association with "And Then I Kissed Her," a reworded cover version of the Crystals song performed by The Beach Boys two years later. Following the use of "And Then He Kissed Me," the Spector-produced sound of Bob B. Soxx & the Blue Jeans with their carefree cover of the 1946 Disney film number "Zip-a-Dee-Doo-Dah" is played as we are shown Lana Clarkson's blonde friend explain in court, "When she had her game face on, she could make anyone believe she was happy. She could light up a room with her smile."

The next section of the film is one of its most remarkable fabricated sequences. Listening to The Righteous Brothers sing the Spector-written and -produced hit "You've Lost That Lovin' Feelin'," we are shown the prosecution describing the path of the bullet. Jayanti then cuts to Spector describing his production techniques: "I was scared shitless. Every record I made was up in the air until the last tag and the last drop of paint." Given the constant connections being made by the documentary, the implication is that Spector was traumatized in the moments immediately after Clarkson's death simply because he feared for his future. A caption from Mick Brown's book then calls the song, "A masterpiece of chiaroscuro, of searing emotional light and darkness, of pain and catharsis. It is the very summit of the producer's art." Again, the words of his description ("searing," "darkness," "pain," "catharsis") are made to seem palpably relevant to the act. The next shot is of Spector looking subdued in court. When, back in a shot of his documentary interview, he explains that to keep the single radio friendly, he lied about its length on its record label, Jayanti cuts to the judge's face looking annoyed. Then when an expert witness says that over ninety-five percent of intra-oral gunshot wounds are suicidal, another Brown caption explains the song has "the theme of yearning transmuted into loss, starkly declaring the evidence of a dying love."

The carefully organized parade of juxtapositions continues. Although some library footage is shown of Tina Turner singing "River Deep, Mountain High," the song is used again on the soundtrack. This time it rings out over images of the court room while Brown's notes read "[i]t's the simulacrum of all Spector's grandiosity, his over-arching ambition. It is all his passion, his thirst for revenge, and his madness. Tina Turner's vocal, monumental in itself, is buffetted and bruised in the tumult of the arrangement." At this point we see Spector grin in court. The caption continues in the next shot, "[t]he wildly colored threads of melody are twisted and bent until their shape and colors are all but lost." Brown adds, as if talking about Spector's own persona, "You can be enthralled by it, moved by it, but you can never love it. The sound is titanic, huge and echoing, an unstoppable hurricane." An expert court witness then explains, "[i]n my opinion there is absolutely no physical evidence. The physical evidence is that she had the weapon. She is the one who fired the gun." Brown's caption answers "but like a hurricane it leaves destruction in its wake. It's a record that sweeps you up into its peculiar psychosis and leaves you stunned and exhausted in its wake." It is as if Spector's arrangement, once again, is seen as symbolic of Spector himself, or at least what we know about him.

At this point Jayanti asks, "Have you ever felt like you've really made it, that you've crossed to the safety zone?" Spector ponders:

> I don't have complete confidence that I've crossed the border and probably won't until I'm dead and buried. I mean, I know I am taught in schools. People come up to me and say, "You've changed my life" and things like that . . . But I still believe that they take Tony Bennett more seriously than they take my art. I still believe that they take Dylan more seriously because he had a social position, a social critique. I still don't think they remember that I wrote "Spanish Harlem." I still don't think that they remember I worked with John [Lennon] and I wrote "Woman is the Nigger of the World."

The documentary then takes its cue from the title of the single that Lennon released in the USA on Apple in 1972 by showing footage of Lana Clarkson's modeling portraits, as an expert witness discusses how competition from younger women means that it is tough for women who sell their looks. A show business agent called as a witness then explains that Clarkson was not just bodacious and curvaceous; she also had great comic timing. The court was shown a video-taped comedy skit of her impersonating Little Richard doing a pitch on the Home Shopping Network. As if to reference claims about musical role, (Clarkson as) Richard is selling something called an Originator. Next we see some strange footage of her removing her Little Richard make-up as she explains, "What inspired it? Life. I met Little Richard backstage at the American music awards." Reporting the moment, Kevin Lally of the Hollywood Reporter explained:

> At first, the dead woman is made manifest in extensive forensic evidence; later, she's characterized by the defense's contention that she was so depressed she committed suicide with Spector's gun. Finally she speaks for herself in a clip film, re-edited by Jayanti to focus on her grotesque impersonation of Little Richard.[30]

This is one of the strangest moments in the documentary as Clarkson talks with her skin mask half peeled off—still, as it were, in black face, so exposing her act as a form of imitation. As Ronnie Scheib noted in *Variety*, "At one point, Jayanti switches on the audio, catching the promotional reel of murder victim Lana Clarkson—a comic actress whose awful Little Richard imitation gains unexpected pathos as it plays to a hushed court audience."[31] While she is relegated to a faceless figure in Spector's myth for most of the documentary, lacking the lucrative and socially rewarding celebrity profile about which she once dreamed, here Clarkson is portrayed by the director not only as an image, but also as a lively voice on the audio track. It is as if for a moment in the documentary she breaks from the anonymity that has sealed her victimhood, but her personality can only be expressed when she looks and communicates through the face of another. The footage raises the issue that Spector himself, as an invisible musician, has often expressed his musical message through African-American performers like Tina Turner.[32] Given the "wall of anger" idea, the footage therefore symbolizes that Spector's life-shaping trauma, the circumstances that precipitated his father's suicide, can only speak to us through his music and tragic flirtation with firearms. Following the haunting Little Richard skit, the documentary continues with Beatles numbers, playing "Let It Be" as the courtroom makes up its mind and then "The Long and Winding Road" as we hear a prosecutor say, "Phil Spector, seconds after the gun shot, literally had the smoking gun in his hand, in his right hand, across his waist. He literally had Lana Clarkson's blood on his hands."

One problem with the distinction between visible and invisible music, at least in Phil Tagg's formulation, is the argument that invisible music invariably tends to operate in a relatively covert manner. Tagg claims that "in *a scopocentric culture such as ours*, visible music draws much more attention to itself than does invisible music, no matter how important or omnipresent the latter may be."[33] Tagg's use of the word "scopocentric" is interesting here as it perhaps implies that we notice the sound bed of invisible music less than moving images. In *The Agony and the Ecstasy of Phil Spector*, because of our familiarity with its wonderfully bombastic sound, the music occupies a very prominent position. Captions featuring Mick Brown's commentary draw further attention to it, sometimes relegating the images to act as a kind of bedding. Whether we see courtroom footage from the first trial with the original soundtrack replaced or photographs as evidence exhibits, it is almost as if the visibility of this footage is in question because it is positioned as a found object in the visual narrative. It is as if *our own* familiarity with the Wall of Sound—now perceived as a wall of denial—acts as a barrier to really seeing (i.e. understanding) the court room as a primal scene, just as it did for Spector. In that sense, beyond the music producer's own monstrosity, Jayanti's agency, as a literally invisible filmmaker (he is off-camera and only heard in the interviews), is put to a dubious end: in the guise of the sycophantic fan he enacts a betrayal that further degrades Spector's image. Even before his final court trial, Spector had therefore in effect already been tried twice: once in court for shooting Lana Clarkson, then in Jayanti's documentary he was prosecuted by his own music. As Bruce Bennett, reviewing the BBC show for the Independent Film Channel explained, "*The Agony and the Ecstasy of Phil Spector* becomes a kind of confessional and accusatory spoken word aria that wanders into the documentary borderlands."[34] Unlike most music documentaries, both its subject and style make it uncomfortable viewing.

Notes

1 See Nick Kent, *The Dark Stuff: Selected Writings on Rock Music* (London: Penguin, 2004), 440.
2 Philip Tagg, "Caught on the Back Foot: Epistemic Inertia and Visible Music," *IASPM@Journal* (2011): 3. http://www.tagg.org/articles/IASPM1106.htm (accessed March 2012).
3 Ibid., 11.
4 Spector's ascent as the "tycoon of teen" heralded the increasing prominence of further invisible musicians as popular music icons. After more producers came DJs and other artful technicians.
5 Tony Visconti, *Bowie, Bolan and the Brooklyn Boy: The Autobiography* (London: Harper Collins, 2007), 14.
6 Kent, *The Dark Stuff*, 440.
7 Ibid., 462.
8 Tom Long, "Film Explores Phil Spector's Madness and Brilliance," *Detroit News* (September 9, 2010). http://www.detroitnews.com/article/20100909/OPINION03/9090320/1034/ENT02/Film-explores-Phil-Spector-s-madness-and-brilliance (accessed March 20, 2012).
9 Kent, *The Dark Stuff*, 463.
10 Dave Thompson, *Wall of Pain: The Life of Phil Spector* (London: Omnibus Press, 2010), 7.
11 James Hoberman, "The Agony and the Ecstasy of Phil Spector, Pop Mastermind and Raging Ego," *The Village Voice* (June 29, 2010). http://www.villagevoice.com/2010-06-29/film/the-agony-and-the-ecstasy-of-phil-spector-pop-mastermind-and-raging-ego/ (accessed March 20, 2012).
12 John McCarthy, "*The Agony and the Ecstasy of Phil Spector*," *Box Office* (July 1, 2010). http://www.boxofficemagazine.com/reviews/theatrical/2010-07-the-agony-and-the-ecstacy-of-phil-spector (accessed March 20, 2012).
13 Laura Clifford, "*The Agony and the Ecstasy of Phil Spector*," undated. http://www.reelingreviews.com/theagonyandtheecstasyofphilspector.htm (accessed March 20, 2012).

14 Chris Foran, "Phil Spector Documentary Finds Darkness Amid the Genius" (January 6, 2011). http://www.jsonline.com/entertainment/movies/113020429.html (accessed March 20, 2012).

15 Stephanie Zacharek, "Questions Remain in Messy, Sordid *Agony and the Ecstasy of Phil Spector*" (June 28, 2010). http://www.movieline.com/2010/06/28/review-questions-remain-in-messy-sordid-agony-and-the-ecstasy-of-phil-spector/ (accessed March 20, 2012).

16 Foran, "Phil Spector Documentary Finds Darkness."

17 Michael O'Sullivan, "*The Agony and the Ecstasy of Phil Spector*," *Washington Post* (December 17, 2010). http://www.washingtonpost.com/gog/movies/the-agony-and-the-ecstasy-of-phil-spector,1176722/critic-review.html (accessed March 20, 2012).

18 Norman Wilner, "*The Agony and the Ecstasy of Phil Spector*," *Now Toronto* (January 27–February 3, 2011). http://www.nowtoronto.com/movies/story.cfm?content=178894 (accessed March 20, 2012).

19 Hoberman, "The Agony and the Ecstasy of Phil Spector."

20 Chris Baldick, *In Frankenstein's Shadow* (Oxford: Clarendon, 1987), 10.

21 Patricia Aufderheide, *Documentary Film: A Very Short Introduction* (Oxford: Oxford University Press, 2007), 2.

22 Hoberman, "The Agony and the Ecstasy of Phil Spector."

23 O'Sullivan, "*The Agony and the Ecstasy of Phil Spector*."

24 Clifford, "*The Agony and the Ecstasy of Phil Spector*."

25 Long, "Film Explores Phil Spector's Madness and Brilliance."

26 Kevin Lally, "*The Agony and the Ecstasy of Phil Spector*: Film Review," *Hollywood Reporter* (October 14, 2010). http://www.hollywoodreporter.com/review/agony-and-ecstasy-phil-spector-29773 (accessed March 20, 2012). Zacharek, "Questions Remain in Messy. . . ."

27 See "The Photographic Message," in Roland Barthes, *Image, Music, Text* (New York: Hill, 1977). 15.

28 Ronnie Scheib, "*The Agony and the Ecstasy of Phil Spector* (Documentary—UK)," *Variety* (October 20, 2009). http://www.variety.com/review/VE1117941421?refcatid=31 (accessed March 20, 2012).

29 Dave Thompson, "'He Hit Me (And It Felt Like A Kiss)': Song Review," *Allmusic Database*. http://www.allmusic.com/song/t1072015 (accessed March 20, 2012).

30 Lally, "*The Agony and the Ecstasy of Phil Spector*."

31 Scheib, "*The Agony and the Ecstasy of Phil Spector* (Documentary—UK)."

32 Jayanti summarized this in one of his questions to Spector: "I thought The Righteous Brothers were black when I first heard them. For a long time I thought it was a black song, and I asked you about that. You said you generally hire black bands, but something about their voice—you were still looking for the great voice. And the great voice was Tina."

33 Tagg, "Caught on the Back Foot," 12 (emphasis added).

34 Bruce Bennett, "'*The Agony and the Ecstasy of Phil Spector*,' a 'Defeat Lap' for the Legendary Producer," *Independent Film Channel* (2010). http://www.ifc.com/fix/2010/06/phil-spector (accessed March 20, 2012).

Chapter 15

Desperately Seeking Kylie!

Critical Reflections on William Baker's *White Diamond*

Sunil Manghani and Keith McDonald

White Diamond (William Baker, 2007)[1] is advertised as a "personal portrait of Kylie Minogue." It was conceived and made by the singer's long-time friend, stylist, and creative director, William Baker. The majority of the film is an intimate, behind-the-scenes account as Kylie Minogue embarks on a "comeback" world tour following an unexpected hiatus due to the diagnosis and treatment of breast cancer.

The film takes its place among a canon of music documentaries which attempt to present a behind-the-scenes portrait of an iconic and enigmatic performer, and is perhaps most comparable to Alek Keshishian and Mark Aldo Miceli's portrait of Madonna in *Truth or Dare* (1991).[2] The association is readily made because of the popular perception of Kylie Minogue as a continuation of a style of female performer influenced by the career machinations of Madonna. The allure of these music documentaries pertains to their attempt to enter the private space of the public performer and reveal an "authentic" portrait of the icon, behind the mask of the artistic construct. This dual representation relies upon the notion of a binary opposition between the carefully choreographed on-stage persona and the back-stage authentic identity; a convention summed up by Michael Chanan as being reliant on the idea that "every habitus has an off stage doppelganger."[3]

Domesticating Kylie

The opening of *White Diamond* shows Kylie Minogue sitting at a counter in a domestic kitchen. She looks relaxed and is free of the glitz and glamor she is otherwise well-known for. On the other side of the counter, just off-camera, William Baker tries to explain the idea he has for the film. In effect, the film begins with a plea for the *real* Kylie Minogue to show herself:

WILLIAM BAKER: So what are your concerns about this?

KYLIE MINOGUE: My concern is you'll have ten million hours of footage on high-definition and I'm not gonna like any of it.

WILLIAM BAKER: [laughs] The look. Why am I getting the look?

KYLIE MINOGUE: You want me to be honest.

WILLIAM BAKER: [laughs] Why is that? Why won't you like any of it?

KYLIE MINOGUE: Because I like to be more private than that. It's only because you're doing it that I'm doing it.

WILLIAM BAKER: I know what I'm trying to get out of you.

KYLIE MINOGUE: But I don't know what I'm prepared to give, so we shall find out.

Kylie Minogue's initial concern appears to be an aesthetic one. She is anxious about how she will "look" in high definition. However, she quickly brings to the fore her more significant concern of privacy, which serves as an important preface to the film. We are made curious as to just how much she is prepared to give. While the documentary comprises mainly candid, hand-held filmwork, a series of staged, beautifully lit interviews are intercut at regular intervals. Filmed in black-and-white (echoing a technique utilized in Madonna's *Truth or Dare*) these inserts connote a confessional, intimate mode of Kylie Minogue with her confidant; differentiating with the footage (in color) of Kylie Minogue on-stage and on the road, or the behind-the-scenes filming that make up the majority of the documentary. The interviews provide meta-narrative and analysis, aiding the conceit that somehow we have gained private access and will learn what Kylie Minogue truly thinks and feels. During one of these sequences, William Baker expresses his own personal frustration:

> People don't see you as the person that you are, the person that is my
> friend, that I love. That really annoys me. I think people see you as a

Figure 15.1 Still from *White Diamond* (2007). Kylie Minogue sits in her kitchen discussing the purpose of the film with William Baker (off-camera).

result of *Neighbours*, "I Should Be So Lucky," Michael Hutchence, gold hotpants, "Can't Get You Out Of My Head," cancer, equals Kylie. Nobody really knows what makes you tick. But I think the time has come to rip the surface away, and go deeper. I think that really scares you.

William Baker's confusion with what he sees as a contradiction between his friend, Kylie Minogue, and her public persona, "Kylie," is a recurring theme. As stylist and creative director, William Baker has been a dominant figure in the creation of the Kylie-myth through its many evolutions. It is also the case that after her illness Kylie Minogue "became quite selective about whom she wanted round her. Her level of privacy was increased," and as a result William Baker "stepped up as photographer."[4] All of which makes his wish to "reveal" the real Kylie Minogue somewhat surprising.

The interplay between black-and-white and color footage italicizes the notion that there is a colorful on-stage and public character and a more authentic and "real" back-stage subject. This relates to Irvin Goffman's concept of dramaturgy, particularly in regards to the presumed division between the publicly aware depiction of oneself and the more private self, free from depiction and bathed in verisimilitude. Goffman states that "a back region or backstage may be defined as a place, relative to the given performance, where the impression fostered by the performance is knowingly contradicted as a matter of course."[5] He goes on to contend that this supposed division is largely a fallacy; that our pragmatic awareness of ourselves means that our behind-the-scenes behaviour is as much a performance in that we are intrinsically aware of its performative value.

If Kylie Minogue is genuinely scared of Baker's intentions in *White Diamond* "to rip the surface away, and go deeper," it is arguably less a fear of revealing herself, than of talking *for* "Kylie." More than anyone, Kylie Minogue knows she is *not* Kylie. In interview, she notes how she assumes a role: "I change characters when I do a photo shoot. It's kind of avoiding being me—which I've become very good at. It's hard for me to explain, but rather than being captured, I become a new character or I choose a facet of me and let [it] take over."[6] In a sense, then, there is no real Kylie, only a series of public performances and textual constructions. Thus, to make a documentary is likely only to reveal there is no *behind the scenes* of a pop star; only a set of cultural arbiters who bring the star to life (which would include Kylie Minogue herself, and her creative director William Baker).

As Richard Dyer puts it: "the whole media construction of stars encourages us to think in terms of 'really'—what is ['x' celebrity] really like? which biography, which word-of-mouth story, which moment in which film discloses her as she really was?"[7] *White Diamond* begins precisely with William Baker posing this question of "really." And Kylie Minogue has herself commented on what it is "really" that people might find so interesting about her. "The closest I can get to understanding it," she suggests, "is if I'm sitting at the dentist and there's a magazine. I will pick it up and work my way through it and find myself saying, 'Are they going out together? Look what she's wearing!' We all like a bit of gossip. It's like looking into people's houses when it's night-time and you can see inside."[8] In this apparently idle moment of flicking through a magazine, Kylie Minogue acts out impeccably the role Roland Barthes described of the "reader" of myths. Different to the cynical and/or analytic understanding of myth of either the producer or decipherer of myths, who "destroy the myth, either by making its intention obvious, or by unmasking it," the reader or consumer of myth focuses on its *dynamic*: "the reader lives the myth as a story at once true and unreal."[9]

The construction of "Kylie" is astute to what is true *and* unreal. It is based upon openly playing with styles, genres, and personas to create a whole hall of mirrors. Each shard of the film *White Diamond* glimmers with new possibilities in "really" finding out something about Kylie Minogue. Yet, as becomes apparent, the film offers a further set of constructions, though, arguably, blended together in a more sophisticated manner.

Text and Agency

In his account of Madonna, John Fiske attributes her success to being an "open" rather than "closed" text; suggesting Madonna is open to be read in different ways, from different points of view, rather than soliciting simply a "preferred" reading.[10] Similarly the presentation of Kylie Minogue in a documentary such as *White Diamond* might be considered to proffer an open text, or at least to offer a metatextual portrayal in that it brings together different levels of textuality. So, for example, we see Kylie Minogue in rehearsal and in performance, we see the familiar tour-bus road movie elements alongside press and fan encounters, all of these are well-worn paratextual products associated with fame. Essentially, however, the different levels come together as a single cultural form, as an official "unofficial" documentary.

When we consider Kylie Minogue's career to date, which, like Madonna's, spans several decades, we can refer to a "large celebrity text" composed of core and secondary texts.[11] Core texts, for example, include her role in the Australian soap, *Neighbours* (circa 1986–1988); her various music albums, tours, videos, and television performances; film roles; appearances at the Sydney Olympics, and Sydney Gay and Lesbian Mardi Gras parties; her collaborations with artists such as Nick Cave; and her fashion and perfume ranges. The "large celebrity text" will produce an extensive range of secondary texts, to include journalistic writings, biographies, documentaries, fanzines, and public relations; a pervasive feature of which is to give the illusion of bridging the divide between person and persona.

The idea of "Kylie" as text is perhaps no better illustrated than with the example of Madonna, at the MTV Europe Music Awards in 2000, wearing a t-shirt with the name "Kylie Minogue" written in glittery text. News media reporting referred to the t-shirt as Madonna's tribute to Kylie. In interviews, Kylie Minogue has oft cited Madonna as an influence, having been in her mid-teens when Madonna was developing her career in the early 1980s. In the same year Madonna appeared in the film *Desperately Seeking Susan* (1985), Kylie Minogue gave her first television singing performance. By the year 2000, she was emerging as a genuine pop icon—by the end of 2002, for example, "she made the news with the announcement that she had leapt from 40th to 25th on the UK list of most popular chart stars of all time."[12]

Yet, a great deal more can be read into *that* Kylie t-shirt. Madonna is well-known for breaking with rules and conventions. In particular, she is known for subverting traditional stereotypes of women; giving rise to a veritable discourse of so-called "Madonnologists," reflecting a "left wing ideology, radical antiracism, extreme feminism lesbian or gay militancy."[13] In wearing the Kylie t-shirt, Madonna made a "camp" gesture. In other words, it functioned as a form of overstated imitation, inversion, and punning. Madonna is associated with "drag" as a form of constructedness and parody.[14] In other words, "Madonna" is a series of styles, codes, and texts, from which she (re)constructs her image, in particular as a deliberately gendered image. It has been said, "she becomes king as she behaves as a queen; she is a woman playing a man playing a woman."[15] In this vein, we can understand the Kylie t-shirt better as an ironic statement, whereby Madonna appropriates, through a mere piece of clothing, the seemingly unconstructed femininity, glamour, and sexuality of Kylie Minogue.

Both Madonna and Kylie Minogue can be situated within the frame of postfeminism. This label is used to define a period after the second wave of feminism, referring roughly to the late 1980s onwards. It is also used to signify a backlash to feminism, and in particular a certain feminist critique of femininity, glamour, sexuality, and consumerism. Postfeminism represents a change in attitude, whereby "no longer is being sexy and interested in clothes an indication of being incapable of independent decision-making or professional advancement."[16] Both Madonna and Kylie Minogue have drawn on sexual imagery as part of a persona, yet equally represent women with agency.

In more radical terms, however, postfeminism is also claimed as a "useful conceptual frame of reference encompassing the intersection of feminism with a number of other anti-foundationalist movements including postmodernism, post-structuralism and post-colonialism."[17] In this sense, the "open" text of Madonna (as Fiske would argue) can be understood in more overtly political terms than could ever be applied to Kylie Minogue. Madonna's shifting persona and image mark a form of deconstruction, being *both* inhabitation and iconoclasm, which seeks (in many cases polemically) to destabilize dominant representations of gender and sexuality. By contrast, Kylie Minogue is associated with fashion, sensuality, and hedonism. Yet, in a Warholian sense, she offers a potentially more beguiling response to the postmodern condition than we might suggest of Madonna. One critique of Madonna, for example, is that her gender bending and transgressive sexual identities are simply a skillful manipulation, emblematic of narcissism at the heart of mainstream consumer society.[18] The argument made is that she "promotes a concern for the cultivation of the 'surface' of the individual, rather than responsibility for the wider community or the common good." As such she can be considered *both* "politically radical (subverting images of male-dominance) and conservative (reproducing dominant ideas about consumer culture and capitalism)."[19]

The inverse to Madonna, Kylie Minogue more readily situates herself within patriarchal structures. In *White Diamond* it is evident the people looking after her career are all men; and elsewhere she has openly described a tendency to have men as controlling figures in her professional and personal life. "I've looked very hard at why I end up in the relationships I do," she explains, "I was always Daddy's girl. He's an accountant and he had always looked after my money . . . He's clever and I respect him. But I am aware that men taking a lead may come from that. I never rebelled."[20]

Like Madonna, Kylie Minogue (with her creative team) produces sophisticated music videos and performances that tap expertly into a rich history of fashion and music genres. Unlike Madonna, the play of signifiers in the elaborate stage shows and performances does not foreground their constructedness. Kylie is no "drag act"; she genuinely revels in the sensuality and glamour of the costumes and dance routines. In terms of postmodern aesthetics we might define Madonna's art as parody and Kylie Minogue's as pastiche. However, despite the frivolity of the Kylie aesthetic, there is arguably something "radical" in its surface nature. Clearly this is not radical in a political or social sense, but rather the idea of the "root of something"; as in mathematics. When the fêted postmodern critic Jean Baudrillard spoke of his own creative *production* of photographs he referred to "a process of capturing things, because objects are themselves captivating," and went on to suggest: "It's almost like trapping things—like trying to catch the primitive dimension of the object, as opposed to the secondary dimension of the subject and the whole domain of representation. It's the immanent presence of the object, rather than the representation of the subject."[21]

Madonna, we could argue, is concerned with the domain of representation. However, the play of styles and surfaces leaves her open to the criticism that she cultivates *only* a surface account of the individual, and lacks true political engagement. By contrast, "Kylie" is primarily (and "primitively") concerned with the immanent *presence* of something; in this case glamour, pop, and sensuality. At risk of pushing the analogy, it is almost as if she is trapped within herself, which in turn, perhaps, makes her so *captivating*. Crucially, however, the "radical" surface of "Kylie" means that Kylie Minogue's (female) agency is perhaps less prominently displayed. Within the music industry, the singer is regarded an astute businesswoman. Yet, as an equally astute artist, Kylie Minogue has courted a "girlie," almost Peter Pan-like youthful image; in her own words, she is a "Showgirl Princess." As Frances Bonner argues, if we only look to the inviting poses of the pin-up "Kylie," we are not going to see the woman behind them. "The present persona of a savvy, sexy woman with agency must be mapped from other parts of her celebrity text onto these, cued by the exaggeration in the poses: alone they are insufficiently anchored to let us read her as a person in control."[22]

White Diamond is of course one deliberate "text' (or "intertext") seeking to map these different "parts" of Kylie Minogue. As noted, William Baker is clear about his intentions "to rip the surface away, and go deeper." We can relate Baker's desire to bring out the *real* Kylie Minogue, the real *woman*, as borne of a frustration he feels in being witness to her agency (from the position of privileged friend), knowing that "Kylie" does not readily allow this to be shown. However, from Kylie Minogue's point of view, we can consider her unease with the documentary to be precisely a mark of her agency. This can be understood as twofold: firstly, the opening scene in which Kylie Minogue sits in her kitchen raising concerns about the documentary, appears fleetingly to reveal the woman behind the persona. It is a candid scene, in which she barely looks like "Kylie." She acts as a kind of executive producer, able to command over the viability of the production. Secondly, at a more fundamental level, whether consciously or not, Kylie Minogue is attuned to "Kylie" as a play of surfaces, which she has carefully maintained through a measured, professional approach to her "work" over many years. *White Diamond* suggests altering that chemistry, which must immediately evoke a tension for the *person* Kylie Minogue; her calculating *other*-half, or doppelganger.

Re-Constructing Kylie

The idea of treating the celebrity as a "text" is useful as a means not to conflate person and persona, as well as usefully demarcating the persona as a "site" of analysis. However, despite the arguments for "open" texts and the difference between preferred readings and "sites of resistance," textual analysis has a centripetal force attributing "units of meaning" with their own intrinsic significance and effects. Michael Warner offers a more expansive notion of a "textual" public sphere as an on-going process of the construction and reflection of public discourse that, whilst invisible, or difficult to pinpoint, is nonetheless very real. "No single text can create a public," he writes; rather it emerges through "the concatenation of texts through time." Thus, "[o]nly when previously existing discourse can be supposed, and when a responding discourse can be postulated, can a text address a public."[23]

In order to fully acknowledge the significance of a public text, emphasis needs to be placed upon texts as the circulation of discourses. The "concatenation of texts" is temporal and structural, better understood from a "constructionist" perspective. An important example of how discourses intersect can be noted with Kylie Minogue's diagnosis and treatment of breast cancer. A study in the *Medical Journal of Australia*[24] shows how news coverage of her illness "caused an unprecedented increase in bookings for mammography."[25] Significantly, the report highlights "[w]hile her celebrity status was a key factor driving the coverage, her age (36 years) and the notion that breast cancer was no respecter of celebrity status, wealth or youth . . . were often emphasised."[26] Thus, while Kylie Minogue was the center of attention, a series of discourses collide, relating to abstract notions of celebrity status, health, wealth and youth. Crucially, an established medical discourse is re-positioned (or at least promoted) through connection with the celebrity "text" of Kylie Minogue. Indeed, the report concludes that "[h]ealth advocates should develop anticipatory strategies for responding to news coverage of celebrity illness."[27]

From a constructionist point of view, given the groundswell of sympathy and the way in which her celebrity status placed such spotlight on the disease, it could be argued the singer's illness was never simply her own, but was articulated through a series of discourses and audiences. In this respect, *White Diamond* can be seen as a pronounced way of reclaiming "lost time." Having collapsed during the Showgirl tour in the UK in 2005, just prior to her cancer diagnosis, the film documents Kylie Minogue's return to the public stage in 2006, only months after going into remission. Following the first performance of her (re-titled) Showgirl Homecoming tour in Australia, we witness Kylie Minogue back-stage exhausted and unable to talk. She lies on a concrete floor, desperate to sleep. These are clearly not the kind of scenes we are used to seeing of the singer. The film is almost a confession of what goes on back-stage, both literally and metaphorically. Crucially, we see a "new," older (and no doubt wiser) Kylie.

The documentary taken as a whole offers a complex portrait, drawing together disparate footage of Kylie Minogue both on-stage (in all manner of outfits) and off-stage rehearsing with dancers; preparing photoshoots and joking with William Baker (typically as the two hang around, bored, waiting for things to happen); as well as the black-and-white-filmed interviews in which Kylie Minogue reflects on the importance of returning to the stage. She notes how the first Showgirl tour was "rudely interrupted" by her cancer diagnosis, and her return to the stage motivated by a natural desire for its completion. Yet, the decision to make a documentary showing a "personal portrait" is more significant. During one of the interview sequences, Kylie Minogue suggests the need to open up:

> After the last couple of years, having had cancer and been through a very different journey . . . I think I felt more exposed anyway. I really felt like I was stripped of everything. So perhaps it is a good time to . . . to . . . be a little more true to myself and share that.

Kylie Minogue calmly verbalizes the fact she had cancer, yet the viewer watches her physically struggle to get the final sentence out that she might now be "more true" to herself, i.e. to allow herself to express more private feelings. The film is of course ambivalent, shifting constantly from the private to the public, potentially representing a new direction for the singer. Yet, we have to remind ourselves, we only really see the back-stage of the "Kylie" tour. Other than the brief, opening sequence in which she discusses the film in her kitchen, and the black-and-white, one-on-one interviews with William Baker, the film remains in the bubble of Kylie Minogue's "on tour" entourage. As such it is a reworking of the *myth* of Kylie—both a renewal of that myth, and a foregrounding of its mediation.

Figure 15.2 Still from *White Diamond* (2007). Kylie Minogue takes a break from her tour, escaping for a few days to a beach.

Figure 15.3 Still from *White Diamond* (2007). Kylie Minogue performing on-stage, in a sequence immediately following the scenes of her on a beach, taking a break from the tour.

Midway of the comeback tour, Kylie Minogue is forced to take a break, escaping for a few days to a beach house. She refers to her body as a "battlefield," yet describes it as "big news" to herself that she was "mature enough and comfortable enough" to take some time out. What follows is a sequence in which "workaholic" Kylie Minogue is able to put aside her stage persona and simply play on the beach. Nevertheless, the sequence is heavily stylized. It is shot as a nostalgic home movie, with Kylie Minogue dancing in and out of the waves and smiling to the camera. There is very little dialogue; instead, like a music video, various shots taken at different times (with different clothing worn, etc.) are edited to one of Kylie Minogue's own tracks, which then segue back into the concert footage. Now as "Kylie," heavily made-up and dressed in a red, sparkling gown, she calls out to the audience: "This is one of my dreams . . ." Neatly edited in this way, our thoughts oscillate as to whether her dream is really the pleasure and simplicity of the beach, or the glamorous life of the stage performer (or both!). In the end, perhaps, *White Diamond* does more to demonstrate Kylie Minogue's professionalism, rather than show us what lies beneath.

Alien(ation) Technique

Kylie Minogue has carefully managed her persona and image over her long career. In the 1980s, her visual image was largely based upon head-and-shoulder shots—emphasising her bright, smiley "girl-next-door" looks, which chimed with her success in the easy-viewing soap opera, *Neighbours*. From the late 1990s onwards, however, her visual image shifts to either detailing her whole body, frequently "contorted into the inviting poses of the pin-up, simultaneously revealing and concealing,"[28] or referring to her body in more abstract and fragmentary ways. The obvious example is the fetish surrounding her diminutive *derrière*, resulting from her wearing a certain pair of ruched, gold lamé hotpants in the music video for "Spinning Around" (2000). Kylie Minogue's youthful face is also frequently commented upon, giving rise to various rumours about cosmetic surgery.

Kylie Minogue's looks have attracted a range of responses, including even the bizarre suggestion that she might be an alien. This was an idea first put forward in an article in the British newspaper the *News of the World*, early in her career, as a way of commenting on her youthfulness, ability to keep slim (without dieting, etc.) and her proportionally large mouth. Yet, much later, in discussing the video for "Can't Get You Out of My Head" (2001), the music critic Paul Morley and the video's director, Dawn Shadforth, draw explicitly upon the idea of Kylie Minogue as being alien and strange in order to comment on her as a creative, experimental artist. In the video, Kylie Minogue brings her face unusually close to the camera lens. In doing so, her face subtly distorts, yet remains glamorous.

Figure 15.4 Still from music video "Can't Get You Out of My Head" (Dawn Shadforth, 2001).

DAWN SHADFORTH: . . . it is quite a wide-angle lens and . . . I just remember the photographer going 'her face can really take it.' And I think it really affected her performance because she is really bearing down, right down the lens and it gives a sort of sense of intimacy and as you say a sort of strangeness . . .

PAUL MORLEY: . . . and it is the side of Kylie that suddenly reveals itself as being experimental, she is prepared to push herself into positions and shapes that might not be conventionally attractive; and breaking out of the idea of being a cuddly Kylie and an everyday Kylie. She becomes alien Kylie as well, I mean, it's such an alien shot almost . . .

DAWN SHADFORTH: She always looks beautiful . . . and yes in an unusual way. And I think that's something that perhaps she was consciously looking for at this point in her career . . .[29]

Kylie Minogue's lithe physique and natural (or "alien") élan, indeed the significance placed upon her body in general, is arguably one significant reason why the reports of breast cancer struck such a powerful chord. However, the exchange between Morley and Shadforth is revealing of Kylie Minogue's own knowing manipulation of her body and image. The idea that her performance close to the camera lens allows for both a "sense of intimacy" and "strangeness" is perhaps emblematic of the "Kylie" aesthetic and again reveals the problem posed by *White Diamond* to undo this logic. And/or, *White Diamond* is yet another example of Kylie Minogue being prepared to "push herself into positions and shapes that might not be conventionally attractive." In Barthes' poststructuralist writings, he refers to the "grain of the voice" as "the body in the voice as it sings."[30] He refers to this as a form of writing, as well as a "hedonistic aesthetics."[31] Beyond the pleasure of consumption, of which we can detach ourselves and acknowledge the quality of a work as something we cannot re-produce, Barthes sought a more fundamental pleasure of the text: "bound to *jouissance*, that is to a pleasure without separation . . . the Text is that space where no language has a hold over any other, where languages circulate."[32] Akin to the performances of Marilyn Monroe, the body of Kylie Minogue appears to come before the voice as it sings. And crucially, in keeping with the play of surfaces described above, there is no separation of languages within a performance. Indeed, part of the illusion of *Kylie écriture* has been to keep the "real" Kylie Minogue out of the frame.

White Diamond breaks with the Kylie "hedonistic aesthetic." Through a series of different framings it foregrounds and reintroduces a separation of text and meaning. In other words, as an overt "portrait" of Kylie Minogue it thwarts the circulation of languages we might otherwise attribute or rather simply experience with "Kylie." In *Heavenly Bodies*,[33] Richard Dyer opens with a portrait of the actress Joan Crawford, taken in the 1970s by the photographer Eve Arnold. The photograph shows two reflections of Crawford in two mirrors. A larger mirror on the far wall shows "the Crawford image at its most finished," while in a smaller one, held in her hand, we can see the texture of her make-up, "we can see something of the means by which the larger image has been manufactured." In other words, the photograph is carefully composed to juxtapose two different views of the one person. As Dyer notes:

> [t]he style and context of the photo encourage us to treat the smaller image as the real one, as do our habits of thought. The processes of manufacturing an appearance are often thought to be more real than the appearance itself—appearance is mere illusion, is surface.[34]

This is precisely the equation we can associate with *White Diamond*, and with William Baker's own professed intentions for making the film.

However, there is a third image of Joan Crawford in the photograph. In the left-hand corner of the image we see the back of her head and shoulders, as she sits holding up the small mirror. Both mirror images in themselves immediately pose a question about the complex relationship of presentation and representation. And both these images return an image of the front of the out-of-focus body of Crawford, whose back is turned towards us. It is perhaps most tempting of all to associate this "vague, shadowy figure" with the *real* Joan Crawford. Yet, as Dyer argues, it is the *three* nested images in combination that make up the phenomenon Joan Crawford, and which perpetuate the insistent question of who it is "really" that draws our attention.[35] Watching *White Diamond*, we are similarly drawn to William Baker's insistent question of who "really" is Kylie Minogue—though in this case there are not

Figure 15.5 Still from *White Diamond* (2007). Cutaway shot, showing Kylie Minogue in her kitchen with William Baker discussing the purpose of the film.

just three juxtaposed images, but a range of scenes played before us, as well as a whole "large celebrity text" that reaches its "crisis" with Kylie Minogue's illness. The film's aesthetic draws parallels with Eve Arnold's photographic work, deliberately foregrounding its own mediation.

The singular "moment" of Kylie Minogue sitting in her kitchen discussing the making of the film might be considered an incident where her "vague, shadowy figure" actually gains focus. For that one moment, as if we suffer amnesia, Kylie Minogue is not the same celebrity we are used to seeing. *White Diamond* is a documentary about amnesia. Her audience must always suffer amnesia *in between* the public performances and appearances (not least during the period of her cancer treatment). As with any star, we do not know where she goes when she leaves the back of the stage, or is seen driven away in a limousine. But, equally, the potential collapse of the person and persona documented in *White Diamond* comments on Kylie Minogue's own amnesia about being a showgirl. *White Diamond* is her (and William Baker's) form of therapy to recover that role. The film is not so far from the plot of Madonna's *Desperately Seeking Susan*. Similarly, it tells a "story" of a fascination with a woman (Kylie Minogue) whom we typically know only through a textual reading. This fascination takes on a whole new dimension because of and following the treatment for breast cancer. From this point, we are afforded glimpses of the woman as if returning from a kind of amnesia. In *Desperately Seeking Susan* the passage is one from voyeur to participant. Similarly, in *White Diamond* we are drawn into William Baker's desperate search to find (for the audience at home) "the person that you are, the person that is my friend, that I love." Above all else, however, Kylie Minogue's initial response would seem to echo repeatedly: "I don't know what I'm prepared to give, so we shall find out."

Coda: Kylie *Écriture*

The underlying dilemma of *White Diamond* is that we do not necessarily want to see Kylie Minogue in her different stages of being "made up"; as with Eve Arnold's photograph of Joan Crawford. Kylie Minogue, herself, is alert to this problem, querying William Baker's wishes to make the film in the first place. Nevertheless, filming is evidently underway in that opening "kitchen" sequence, eventually yielding the feature-length documentary in which *both* "Kylie" and Kylie Minogue are (re-)framed. They are *in the frame* for being a Showgirl Princess *after* surgery. They are also *in* the frame of the movie screen as a commodity, portraying Kylie as an authentic "good," borne of Kylie Minogue's deeper substance.

As frames within frames, *White Diamond* contrasts with (or at least foregrounds) the hedonistic aesthetic we usually associate with "Kylie" and pop music more generally. Instead, the documentary offers a genuinely new appraisal, though fittingly, perhaps, it further demonstrates the singer's willingness to reinvent herself, to be ahead of the curve. Despite the inevitable failings of *White Diamond* to "really" offer a personal portrait, the documentary reveals a new articulation of *both* person and persona, a new *Kylie écriture*. Filmed in close-up, in black-and-white, Kylie Minogue reflects on what "it" all means having come through the treatment for breast cancer:

> Yes, you could look at it as just a show, but it's not just a show to me. That's my work. It's my passion. And it gives so much to so many people. Myself included. I didn't come through all of that [her treatment for cancer] and think, 'That's just frippery, show,' 'Pop what?' No, I thought there was something that connects with people. I certainly wasn't ready to give that up after that experience because it actually means more to me.

Kylie Minogue has gone on to release yet more lavishly produced albums and elaborate tours, notably the Ziegfeld Follies and Greek mythology-inspired stage spectacle of her chart-topping album *Aphrodite* (2010). However, in 2012, to celebrate twenty-five years in the music industry, Kylie Minogue eschewed all such spectacle with her so-called Anti-Tour. Performing to her most loyal fans at a few select, "intimate" venues in Australia and England, her set list comprised almost exclusively of B-sides, demos, and rare tracks. The Anti-Tour marks a continuation of the project begun in *White Diamond*. At the Manchester Academy, for example, Kylie Minogue was able to converse with the crowd about people she misses, about her illness, and reminisces of past shows in Manchester (at the big arena). She also spoke of her family (dedicating a song to her father) and was able to talk of William Baker as if he were a friend of the audience. Kylie Minogue has lost none of the passion for her work, but she has also seemingly made it more "meaningful," for herself and her audience. It is not necessarily that she is prepared to give away any more of her "true" self, but she is seemingly now set upon a trajectory that allows a more subtle aesthetic blend of "person" and persona.

Notes

1 *White Diamond* was produced by EMI Records.
2 *Madonna: Truth or Dare* (Alek Keshishian and Mark Aldo Miceli, 1991).
3 Michael Chanan, *The Politics of Documentary* (London: BFI, 2007), 226.
4 William Baker in Simon Sheridan, *The Complete Kylie* (London: Titan Books, 2012, revised edition), 261.
5 Irvin Goffman, *The Presentation of Self in Everyday Life* (New York: Anchor Books, 1959), 112.
6 Kylie Minogue in Julie Aspinall, *Kylie: Queen of the World* (London: John Blake, 2008), 135.
7 Richard Dyer, *Heavenly Bodies: Film Stars and Society* (London: Routledge, 2004), 2.
8 Kylie Minogue in Aspinall, *Kylie*, 136.
9 Roland Barthes, *Mythologies* (London: Vintage Books, 2009), 153.
10 John Fiske, *Understanding Popular Culture* (London: Unwin Hyman, 1989), 124, 145–146.
11 Frances Bonner, "The Celebrity in the Text," in Jessica Evans and David Hesmondhalgh (eds.), *Understanding Media: Inside Celebrity* (London: Open University Press, 2005), 82.
12 Ibid., 83.
13 Georges-Claude Guilbert, *Madonna as Postmodern Myth: How One Star's Self-Construction Rewrites Sex, Gender, Hollywood and the American Dream* (Jefferson: MacFarland & Company, Inc., 2002), 2.
14 Ibid., 111–147.
15 Cathy Schwichtenberg cited in ibid., 118.
16 Bonner, "The Celebrity in the Text," 86.
17 Ann Brooks, *Postfeminisms: Feminism, Cultural Theory, and Cultural Forms* (London: Routledge, 1997), 1.
18 Douglas Kellner, "Madonna, Fashion, and Image," in *Media Culture* (London: Routledge, 1995), 263–296.
19 Nick Stevenson, "Audiences and Celebrity," in Evans and Hesmondhalgh, *Understanding Media*, 157–158.
20 Kylie Minogue in Aspinall, *Kylie*, 114.
21 Jean Baudrillard, "The Ecstasy of Photography," in Nicholas Zurbrugg (ed.), *Jean Baudrillard, Art and Artefact* (London: Sage, 1997), 33.
22 Bonner, "The Celebrity in the Text," 84.
23 Michael Warner, *Publics and Counterpublics* (New York: Zone Books, 2002), 90.
24 Simon Chapman, Kim McLeod, Melanie Wakefield, and Simon Holding, "Impact of News of Celebrity Illness on Breast Cancer Screening: Kylie Minogue's Breast Cancer Diagnosis," *Medical Journal of Australia* 183, No. 5 (2005): 247–250.
25 Ibid., 247.
26 Ibid., 248.
27 Ibid., 250.

28 Bonner, "The Celebrity in the Text," 84.
29 Paul Morley and Dawn Shadforth in conversation, *Pop, What is it Good For?* (BBC Four, 2008).
30 Roland Barthes, *Image-Music-Text* (London: Flamingo, 1977), 188.
31 Ibid., 163.
32 Ibid., 164.
33 Dyer, *Heavenly Bodies*, 2004, 1.
34 Ibid., 1.
35 Ibid., 2.

List of Contributors

Christopher L. Ballengee is a PhD candidate in Ethnomusicology at the University of Florida and adjunct music instructor and sound engineer at Santa Fe College in Gainesville, Florida. His research focuses on music in the Caribbean, especially Indo-Trinidadian tassa drumming. Christopher is currently shooting a documentary on tassa musicians living in Florida, is a film and video reviewer for *Notes* (the journal of the Music Library Association), and has presented videos and papers at various conferences in the United States and internationally.

Andrew Burke is an Associate Professor in the Department of English at the University of Winnipeg where he teaches Critical Theory and Cultural Studies. His work has appeared in journals such as *Historical Materialism*, *Screen*, and *New Cinemas* and has covered a wide array of topics, including the film essays of Patrick Keiller, the music and film work of the pop group Saint Etienne, and the gallery work of Douglas Coupland. His current project is on the representation of memory and modernity in contemporary British cinema.

Oliver Carter is a Lecturer in Media and Cultural Theory at the Birmingham School of Media, Birmingham City University, where he convenes modules in media, communication and creativity. Oliver is also a doctoral student, researching the political economy of European cult cinema fan production, and is interested in how the boundaries between amateur and professional media production are becoming increasingly blurred. Oliver is also a contributing author to the book *Media Studies: Text, Production and Consumption* (Pearson Longman, 2009). Oliver blogs at www.olivercarter.co.uk.

Sam Coley, Senior Lecturer in Radio at Birmingham City University, was the co-investigator for radio and development in the AHRC KTF scheme run by "Interactive Cultures" (http://interactivecultures.org/) between 2008 and 2009. Sam teaches radio production, documentary making, commercial production and digital editing skills. He has a background in both UK and Australasian radio industries and has worked as creative director for the Northern Region of New Zealand's TRN Radio Network. Sam is a regular documentary producer for Radio New Zealand and is currently researching the uses of radio as an educational tool in developing countries. Examples of Sam's production work can be found at www.samcoley.com.

K. J. Donnelly has written widely on the subject of film music and music in films. His major publications include *British Film Music and Film Musicals* (Palgrave, 2007), *The Spectre of Sound: Film and Television Music* (British Film Institute, 2005), *Pop Music in British Cinema: A Chronicle* (British Film Institute, 2001), and the edited collection *Film Music: Critical Approaches* (Edinburgh University Press and Continuum, 2001). Kevin's forthcoming books include *Occult Aesthetics: Sound Synchronization and Film* (Oxford University Press) and *Tuned to the Future: Music in Science Fiction Television* (Routledge, co-edited with Philip Hayward).

Mark Duffett is Senior Lecturer in Media and Cultural Studies at the University of Chester where he has taught for over a decade in the areas of popular music, media studies and fan culture. Mark has written articles for various journals including *Popular Music*, *Popular Music and Society*, *The Journal of Popular Music Studies*, *Convergence*, *Information* and *Culture and Society*. His recent publications include chapters on The Sex Pistols in *Popular Music and British Television* (Ashgate, 2010) and on race in *Kraftwerk: Music Non-Stop* (Continuum, 2010). Mark is currently editing a book on popular music fandom for Routledge and working on a textbook about media fandom for Continuum.

Robert Edgar is Head of the MA programs in Film and Documentary at York St John University. He has research interests in postmodernism and cinema, theories of comedy, screenwriting, and directing. Publications include *Screenwriting* (AVA, 2009) and *Directing Fiction* (AVA, 2010). Recent research projects include work on Hitchcock and Herrmann, contemporary television, and *Top Gear*.

Kirsty Fairclough-Isaacs is Lecturer in Media and Performance in the School of Media, Music and Performance at the University of Salford. Kirsty has written on celebrity, stardom, makeover culture, and post-feminism. Current research is centered on female celebrity and discourses of aging in Hollywood. She has most recently published in *Celebrity Studies*, *Genders* and *Feminist Media Studies*.

Michael Goddard is a Senior Lecturer in Media Studies at the University of Salford. His current research centers on Polish and European cinema and audiovisual culture, he has published the monograph *Gombrowicz, Polish Modernism and the Subversion of Form* (Purdue, 2010) and has completed a book on the cinema of the Chilean-born filmmaker Raúl Ruiz. Michael has also co-edited volumes on East European subcultures, and The Fall and two volumes on noise with Benjamin Halligan, as well as an issue of *Fibreculture* on Media Ecologies. Michael is now conducting a research project, Radical Ephemera, examining alternative media ecologies in film, television, radio, and radical politics of the 1970s. Michael is co-editor of *Studies in Eastern European Cinema* (Intellect).

Ailsa Grant Ferguson is a Research Associate in Shakespeare at King's College London and is a member of the London Shakespeare Centre. She has a PhD from the University of Bristol specializing in countercultural film appropriations of Shakespeare. Her research and teaching are in the fields of both early modern literature and screen adaptation and her recent and ongoing research projects include: the commemoration of Shakespeare since the nineteenth century, counterculture and subversion in Shakespearean performance, and Shakespeare in conflicted spaces.

Jon Hackett recently completed his doctorate at the University of Sussex, where his first thesis supervisor was Professor Geoffrey Bennington (one of the foremost translators and commentators on the work of Jacques Derrida). Jon has been a course convenor at the University of East London, has taught at Goldsmiths and Université Paris 13, and currently teaches in the area of Film Studies at St Mary's College, Twickenham.

Benjamin Halligan is the Director of Postgraduate Research Studies for the College of Arts and Social Sciences, University of Salford. Publications include *Michael Reeves* (Manchester University Press, 2003) and, with Michael Goddard as co-editor, *Mark E. Smith and The Fall: Art, Music and Politics* (Ashgate, 2010), *Reverberations: The Philosophy, Aesthetics and Politics of Noise* (Continuum, 2012) and *Resonances: Noise and Music* (Continuum, 2013), in addition to numerous articles and chapters on audiovisual practices.

Erich Hertz is an Associate Professor of English at Siena College in New York where he teaches courses in contemporary culture, film, and literature. Erich has published on Adorno, Benjamin, Surrealism, and contemporary Scottish fiction. He is currently co-editing a volume entitled *Write in Tune: Contemporary Music and Fiction*.

Paul Long is Reader in Media and Cultural History, and Associate Director of the Birmingham Centre for Media and Cultural Research, at Birmingham City University. Paul's current research concerns crowd-curation in the art world and below-the-line work in the cultural industries. He is the author of *"Only in the Common People": The Aesthetics of Class in Post-War Britain* (Cambridge Scholars, 2008) and co-author, with Tim Wall, of *Media Studies: Texts, Production and Context* (Pearson Longman: second edition, 2012).

Sunil Manghani is Reader in Critical and Cultural Theory at Winchester School of Art. He has published in *Theory, Culture and Society, Film International, Invisible Culture, Journal of Visual Art Practice, Culture, Theory and Critique*, and *Parallax*. He is the author of *Image Critique and the Fall of the Berlin Wall* (Intellect, 2008) and the textbook *Image Studies: Theory and Practice* (Routledge, 2012) as well as editor of *Images: A Reader* (Sage, 2006) and *Images: Critical and Primary Sources* (Berg, 2012).

Keith McDonald holds a PhD from Birkbeck College, University of London, and is Senior Lecturer in Film, Literature and Media, York St. John University. His publications appear in *Children's Literature in Education, Biography: An Interdisciplinary Quarterly* and *The Irish Journal of Gothic and Horror*. Keith is author of *Film and Television Textual Analysis* (Auteur, 2006) and is currently working on a book for Continuum Press regarding the work of the Mexican director and screenwriter Guillermo del Toro.

Jeffrey Roessner serves as Dean of Arts and Humanities at Mercyhurst College, where he teaches in the areas of contemporary literature and creative writing. He has published on John Fowles, Angela Carter, Jeanette Winterson, R.E.M., and The Beatles, among others. He also authored the songwriting book *Creative Guitar: Writing and Playing Rock Songs with Originality* (Mel Bay, 2009).

Michael Saffle earned his Ph.D. at Stanford University and taught there for a year before accepting an appointment at Virginia Tech. His work has appeared in the *Journal of the American Musicological Society, Acta Musicologica, Notes, Asian Music, IRASM*, and the *Leonardo Music Journal* as well as the *Journal of Popular Film and Television* and *Music in Television*, edited by James Deaville. Saffle's books include *Franz Liszt: A Guide to Research*, revised and republished by Routledge in 2004 and again in 2009. As a scholar he has held fellowships from the Fulbright and Humboldt Foundations as well as the American Philosophical Society and the Virginia Foundation for the Humanities and Public Policy. In 2006, on his sixtieth birthday, Saffle was honored with a Festschrift published as a special *Spaces of Identity* issue.

David Sanjek was the Head of the Popular Music Research Centre in the School of Media, Music and Performance at the University of Salford. David had previously served as the Director of the Broadcast Music Incorporated Archives in New York, and as advisor to The Rock & Roll Hall of Fame, The Rhythm & Blues Foundation, The Blues Foundation, the Experience Music Project Museum and on several committees for the National Academy of Recording Arts and Sciences. David was a world recognized authority on music archiving and was published widely and extensively on popular music and film.

Tim Wall lectures in Radio and Popular Studies and is Director of the Birmingham Centre for Media and Cultural Research, Birmingham City University. His aim as a researcher is to understand the relationship between the media, technology, and culture; his aim as a teacher is to get students researching and thinking for themselves. The second edition of his well respected book, *Studying Popular Music Culture* (Hodder Arnold) was published in 2012.

Emile Wennekes is Chair Professor of Post-1800 Music History and former Head of School, Media and Culture Studies, at Utrecht University, the Netherlands. Emile has published on diverse subjects including Amsterdam's Crystal Palace, Bernard Haitink, Bach and Mahler receptions, and contemporary music in the Netherlands (some books are available in translation: in six European languages and Chinese). Emile previously worked as a journalist for leading Dutch dailies and was artistic advisor and orchestral programmer before intensifying his academic career. His current research focuses on the remigration of musicians after the Second World War as well as on "mediatizing music." Emile chairs the study group Music and Media under the auspices of the International Musicological Society.

Julie Lobalzo Wright completed her doctorate in Film Studies at King's College London. Her work focused on crossover stardom through an examination of male popular music stars in American and British cinema, and her current research is centered on masculinity and popular music.

Index

Tommy (Russell, 1975) 110, 171, 177
Tonite Let's All Make Love in London (Whitehead, 1967) 4, 109

University of Florida, the 195, 196, 197, 202, 203, 204

Warhol, Andy 16, 18, 118, 119, 121,133, 223
Warner Brothers 93, 100, 101, 102, 104
Westwood, Vivienne 147, 149
Woodstock (Wadleigh, 1970) xii, xiii, 3, 5, 43, 44, 47, 48, 54 n.35, 71–72, 73, 74, 75, 77, 78, 79, 80, 81, 82, 84, 88, 93, 100, 101, 102, 108, 109, 162, 171

Wadleigh, Michael 3, 43, 71, 73, 78, 82, 88, 93, 100, 162, 171
"wall of sound" 206, 208, 210, 211, 212, 213
Wilson, Tony 133, 134, 135, 136–137, 138
White Diamond (Baker, 2007) 219–234
Who, The 110, 159, 171

Yessongs (Neal, 1973) 174, 176, 177, 179
YouTube 56, 58, 61, 65, 66, 155, 175

Zappa, Frank 1, 30, 48, 111, 161, 162
Zedd, Nick 118, 126, 128